SALT IN THE BLOOD

JAMES MILLER

CANONGATE

First published in Great Britain in 1999 by
Canongate Books Ltd
14 High Street
Edinburgh EH1 1TE

ISBN 0 86241 836 4

British Library Cataloguing-in-Publication Data
A catalogue record for this book is available on request

Designed by Mark Blackadder

Printed and bound in Italy

SALT IN
THE BLOOD

SCOTLAND'S FISHING
COMMUNITIES PAST
AND PRESENT

SCOTLAND'S FISHING COMMUNITIES PAST AND PRESENT

CONTENTS

PREFACE

One day in the summer of 1995 I found myself wandering around the busy harbour at Fraserburgh. A large modern fishing vessel was unloading her catch of herring. A system of pipes sucked the fish from the hold and spewed them into plastic crates which were shuttled off on a forklift truck into the back of a waiting juggernaut. The fish came in a steady stream, a silver river of bodies. Each crate was filled in seconds and two men were kept busy shovelling ice into them. One or two older men, perhaps retired fishermen, watched, and one fellow gathered a few of the fish that had spilled on to the quay and took them, hanging from the handlebar of his bike, home for a fry.

This scene is the modern equivalent of what is familiar from the black-and-white photographs of many of Scotland's harbours in the late nineteenth and early twentieth centuries, except that in the old pictures the herring are being swung ashore in baskets, and armies of gutters, nearly all women, are waiting to receive them and begin the process of salting and packing. I did not know the size of the catch I was seeing in Fraserburgh but the stream of herring seemed unending, as if one vessel had swept up in one excursion what several zulus or drifters would have considered a week-long bonanza.

The Scottish fishing industry, as epitomised by the *Julie Anne* (for that was the vessel's name), is now a high-tech operation. The fleet's catching power is beyond the dreams of the fishermen of my grandfather's generation. Steel, synthetic fibres and electronics have supplanted the timber, tar and hemp and the compass lit by a paraffin lamp that he knew. The sea is the same, but the fish have become fewer. The *Julie Anne* is a Gardenstown boat. On the day before I had been to Gardenstown, or Gamrie, to give it its local name, one of the many picturesque fishing villages that dot the fringe of the Moray Firth. The harbour had been filled with bobbing craft and out on a pole in the bay the Canadian maple leaf flag had fluttered lazily in the sun. The *Julie Anne* would not be able to dock there. This I found symbolic, a little sad but also reassuring. The high-tech fishing industry needs elaborate, extensive shore facilities and it can find these in only a few harbours. The men who crew the fleet, however, still come from all the little places and paint the names proudly on their vessels as their home ports. I felt that the fishing communities are still alive, reduced but still vibrant. The maple leaf

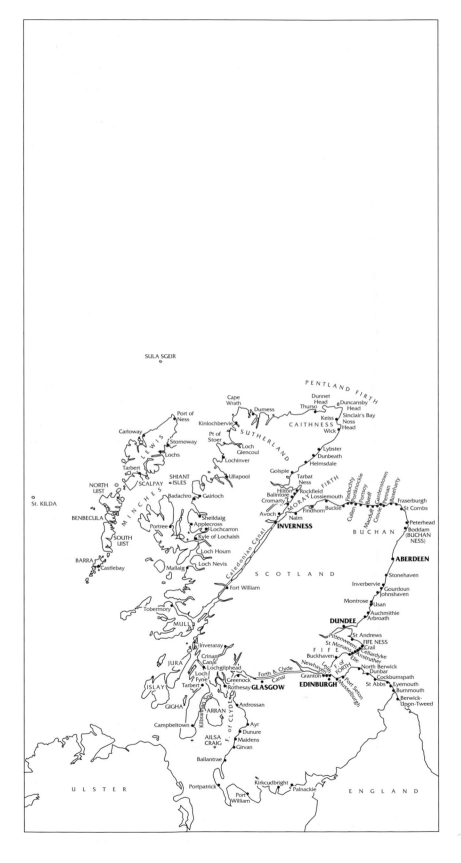

is a symbol, though, of deeply felt grievances in these communities. It was flying in Gardenstown and in many other places around the Moray Firth that summer because Canadian fishermen had recently repulsed Spanish boats from fishing off their coast, and, because of the Common Fisheries Policy, Spanish fishermen have not always been very popular among Scottish fishermen in recent years. This competition for dwindling stocks is another aspect of the fishing that would have been a surprise to my grandfather.

Travelling around the knuckle of Buchan, I thought of the sea and the fishermen and my own heritage, and the idea for this book slowly took form. Was I witnessing the decline of the type of community that had produced me, and how had this come about? I felt I knew bits of the story, I wanted to know more.

There have been many books about the fishing but generally they take as their subject an isolated aspect of it – the story of one particular harbour, of one type of fishing, of one stretch of coast or of one period in history. Some of these have become classics in their field and are widely known, others have been published locally. I collected and read as many as I could lay hands on. All are listed in the Bibliography but a few deserve special mention here: Peter Anson's *Fishing Boats and Fisherfolk on the East Coast of Scotland* (1930) is now rare and much sought after; Iain Sutherland's *Wick Harbour and the Herring Fishing* (1984) and *From Herring to Seine Net Fishing on the East Coast of Scotland* (1985) are definitive works; Alistair Goodlad's *Shetland Fishing Saga* has become a standard history of the northern islands' fishing up until the 1960s; as has Angus Martin's *The Ring-Net Fishermen* (1981) for the Clyde area. More academic treatments are found in Malcolm Gray's *The Fishing Industries of Scotland 1790-1914* (1978) and James Coull's *The Sea Fisheries of Scotland* (1996). Several fishermen have recorded their personal stories and left us a valuable legacy: for example, Peter Buchan's *Collected Poems and Short Stories* (1992), Tom Ralston's *My Captains* (1995) and William (Pilot) Stewart's books about Lossiemouth. This book is not intended to replace any of these but rather to complement them, to present in one volume the overall pattern of history into which they fit.

There are many aspects of the long saga involving people and the sea that I have had to omit or mention only in passing. With their knowledge of the sea and small boats, fishermen made ideal smugglers: there is a tradition that at one time as much of Eyemouth existed underground in the form of tunnels and cellars as could be seen above, and John Thomson in *The Smuggling Coast* (1989) reckoned that smuggling was second in importance after agriculture to the Solway economy in the eighteenth century. Fishermen also served as pilots for merchant shipping and this became an important ancillary occupation in, for example, the Pentland Firth area in the nineteenth century. Whaling was commercially significant for some ports such as Aberdeen, Peterhead and Dundee; and fishermen

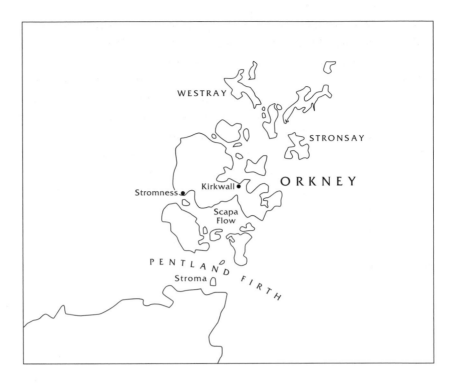

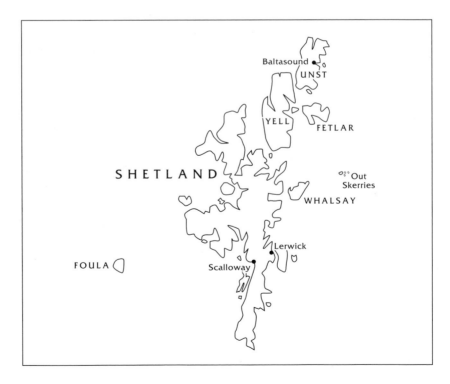

must have been a prime source of skilled manpower in this business. I have made little mention of salmon fishing and none of fish farming.

As I travelled around Scotland, I began to feel that the story of the fishing communities, of their rise and of the present threats to their future, was not fully appreciated by other sections of the nation. The sea has always been vital to Scotland – as a source of food and as a fount of inspiration for her culture and the work of her artists and writers through the centuries – but still it remains a mystery, a powerful elemental force we do not understand. Fishermen perhaps come closest to any kind of real understanding of the nature of the sea. Yet fishing happens far from the eyes of landsmen; the communities comprise a closely-knit brotherhood and sisterhood of the sea; in numbers they are no longer so many. Most people see fish on supermarket counters very few see the heaving waves where the fishermen work. If the fishing communities of Scotland disappear, the nation will have lost an asset beyond price.

J.M.

ACKNOWLEDGEMENTS

I could not have written this book without the help of a great many people and I hope I have not omitted anyone in the following list. First, my thanks must go to the many men and women who entertained me in their homes or work-places with unfailing hospitality and freely gave me the information that is the vital heart of this book. They are: George Alexander, Gardenstown; William Anderson, Whalsay; Norrie Bremner, Wick; Frank Bruce, Macduff; Alec Buchan, Peterhead; Peter Burgon, Eyemouth; George Christie, Aberdeen; Coull Deas, Cellardyke; Gordon Easingwood, Dunbar; Gordon Fraser, Balblair; John Goodlad, Lerwick; Jimmy Gregor, Macduff; Dodie Gunn, John o' Groats; Sandy Hepburn, Gardenstown; Jackie Johnstone, Palnackie; Dr Nick Lake, Inverness; David Lees, Dunbar; George Leiper, Aberdeen; Duncan McArthur, Campbeltown; Angus McCrindle, Girvan; Donald MacDonald, Golspie; James MacDonald, Campbeltown; the late Alfred Mackay, Wick; Dr Calum Mackay, Scrabster; David John Mackenzie, Wick; Murdo Maclennan, Lochs; Hector Macleod, Kyle; Andrew Mearns, Ferryden; Sandy Miller, Hopeman; William and Madge Mitchell, Inverness; Bill Murray, Hopeman; Dr Ian Napier, Scalloway; Peter Patterson, Eyemouth; Cephas Ralph, SFPA, Inverness; Tom and Ina Ralston, Lundin Links; John Robb, Newhaven; Duncan Sandison, Unst; Tom Shields, Girvan; Angus Sinclair, Stromness; Iain and Isobel Smith, Ferryden; Iain Smith, Newhaven; Margaret Smith, Banff; Ian Stephen, Stornoway; Captain Robbie Sutherland, Stromness; John Swankie, Arbroath; John Thomson, Lossiemouth; Alex Watson, Cellardyke; William West, Macduff; Andrew Williamson, Lerwick; Jim Wilson, Newhaven; George Wood, Aberdeen; and George Wood, Macduff.

Many friends helped me with accommodation and contacts and I owe them a special thank you, particularly Donald and Jean Campbell, Edinburgh; Gerry and Peggy McGhee, Monifieth; Robert and Nora Manson, Lerwick; Angus and Judy Martin, Campbeltown; and Ian and Barbara Stephen, Stornoway.

Scotland's fishing story is well covered in a string of museums and libraries around the country and here, too, I met with a generous willingness to help: a special thanks to Aberdeen City Library; Burravoe Museum, Yell; Dunstaffnage Marine Laboratory; Eyemouth Museum; Gairloch Heritage Museum; Inverness Public Library; Lerwick Public

Library; Lossiemouth Fisheries Museum; McKechnie Institute, Girvan; Montrose Museum; Nairn Fishertown Museum; Newhaven Heritage Museum; Scottish Fisheries Museum, Anstruther; Signal Tower Museum, Arbroath; Stornoway Public Library; and Wick Heritage Centre.

Mark Cross, Moray Council; Brian Frater, Borders Council; Sandra Linton, Fife Council; Ross Macdonald, Aberdeen City Council; Iain Macleod, Western Isles Council; and Gordon Summers, Angus Council, were generous with information about local-authority involvement in fishing. Rachel Benvie, Montrose; Tom Bryan, Strathkanaird; Robert Cardno, Peterhead; Dave Clark of the RNMDSF, Eyemouth; Howie Firth, Kirkwall; Jim Henderson, Golspie; Steve Humphries of Testimony Films; Margaret King, Arbroath; Margaret Ann Macdonald, Inverness; Dr Finlay Macleod, Lewis; Elisa Miller, Thurso; Kate Newland, Anstruther; and John Pick, Castle Douglas, all helped me with contacts and information. G.W. Craig of the SFPA and Helge Sørheim, Sunnmøre Museum, Norway, were helpful in their areas of expertise. I owe thanks to Dick Rayner for expertly dealing with some photographs for me. Tom Ralston kindly read much of the text and gave me some valuable advice.

Finally, I would like to acknowledge financial support from the Scottish Arts Council towards the costs of research; and the continuing and encouraging support of my agent, Duncan McAra. None of those named above is responsible for any errors in this book; these are all my own work.

J.M.

ILLUSTRATION ACKNOWLEDGEMENTS

The author is grateful for permission to use the illustrations on the pages indicated to the following: The Abbot of Nunraw, Sancta Maria Abbey, for pages 3, 99, and 231; Aberdeen Maritime Museum for pages 50, 113, 114 (A Scots woman gutting herring.), 124, 149, 151 and 239; Aberdeen University Library, the George Washington Wilson Collection, for page 72. Mr William Anderson, Whalsay, for pages 144, 145 and 156; An Eolas, Stornoway for page 29; Angus Council, Cultural Services, for pages 32, 47, 48, 51, 78, and 175; BBC Publications for the pictures by Eldon Moore on pages 115, 119 and 123; Caithness Area Council, Highland Council, for page 38; the Cowie Collection, University of St Andrews, for page 108; Johnson Controls, Dounreay, for page 67; Mrs Liz Duvill, Gairloch, for pages 89 and 176; Gairloch Heritage Museum for page 35; the Wick Society for pages 17, 30, 71, and 87 from the Johnston Collection; Mr George Leiper, Aberdeen, for pages 56, 116, and 131; Lossiemouth Fisheries Museum for page 13; Mr Angus McCrindle, Girvan, for page 157; Mr Murdo Maclennan, Lochs, for page 165; Moray Council Museums Service for page 213; the Trustees of the National Gallery of Scotland for page xiv; Mr Clive Richards, North of Scotland Newspapers, Wick; Mr John Robb, Newhaven, for pages 126, 128, and 129 (The trawler *Arctic Hunter*, Crew of the trawler *Malcolm Croan*.); Scottish Fisheries Museum, Anstruther, for pages 6, 12, 88, 104, 106, 110, 111,118, 129 (The Crew of a trawler having a meal.), 133 (*The St Kilda.*), 141, 154, 169, 170, 181, 190, 232 and 235; Scottish Fisheries Museum and Mr James Allan, St Monans, for page 114 (Fishermen man a three-pounder gun.); Scottish Fisheries Museum and 'Chapman', Kirby, for page 15; Scottish Fisheries Museum and Mr Tom Easson for page 159; Scottish Fisheries Protection Agency for pages 161, 177, 180, 201, 216 (SFPA Crown Copyright - no reproduction without permission); Scottish Fisheries Museum and Rosemary Galer for pages 133 (John Thomson in the wheelhouse of the *St Kilda.*) and 192, and for permission to use the picture by the late Mr. Reg Weir on page 167; the Shetland Museum for page 26; and Mr George Wood, Aberdeen, for page 121.

CHAPTER ONE

THE OLD COMMUNITIES

A society quite distinct

When Alexander Whyte, the parish schoolmaster of Gamrie on the Banffshire coast in the 1840s, described the fishing village of Crovie he wrote that it was 'like a brood of young sea-fowl nestling with their heads under their dams'.[1] It was an apt image for the row of houses in the tiny settlement, each with one gable to the sea and the other tucked against the steep brae behind. Crovie and the larger neighbouring village of Gardenstown a short distance to the west look out to Gamrie Bay. On either side steep headlands cut off the view and on a misty morning there seems no other world than the grey ocean stretching away northwards. In Whyte's day there were many villages and fishertouns right along the east coast of Scotland, from Burnmouth almost on the English border to Thurso in the north. Few had such a spectacular setting as Gardenstown and Crovie but they had much else in common. The houses tended to be similar – small, often single-storeyed but with lofts for the storage of nets and gear, and set close to each other. In many of the villages laid out by lairds keen on what they termed 'improvement', there was an element of planning, clearly

(Opposite) The Newhaven fisherwoman, Mrs Barbara Flucker, opens oysters in this calotype portrait by D.O. Hill and R. Adamson in the 1840s.

The old fishertoun at Gardenstown, with its cottages gable on to the sea, lies to the west of the harbour.

visible in the way regular lanes led to the seafront but in others the buildings were set down at all angles to create among themselves little courts and open spaces. The visitor now enjoys this irregular planning with the buildings set about with such characteristic features as tarred wooden sheds with brightly painted doors and window frames, piles of creels and bits of nautical bric-à-brac.

As the fisher families looked to the sea for their living, gardens were generally tiny, if they existed at all; and in some of the later, planned villages it seems as if the space was deliberately divided into small plots, probably because it was reasoned that the tenants would have little inclination for cultivation and that as many feus as possible should be squeezed from the available space. This did not seem to matter to the fisher people: after all they had the boundless ocean on their doorsteps, sometimes literally, and at sea they were used to spending long periods in the cramped surroundings of their boats. In the herring boom of the nineteenth century, when a great deal of building went on, some improbable places were pressed into service as havens and settlements, leading James Bertram to observe in 1865 that it was 'curious to notice the little quarry-holes that on some parts of the Moray Firth serve as a refuge for boats'.[2] The siting of house and haven as close as possible was encouraged by the fact that fishermen had to carry bulky, heavy gear to and from the boats. Where the fishertouns were part of a larger settlement, as at Cullen, Nairn and Avoch, the intimate cheek-by-jowl character of the housing was nevertheless preserved and the fishertoun is easily recognised as distinct from the adjacent streets of the landsfolk. The haphazard layout of lanes and houses could make finding the way difficult for a stranger — part of Nairn's fishertoun was nicknamed the 'bagnet' because it was easy for a visitor to get lost and not find the way out.[3]

Not all the fishing settlements adhered to this traditional pattern. The planned towns built by the British Fisheries Society and other improvers followed the fashionable principles of their day where space allowed. Ullapool, the Pulteneytown area of Wick, and Lossiemouth, for example, have spacious streets laid out in a grid, although in most of them at least a faint echo of the older fishertoun can be sensed in odd corners where the local topography has encouraged a more characterful bit of town planning. In Thurso the modern council housing in the Fisherbiggins area maintains the irregular layout of the older fishertoun.

A unique fishing community was established in the village of Footdee, or Fittie as it is known locally, on the north side of the mouth of the Dee at Aberdeen; it was described by James Bertram:

> The square of houses ... are peculiarly constructed. There are neither
> doors nor windows in the outside walls ... and none lives within the
> square but the fishermen and their families, so that they are as
> completely isolated and secluded from public gaze as are a regiment
> of soldiers within the dead walls of a barrack ... the total population

Peter Anson's drawing of Pennan.

of the two squares was 584 — giving about nine inmates for each of
these two-roomed houses ... [some families occupied only one
room]. There are thirty-six married couples and nineteen widows in
the twenty-eight houses; and the number of distinct families in them
is fifty-four.

At that time, the 1860s, the Fittie fishermen were poorer and less enterprising than other fishermen, it seemed, and were working with old boats
not too far from shore. They were regarded as peculiar, dirty and backward
by other Aberdonians but the truth was otherwise, as visitors to the squares
found for themelves, and when a fisherman was lost at sea his dependants
were adopted into the families of his neighbours.

In the Hebrides, Orkney and Shetland and along the west coast, a few
planned villages such as Shieldaig were created as fishing communities but

here fishing was intimately woven into a pattern of life that drew from land as well as from sea. Fishertouns on the east-coast pattern never emerged, although towns and villages in the northern isles show some of the same features, especially Stromness, Scalloway and Lerwick's 'sooth end'. Fishing and crofting were activities spread across almost the entire community. On the west coast of the Highlands, fishing was combined with agriculture in the yearly round. For example, in the parish of Lochcarron, 'all the common tenants upon the shore towns are fishers. Every town [that is, crofting township] has two or three boats, or more ... They kill several kinds of fishes with the hand line ...'[4] Further south, in Applecross, where the fishing was for local needs, 'Each principal farmer hath generally a boat of his own; and among the lower class either two, three or four make a joint purchase'.[5]

The rhythms of life in the fishing communities were those of the annual migrations and appearances and disappearances of the fish shoals grafted on the shorter, more predictable changes of moon and tide. The weather was an unreliable dice-throw, a providential force that could keep or destroy the promise of the seasons. The nature of their calling imposed on the people in the fishertouns a distinct way of life. 'It is well known that scarce any but the children of fishermen follow the occupation of their fathers,' commented the minister of St Cyrus in describing the people of Milton, 'and that they are a distinct tribe, by their manners, and by inter-marrying only with each other'.[6] This separateness of the fishing communities persisted for a long time and still does in some significant ways. In the 1840s, the fisherfolk of Whitehills were 'a society quite distinct from the agricultural labourers residing in the same village, intermarrying almost exclusively among themselves, or occasionally with neighbouring seafaring communities. Hence they may be generally distinguished ... by their personal appearance, their complexion being clear, and their females possessing superior comeliness'.[7] Of the east coast fishertouns, the minister of Buckie could write: 'The intercourse of the fishertowns with the country is frequent and easy; nevertheless the difference in language and in manners is striking ... They go to sea as boys, become men at eighteen and marry soon after; for it is a maxim with them, apparently founded in truth, that no man can be a fisher and want a wife. They generally marry before 24 years at farthest; and always the daughters of fishers from 18 to 22 at most. The fisherwives lead a most laborious life ...'[8]

It was this 'laborious life' of the fisherwives that encouraged marrying only within the communities. No woman from outside would, or was even considered physically and psychologically able to cope with the stresses and the workload involved in the standard practice of line fishing – gathering bait, sheeling mussels, working with sharp hooks and trudging miles to sell her husband's catch day after day.

The practice of intermarriage within fishing families led to the people in the touns sharing a small stock of surnames. Certain names have been associated now with particular places for many generations: for example,

Burgon with Eyemouth; Patience with Avoch; MacLeman in various
spellings with Avoch and Fraserburgh; Coull and Tait with the Buchan area;
and Ralph and Bochel with Nairn. In the village of Downies, to the south
of Aberdeen, 236 of the 249 inhabitants in 1870 shared four surnames –
Wood, Main, Leiper and Knowles – and the other thirteen households were
not connected with the fishing.[9] 'The different divisions of Buckie are
inhabited by different clans,' observed Bertram, 'on the west side of the
river or burn there are none but Reids and Stewarts, while on the east side
we have only Cowies and Murrays.' Of the fifty-seven men listed in the
cashbook of the Nairn Fishermen's Society when it was founded in 1767,
thirty were called Main; and there were five Wilsons, five Jamesons, four
Barrons, four Ralphs and three Storms, with a few others represented by
one person.[10]

In Gardenstown in the early 1900s, Peter Anson listed 17 families called
Nicol, 19 Wisemans, 26 Wests and 68 Watts; in Banff 27 Woods; in
Portknockie, 20 Piries, 24 Slaters, 47 Woods and 89 Mairs; and so on.[11] In
this situation the use of by-names, nicknames or tee-names became a
necessity. It was common for men to be known by the name of their boat
but many more tee-names were more imaginative: Anson's list for Buckie in
the 1920s is probably typical: Bo, Bodger, Bosan, Bullan, Cockie, Codlin,
Con, Costie, Coup, Curly, Doddam, Doddle Diddle, Dosie, Dumpy, Fling,
Fosky, Kander, Latin, Miss, Pendy, Shakes, Stripie. The Newhaven people (or
'Bow-Tows') used tee-names but also came up with another solution to the
problem: married women continued to be known by their maiden name
and a man's name could be followed by his wife's surname.[12]

The origins of tee-names have usually been forgotten as they have been
passed down through generations and some have acquired a semi-official
status and can be used in addresses and on public occasions. But their use
needs the kind of knowledge acquired only by being born and brought up
in a place. Some names could be spoken in the owner's presence, others
most decidedly could not and in this social minefield the stranger was well
advised to use only baptismal names. A number of the fishermen I spoke to
told me their own tee-names and described how they have been passed
down through father and grandfather in some instances. In Ferryden,
Andrew Mearns told me how once a coastguard came down and asked for
a Mr Bogey, unaware that this was not his real name. 'Maybe he smoked
Bogey Roll, I don't know how he got it,' said Andrew. 'There was a skipper
who had a crew that was lazy, and he had a name for each of them, called
after fish – there was Whiting, Flukey, Ling, Lingie, I forget the rest.'

Some surnames are found over long stretches of coast – there are
Mains, Watts, Wests and Taits all around the north-east, evidence for the
coastwise migration of fisher people as different settlements were founded
and flourished. The origins of such names are not really known: some are
held to derive from Norse – Main from Magnus, Ralph from Hrolf. Legends

account for others: bearers of the rare surname of Storm in Nairn are descended from a baby boy who alone survived the wreck of a foreign vessel, drifted ashore in a box and was brought up by a fishing family.[13] A small boy was the sole survivor of a foreign vessel wrecked on Westray in the 1730s. The only clue to the ship's origin was a piece of wreckage with the name Arkh-Angell. The boy grew up as an Orcadian with the name of Archie Angel and for some generations there were people called Angel on Westray; a modern fishing boat bears the name *Arkh-Angell*.[14]

The distinctiveness of many of the fishertouns themselves gave rise to traditions of foreign origin, as in the case of Newhaven. It is held that the villagers are descended from Flemish craftsmen brought to the area by James IV to build his warship, the *Great Michael*, between 1507 and 1511.[15] None of

The fishertoun of Cellardyke, Fife. A rough sea coming right up the beach in front of the village.

the Newhaven fisher names directly supports this idea. These are nearly all of Lowland origin and the only one with a possible Flemish provenance, Flucker, is recorded in Fife as early as 1275.[16] However, surnames changed easily in the past and there may be some substance to the tradition. In the *Old Statistical Account*, the author of the Buckhaven entry recorded the local belief that the original inhabitants had come from a Dutch ship stranded on the coast in the reign of Philip II (1556-98): 'By degrees they acquired our language and adopted our dress, and for these threescore years past, they have had the character of a sober and sensible, an industrious and honest set of people,' he wrote, and went on to note their particular custom whereby brides 'of good condition and character' wore an ornamental girdle or belt at their weddings and passed it down to other brides as a mark of esteem.[20] Rosehearty is held to have been founded in the fourteenth century by a party of Danes.[17]

A number of stories used to circulate on the Black Isle to explain why the fisher people of Avoch spoke so differently from their neighbours: these included the coming of 'foreigners' from England in the Middle Ages, the people being descendants of Cromwell's troops stationed in Inverness in the seventeenth century, or of Norse settlers, or of wrecked Breton fishermen.[18] The Avoch form of Scots fits neatly into a spectrum of dialects found from Caithness to Buchan and, although some 'foreign' genes may be present, it is far more likely that the original fishers who settled here, as a Scots-speaking enclave in a predominantly Gaelic region, came from somewhere east along the Moray Firth. There were Patiences in Avoch in the early 1700s – a George Patience, son of William Patience, was christened there in 1727[19] – and Lewis Patience thinks his surname may have a French origin.

The distinctiveness of the fisher people sometimes led to them being looked down on by their neighbours. Golspie's fishertoun was marked by the use of Gaelic and the smell of smoked fish clinging to the inhabitants' clothing; in turn, the fishers called their non-maritime neighbours *tuath*, meaning 'peasantry' or 'tenantry', a subtle reference to the fact that the fishers enjoyed a freedom that had eluded their self-proclaimed betters – the sea's harvest enabled the thrifty fisher people to put away enough money to buy their homes when the other villagers remained tenants of the ducal estate of Sutherland.[20] The hardy independence shown by the fisher people appears to have irked some of their supposed social superiors. In his description of Cullen in 1842, the Revd George Henderson wrote with what may be slightly grudging approval:

> In consequence of the fluctuations to which his calling is liable, it is impossible to calculate precisely a fisherman's annual gains, but … there are comparatively few of the working classes in Scotland whose labours are so amply remunerated as those of the fishermen on this coast … The almost invariable habit which prevails, of intermarrying with those of their own craft, and the no less general practice which obtains, of every fisherman's son following his father's occupation, prove very serious drawbacks to the progress of this order of the community in the march of improvement; having the effect of rendering them a distinct class of society, with sentiments, sympathies and habits peculiar to themselves.[21]

A fishertoun in every parish

Alexander Hepburn observed in 1721 that there were one or two fishertouns in every coastal parish in Buchan.[22] Some of the villages were in existence before 1500, as James Coull describes in *The Sea Fisheries of Scotland*, but, at various times, plans were hatched, sometimes as the initiative of a laird, at other times as government policy, to develop fisheries and these often included encouraging the coastwise migration of fisher people. In 1677 Portknockie was founded by men from Cullen; a woman called Kattie [sic] Slater, who died in about 1770 at the age of ninety-six, could recall how her father had built the first house in the village and how she had been brought to it as an infant from Cullen rocked in a fishing scull instead of a cradle.[23] In 1716, Thomas Ord created Findochty by settling it with thirteen fishermen and four boys from Fraserburgh and, in 1727, Findhorn men moved to Portessie.[24] At the end of the seventeenth century, there was only one fishing boat in Avoch but by the 1790s an entire seatown, home to 'ninety-three families', presumably mostly fishers, had grown up, the families moving in from other parts of the Moray Firth coast.[25] Macduff grew from a small place in 1732 with only a few fisher houses to a large village of 1000 people by 1790, with well-laid-out streets and a harbour on which the laird, Lord Fife, had already spent £5000.[26] In the parish of Lonmay, Mr Gordon of Buthlaw built a fishing toun in the late 1700s of twenty tiled houses in two rows.[27] Eight fishermen in Elie were granted rent-free houses on the condition that they supply the town with fish at least three times a week.[28]

The Duke of Argyll brought a number of families from Shetland and northern Scotland to the Ross of Mull in the mid-1700s to teach his tenants the curing of herring.[29] The fisher people at Stotfield, the forerunner of the Lossiemouth community, came originally from Findhorn and, after the disaster in 1806 when many fishermen were lost, eight families came from the east, from the Buckie area, to regenerate the fishing, among them Campbells, Gardens and Thomsons.[30] Coull was a prominent surname in Ferryden and said to originate from the Moray Firth coast.[31] Emigration of Scots-speaking families from the south-west to south Kintyre was encouraged during the seventeenth and eighteenth centuries – one result was the erosion of Gaelic and another was the creation of a fishing community of mixed Highland-Lowland blood, particularly in the 'new' towns of Campbeltown, Tarbert, Inveraray and Ardrishaig. People also emigrated from Northern Ireland to Kintyre to join in the fishing, and another migration route lay between Carradale and Skye, whence men regularly came to Carradale to work at the driftnetting during most of the nineteenth century.[32] Madge Mitchell told me she could not be sure where her people in Portmahomack came from but she thought they moved round the coast and settled there: 'My mother's people were called Mitchell. Rockfield was mostly all Mitchells. We were related to the Skinners in Balintore. My grandparents spoke Gaelic but they were the last generation that did.'

In some localities fisheries declined in the late eighteenth century: one such place was Johnshaven, from where families moved to Montrose.[33] Harrassment by press gangs was one cause put forward for decline; fishing communities were obvious targets for recruitment into the Royal Navy. Newhaven supplied many men in the seventeenth century but the press gangs forcibly taking men to serve in the defence of the realm became more active along the Scottish east coast in the latter 1700s, especially after a naval base was established at Leith. Although many had protection from naval service, fishermen were a natural source of skilled manpower for the fleets fighting Napoleon. The press gangs operated as far north as Shetland where the passing whaling and trading fleets also offered a supply of prime seamen. Not all the decline in some fishing villages could be ascribed to this source, however, and the minister of Nairn complained that the number of boats in the town had decreased by the 1790s because younger fishermen had been encouraged to flit elsewhere.[34] At the beginning of the eighteenth century there were reputed to have been three fishing villages in the East Lothian parish of Whitekirk and Tyninghame but these were gone by 1790.[35] Inverbervie had no fishermen in 1793, a state of affairs existing since 'beyond the memory of man' although lines, hooks and shells dug up in the town indicated that this had not always been the case; and the minister thought that the fishermen had flitted to Gourdon in some past time.[36] In Gourdon itself the number of fishermen had fallen considerably in the latter half of the eighteenth century.[37] Rarely could a fishing settlement disappear in more dramatic fashion: the original village at Findhorn was drowned in the course of the single tide that created much of the present Burghead Bay in 1701.[38]

In 1705, two fishermen called Cargill left the village of Auchmithie and, with the encouragement of the Arbroath magistrates, moved into that town where a new harbour had been built. The Earl of Northesk, however, did not want 'his' fishermen to move from his estate and sought redress in the courts. The Edinburgh court upheld his claim that the fishermen were his serfs and they had to move back to Auchmithie. The Act used by the Earl to reclaim 'his' fishermen was repealed in 1799 and in the decades thereafter the Auchmithie folk were able to move to the town, where the Council offered them land to settle in the area now called the 'fit o' the toon'.[39]

In his study of the fishing villages of the Knuckle, the extreme corner of the north-east from Fraserburgh round to the mouth of the river Ythan, David Summers has described how a number of fishing settlements were born, flourished for a time and then died as circumstances changed. The village of Rattray disappeared when the tidal area that allowed access for the boats became buried under sand dunes but, in 1721, not long before it ceased to exist, it was described as famous for cod. The village of Boatlea was home to eleven families in 1696 but by the mid-1700s the people were moving to Drumlinie and the foundation of St Combs in 1785 encouraged more to move; by 1803 or shortly afterwards, they were all gone. Botany was set up in 1795, the name an ironic comparison between the living conditions in this unpromising spot and the new penal settlement in Australia, but by the mid-1800s the folk had moved, mainly to the new village of Burnhaven. Buchanhaven became absorbed into the growing Peterhead. Fishers also moved from Burnhaven, chiefly to Peterhead, towards the end of the eighteenth century. There was migration from the villages of Old Castle and Collieston, in 1696 the largest fishing settlement on this stretch of coast, to Torry in about 1900. This fate was not shared by all the north-east villages; Cairnbulg and Inverallochy both existed in the sixteenth century and continue to be the homes of fishermen to this day. St Combs, founded as a planned village by Charles Gordon of Cairness in 1785, and its immediate neighbour Charlestown, founded just after 1800 when some people moved there from Boatlea, likewise have survived. Whinnyfold, one of the country's clifftop fishing villages, exists still, as does Boddam, though its glory as a fishing settlement has passed and its small harbour, the most easterly in Scotland in the lee of Buchanness, had only creel boats on my last visit.

The exploitation of the sea was of particular importance in the economy of the folk that inhabited the smaller islands around the coast. Some of these islands are now empty of people but the communities on others have shown great resource in adapting to modern fishing methods to provide themselves with a way of life that is often perceived by outsiders as very desirable. Westray in Orkney is home to a number of modern boats, as are Whalsay and the Out Skerries in Shetland. In the Hebrides, the inhospitable lump of Scalpay, where the Ice Ages scraped away most of the soil, was settled in the 1840s after people were cleared from Pabbay, Uist and Harris by the landowner. The hapless settlers had nothing to turn to but the sea and, after some initial help, a Scalpay man began curing herring in 1856. By the end of the century the island had nine curing stations and the Scalpachs had become adept fishermen, as they remain to this day.[40] Fishermen from Eriskay likewise used the sea to support their communities. Moving people from the land to the coast, where it was planned they would make a living from fishing, was an integral part of the policies of some landlords during the Highland Clearances, which took place mainly in the first decades of the nineteenth century. In a few places, such as Golspie and Helmsdale, the policy had some success but in many others the people, often without any previous experience of the sea, did not fare well. Stroma was famous for the skill of its fishermen and for the type of yole they built to use in the turbulent currents of the Pentland Firth but the island has had no permanent population since 1964. Foula fishermen took part last century in the Shetland *haaf* fishery but there, and on another famous island, St Kilda, lack of a good harbour prevented the development of anything grander than local fishing for subsistence, although the people there, as in many northern islands, ate seabirds and their eggs in their diet.

Yellow butterflies

Fishing was always a dangerous occupation. The work was arduous and uncomfortable and yet a number of factors operated to ensure that it never lacked for willing labourers. Sons generally followed fathers to the sea, obeying the rule that occupations passed from generation to generation; when the opportunities for formal education were limited, the apprenticeship of the fishing was a substitute, but even now in fishing communities the call of the sea is heard in each generation – 'salt in the blood,' as the saying goes. The sea can also satisfy, as few other callings can, the keen seeking of adventure that young men display, and there is also a pride in being a member of a crew where every man counts, where dangers and good fortune are equally shared. The threat of the sea also draws people together; Gordon Fraser put it as 'They live with danger, they're waiting for it to happen all the time'. Gordon recalled for me an incident from his time at sea when their boat was stormbound in Stromness by a northerly gale that was strong enough to force men to crawl along the pier, and hearing over the radio maydays from boats still at sea and being unable to do anything to help – 'It was one of the saddest things, but that's the way it goes.'

The men at sea were half of the fishing community. The other half, the women, shared the hardships and the success. In the seasons when the men were away for long periods, the women had to take responsibility for running the home and bringing up the family and, when disaster struck, the women bore the grief and struggled on to provide for the family, as the words of the north-east song 'The Bonnie Fisher Lass' have it:

> When faither's oot upon the sea
> We're oot upon the pier,
> For we maun dread in terror
> And we maun dread in fear,
> Lest he should meet a watery grave
> And be taken frae oor grasp,
> And we'd wander broken-herted,
> Said the bonnie fisher lass.

In Torry, it was not uncommon for fishermen to be away from home for most of the year and in their absence the wives kept the families running. 'In any three-week period,' said George Wood, 'my father would be at home at the most only three nights.' Before the Second World War, the men did not take holidays, apart from a break over Christmas and New Year, and they stayed ashore only if they were ill. Although some trawlers and liners had radios, they seemed to have used them to call home only during 'something really serious' and often a family member could fall sick and recover without the father's knowledge. 'My grandfather was at Rockall in 1929 when my father's sister took ill and died,' said George, 'and he didn't know until he came home, as there was no radio on the boat. That put a strain on folk but a lot of them had their kin nearhand. It was a lot easier if you came from a fishing family. A toonser [the Torry expression for people from other parts of Aberdeen] who married into a fishing community was like a fish out of water.'

The women were of direct, practical help, part of a family team. The line fishermen who operated from home on a daily basis could not have fished without the back-up of their wives and children who collected and prepared bait, sorted and cleaned the lines, baited the hooks and, in places where harbours did not exist, carried their men to and from the boats so that they could at least start their working day dry. In the fishertouns where white fish were the main catch, they also took on the vital job of marketing. In the past, the fishwife with her creel kept most of the rural communities and small towns in eastern Scotland supplied with fresh food (in the south-west, Ayrshire and Fife male hawkers with carts did the job of selling from door to door), and today vans from some of the north-east villages travel throughout the Highlands on the same errand. In Golspie, as elsewhere, the women of the fishertoun divided the countryside so that each had a district as her patch. Donald MacDonald's grandmother sold in the east end of Golspie village, a Mrs Sutherland took the train to Bonar Bridge, and other women went up to Rogart and Lairg. Fish were usually sold for cash but some could be bartered for eggs or a hen. This pattern of selling continued until quite recently in a few instances but was generally replaced in the nineteenth century by the consigning of fish by train to the larger southern markets in, for example, Glasgow.

In the 1790s, the women of Fisherrow, near Musselburgh, were noted for carrying all manner of goods to Edinburgh but among them the fishwives formed a distinct group, numbering ninety in the list of incorporated trades:

A Fisherrow fisherwoman in traditional costume.

> The fish-wifes, as they are all of one class and educated in it from their infancy, are of a character and manners still more singular than [the other women carriers] and particularly distinguished by the laborious lives they lead. They are the wives and daughters of fishermen, who … four days in the week … carry fish in creels to Edinburgh … when the boats come in late to the harbour in the forenoon, so as to leave them no more than time to reach Edinburgh before dinner, it is not unusual for them to perform their journey of five miles, by relays, three of them being employed in carrying one basket, and shifting it from one to another every hundred yards, by which means they have been known to arrive at the Fishmarket in less than three-quarters of an hour.[41]

A footnote in the *Old Statistical Account* states that three of the women carried 200 lb of herring each in five hours over the 27 miles between Dunbar and Edinburgh. It became the custom for some Fife boats to land their catches at Fisherrow and sell them to the fishwives there rather than sail on to Leith, as this allowed the Fife men time to get home again on the same day. The 'peculiar' manners of the Fisherrow women included their fondness for golf and, on Shrove Tuesday, the married women played the unmarried women at football. 'It is remarkable', wrote the minister, 'that though a considerable degree of licentiousness appears in their freedom of speech, it does not seem to have tainted their morals … there being no class of women, it is believed, who offends less against the seventh commandment, excepting in words, than they do.'

Something of the confidence and competence of the women can be sensed in the photographs taken by David Octavius Hill and Robert Adamson in the 1840s in Newhaven. They pose with proud, calm faces for the camera in their distinctive striped skirts, dark capes and headscarves, wearing white stockings and shoes like slippers, and displaying the creels of their trade. The women of Newhaven had particularly colourful costumes of white flannel skirts with red stripes under an outer petticoat with yellow stripes on the inside; the sides of the petticoat were turned up to show the stripes and this striking design, topped off with elaborately patterned shawls and blouses, earned them the nickname of 'yellow butterflies'. The

Lossiemouth fisherwomen in about 1900.

costumes were based on the working clothes of the late 1700s and were sometimes handed down through generations, with the most colourful rigs being reserved for gala occasions and worn, for example, by the women in the Fisherlassies' Choir and the Fisherwomen's Choir. The romantic appeal of the Newhaven community for painters and photographers was captured in Charles Reade's novel *Christie Johnstone* (1853).

The Newhaven and Fisherrow women worked in groups of five or six to buy a box of fish at the quay and then divide it amongst themselves, asking a neutral passer-by to use the women's individual tokens, which could be a button or a thimble, to mark the divisions, in a manner used elsewhere by the fishermen themselves to share out a catch; this process was called kyling. Then each woman with her chosen share would load her creel and set off, the laden creel and smaller basket called a scull, perhaps in total one hundredweight of wet fish, on her back, the weight taken on the forehead with a headband. Bertram thought most of them possessed a strength 'with which no prudent man would venture to come into conflict'; through having to bargain with their customers they were 'rough and ready in speech' but 'honest, outspoken, good-hearted'. They were tough but the carrying of heavy loads exacted its toll in back and neck problems in later life.

In the north-east the fishwives from different villages had distinctive patterns for their plaids: red and black dice in Inverallochy and Cairnbulg, blue and black in St Combs, black and white in Broadsea, grey and white in Pitulie and, in Rosehearty, what Christian Watt described as 'natural and brown'. Christian Watt was born in the village of Broadsea beside Fraserburgh in 1833 into a fishing family. In later life, she recorded much of her experience in what is now known as *The Christian Watt Papers*. 'I hated the small lines,' she wrote, 'for this meant so much more work for the adults, sheeling the mussels, baiting the lines and wupping on tippings. My parents' day began at three in the morning and often ended at midnight; as my brothers grew up they had to do a lot of the work. I have seen both of my parents fall down with exhaustion at the end of the day, after my father had come in from the sea.' Her mother had a fish round in some of the country villages inland from Broadsea, in what they called the 'near country', and Christian took over some of the round when she was nine years old. In August each year many of the fishwives of the north-east went up to 'the far country', the glens of the Grampian mountains, to sell the white fish caught and cured during the summer; with their bairns, they stayed in barns cleaned up for their arrival. The Watts went to the upper reaches of the Dee: 'My mother, my two youngest brothers and I always went to the barn at Corrybeg ... We paid a small rent for the barn where we slept, and our food was cooked on a fire outside. We had a lot of orders to deliver on our way out ... We stayed two weeks till all our cure was sold. McGrigor, the horse hirer at Strichen, took about ten tons of fish inland for us.' Here, near Crathie, Christian and her companions in their fisher clothes met the Queen and the Prince Consort one day – Christian thought Albert was pleasant but Victoria 'looked so sour you could have hung a jug on her mouth'. The fisher women were soon to be forbidden free access to the glens to sell their fish, as it was judged their walking through the hills would disturb the deer stalking. The encounter with Prince Albert led to a group of fisher people, including Christian's parents, being invited to the Great Exhibition at Crystal Palace in 1851 where they put on a display of net-mending, mussel-sheeling and line-baiting for the metropolitan public. In a similar way, Newhaven women took part in the Fisheries Exhibition in London in 1881 and the Boulogne Fisheries Exhibition in 1923.

The coming of the railways had a major impact on their lives, for the

Newhaven fishwives were now able to travel to all the inland towns to sell fresh fish, so much so that Bertram thought many towns 'better supplied with fish than the villages where they are caught'. The Arbroath fishwives with their 'rip' of smokies, weighing up to 60 lb, and a 'bow' of other fish, could take the train to Dundee, Forfar or Perth.[42] Throughout the latter half of the nineteenth century, as the selling of fish wholesale by auction and the rapid transport of produce to large urban markets developed, the fishwife hawking with her creel became more and more a picturesque memory. Many of the women opened fishmonger shops or stalls in retail markets. A

Selling seafood at the back of the Caird Hall, Dundee.

few kept up the old practice well into recent times: a friend who grew up in Trinity near Newhaven in the 1930s remembers a fishwife coming to the door and filleting the fish for the customer on the doorstep with a knife and board she carried specially for the purpose; and in fact the last Newhaven fishwife, Esther Linton, did not lay up her creel until 1974 at the age of seventy-eight; she died in 1989 at the age of ninety-three.[43]

Women also played a vital part in the great herring fisheries. Their capacity for long hours of hard work and their nimble fingers made them ideal gutters and during the herring season armies of women followed the fishing fleet to the Western Isles, to Shetland, Wick, the north-east, and the ports in eastern England – but their story properly belongs to a later chapter.

It is small wonder that fishing communities evolved customs and practices that marked them out distinctly from other sections of society. The sea imprinted itself on the people in a way that transcended national boundaries. Bertram observed in 1865 that the fisher-folk in northern France showed remarkable similarities to those in Scotland: 'Wherever I went I found the fisher-folk to be the same, no matter whether they talked a French patois or a Scottish dialect … The manners, customs, mode of life, and even the dress and superstitions, are nearly the same on the coast of France as they are on the coast of Fife.' Peter Anson also wrote in the 1930s of the fishermen of Brittany, England and Scotland as being similar in many ways.[44] George Christie told me how his grandfather had been on one of the Aberdeen trawlers sunk by a U-boat off Shetland in the First World War; the U-boat skipper let the fishermen escape in their lifeboats before putting the trawlers to the bottom, saying that his own people were fishermen in Cuxhaven and he didn't make war on such men.

Fishermen could be easily recognised by their modes of dress. The importance of warm, weatherproof clothing at sea should need no emphasis but ashore the fishermen also affected their own fashions. The hazard of hypothermia from wet clothes and exposure to the wind gave rise in many places with no proper harbours to the custom of the womenfolk, their skirts tucked up around their thighs, carrying their men to the boats through the surf so that, at least at the start, the men would be dry. The Hill/Adamson calotype photographs of Newhaven fishermen in the 1840s show the shore-going rig – waistcoats and short jackets, with white trousers, shoes and a variety of hats, glistening and almost certainly tarred. At sea, the men wore garments treated in various ways to make them waterproof. Before the advent of oilskins, fabric might be coated with linseed oil or an oak bark mixture – in Newhaven such clothes were called 'barkit'. Thigh boots made from leather were almost universal. The leather was frequently treated to keep it supple and waterproof. In Argyll crofting communities, as elsewhere, cod livers were melted down for this purpose. Sometimes this was mixed with lard, polish or a little tar. Flannel under-garments, waistcoats, thick jerseys or ganseys, thick blue trousers and heavy jackets were worn. Scarfs kept water from going down the neck. Hats varied

– wide-brimmed 'minister's' hats, cheese-cutters, bonnets – and sou'westers were put on in bad weather. Sea-going wear often had no buttons where lines could easily catch in them. Rubber boots made their appearance in the 1930s and by this time oilskin smocks, usually bright yellow in colour, were also common. Even in the 1950s, fishermen ashore could be recognised from their clothes. Fashions varied from place to place but generally for formal wear they favoured dark-blue, double-breasted suits and flat bonnets. The serge trousers usually had a generous cut. Many older fishermen considered themselves to be properly dressed in their jerseys or ganseys. Writing of the 1920s, Peter Anson said that a fisherman's

Wick skipper Donald Wares in dress gansey and shore-going bowler hat in the 1880s.

home district could be told from the style of his gansey. Fisherwives trudging around the countryside with creels of fish were often noted to be knitting as they walked, and the ganseys were the product. Again fashions varied from place to place but they often had shortish sleeves without cuffs, high tight collars, a row of two buttons at the side of the neck, and series of patterns in the stitching. Flag, chevron, zigzag, cable, double cable, moss and rope were some of the names for these and there is truth in the old saying that a drowned man could sometimes be identified by his gansey.

Cauld iron

Some fishing communities marked rites of passage with particular customs. Initiation ceremonies among the men seem to have been rare – perhaps being seasick and cold was considered initiation enough – but one has been recorded. As Anson, taking his information from *An Old-Time Fishing Town: Eyemouth* by D. McIver, describes it, it has echoes of freemasonry:

> The boat's crew assembled in one of the many public houses. The boy was placed with his back against the wall. Immediately above him hung a rope with a noose from a block and tackle. The rope was passed round the lad's neck. Close to him was a salted roll and a jug of beer. He was ordered to eat the roll. If he hesitated, one of the men tightened the noose by pulling the rope. As the boy tried to eat the salt roll, the skipper threw beer over his face. Another man sprinkled his legs, while two more repeated the words 'weather' and 'lea'.

The ceremony, after which the boys were treated as grown-up men, was accompanied by the singing of verses such as:

> From St Abb's Head tae Flambrough Head,
> Whan'er ye cut, be sure ye bend,
> Na'er lea a man wi' a loose end.

There were also many customs observed in relation to weddings. In the nineteenth century it was common for many marriages to take place at the end of the herring fishing, and several weddings might take place on the same night. These were 'penny weddings', at which each guest chipped in some money to pay for the food and drink. Weddings usually took place on a Friday, an exception to this day being held as unlucky, so that the revellers could have Saturday and Sunday to recover before venturing to sea once more. Bertram described the nuptial celebrations in Newhaven:

> All the delicacies which can be thought of are procured: fish, flesh and fowl; porter, ale and whisky ... not forgetting the universal dish of skate, which is produced at all fisher marriages. After dinner comes the collection, when the best man, or some one of the company, goes round and gets a shilling or sixpence from each ... all are welcome who like to attend, the bidding being general. The evening winds up, so far as the young folks are concerned, with unlimited dancing.

Weddings at Collieston were graced by the dancing of the lang reel, usually on the links at the end of the sands of Forvie, in which all the guests took part. Many of the fishing communities still hold special gala days in the

summer with the crowning of gala or herring queens and processions. The
Fishermen's Walk in Musselburgh is a noted event.

A large repertoire of taboos and superstitions were observed in the fishing communities, and the phenomenon figures in many books. Some beliefs were local, many were common to all European seafarers. The fisher people's world was riven with uncertainty. No wife or mother could be sure that they would see their men again after they left the house each day. No fisherman could be certain he would make it back to a safe haven, just as no man could be sure when he shot a net whether it would come up empty or bulging with fish. In probably no other peacetime occupation or social group was there this level of what you could call luck or Providence and many customs were geared towards tempering the risks, producing a range of beliefs, practices and super-stitions that formed a kind of cement in the mindset of the fisher community. Many of the superstitions are no longer observed but older fishermen can recall some of them being practised until quite recently.

Some animals and their common names were taboo, in particular the pig, the rabbit, the hare, less commonly the swan, and the salmon. These were referred to, if they were mentioned at all, by other names, such as 'himsel' for the pig, 'red fish' for salmon and 'langlugs' for the hare, and inadvertent use of the wrong word would provoke the response 'cauld iron' and the touching of the nearest piece of ferrous metal. Martin Martin noted in the 1690s several words that Hebridean seafarers were careful never to use.[45] Shetland fishermen preserved many old Norse words in their own sea language.[46] When Donald MacDonald, still a young lad, produced as his 'piece' a cold rabbit leg, one of the crewmen 'almost had a heart attack'. Boats were never turned anti-clockwise, against the sun, and many skippers took particular care to observe this.

Many of these superstitions can be traced back to belief in witchcraft and a collective term for them in Scots – 'freets' – is derived from the word 'fruit', meaning the good essence in an object that could be stolen by a witch or evil spirit. What is interesting is that these superstitions which were once probably much more prevalent in society at large survived longer in the fishing communities. Alfred Mackay who fished out of Wick on herring drifters in the 1930s told me how, on a night when the catch was poor, he saw men make an effigy of a human, hang it over the stern and burn it, a procedure called 'burning the witch' and still being practised to some extent in the 1940s. There are many records of effigy burning from other parts of Scotland. Another custom Alfred witnessed was to coat pennies with bright metallic paint and throw them over the side, saying 'If we canna catch ye, we'll buy ye.'

The superstition concerning the salmon may have its origins in ancient Celtic beliefs but it may have been reinforced by the legal constraints surrounding the right to catch this fish in inshore waters, it often being the sole prerogative of the laird, and the risk of being accused of poaching. Other taboos covered women and ministers. Certain women brought bad luck and men would avoid them on their way to sea, surely another echo of witchcraft. The taboo against ministers is also probably linked to the spirit world, although some fishermen would maintain that sufficient explanation lies in the fact that, when a fisherman was lost, it was the minister who usually broke the sad news to the relatives. It is a curious superstition, in that many of the fishermen were particularly religious in the past and regularly attended divine service. Some beliefs were associated with numbers but this was not confined to fishermen. In Orkney a young fisherman pointed out to me that many of the islanders like to choose registration numbers for their boats with digits that add up to thirteen.

In Lewis, Murdo Maclennan told me some stories from his own experience:

> They [the Lewis fishermen] wouldn't name a rabbit at all, they called them 'these four-legged creatures'. Some folk, if they met a certain woman on their way to the boat, would turn back. I never believed in these things. I think some of the women here, when the time came for the boats to go to sea, would leave their crofts and go inside so the men wouldn't be meeting them. I remember getting a salmon, a good three or four pounder, in the herring net. Boy, did we enjoy it. Some of the older hands said, 'That's your fishing gone.' But we had the salmon for our tea and that night had one of the best landings we ever got.
>
> If they saw a minister on the pier, that was deadly. It was fatal to see a minister on the pier. I mind one of the east coast boys telling me – they were fishing in Barra. The skipper had told the cook to get a paper, a daily paper, when the mailboat came in. The cook dozed off and he forgot about the paper. But anyway he woke up and when he looked up the shop had closed and the mailboat had gone, and he went up to the pier and, who was standing there, but the priest who was down for a walk. They started talking and the cook said that he was too late to get a paper. The priest put his hand in his pocket and said, 'There's a paper for you, don't worry.' When the boat was going to sea, the skipper asked for his paper. The cook handed it over and said he had got it from the priest on the pier. The skipper nearly jumped overboard. Anyway, they carried on to the fishing grounds and what a night – there was a mixture of small herring and big herring, and the nets were full up, and the skipper told the cook on the following day to get away to the pier and when you see that priest tell him that you want a paper and that when he prays tonight he should say to the fellow up above to keep out the small ones.
>
> I knew a fellow in Stornoway who hated ministers coming round. An old minister we knew well used to come to our boat quite often to get a few herring, and this fellow said, 'That's deadly, anyway.' One day we weren't aboard but this fellow was – and the minister asked for a few herring, and he had to go to meet the minister and give him a few herring. When we came back, he said 'Oh, that

minister was down. He's a nice man, he was talking to me and he wished us well.' That night we got stuck into a good shoal and after that this fellow was the first on the pier looking for the minister.'

In Caithness, Dodie Gunn remembered that his father, if he saw a certain woman when he was going to the sea, would turn back. 'Another fellow, he was a teacher but he was the most superstitious man you ever saw in your life,' said Dodie. 'He swore every old woman turned into a hare. That was the worst thing a fisherman could ever cross.' William Mitchell in Inverness recalled for me how when he went fishing with some of his relatives out of Portmahomack as a boy he was quite sharply reminded not to whistle. It was common to play tricks on superstitious men: one day a man I knew dropped a dead rabbit into the sea right where he knew the seine net being towed in the vicinity would catch it; and when the skipper of the seiner hauled and saw the rabbit, he steered for home as fast as he could go. Many fishermen made jokes about the taboos: it was customary on one Wick boat to have ham and eggs every morning and the skipper out of mischief would ask aloud, 'I wonder how many hundredweight of himsel we've eaten now.'

For all the joking, the concept of luck seems to have had a real place in the fishermen's way of thinking. There are many instances of one boat filling her hold while another nearby remained empty. No doubt the idea of luck made some sense of the inexplicable and unexpected. It may have served another purpose: as the records of successful fishermen show, there were men who were very skilled at the job and regularly caught more than their fellows; in a close-knit community, it may have been better to ascribe success to luck rather than impugn a less successful neighbour's skill. George Leiper gave an interesting reply when I asked him if he had enjoyed his time at sea – 'Yes, I did, for a simple reason – that I was reasonably lucky.' He went on to tell me the following story about a fellow skipper who worked great lines in the North Atlantic:

> We came up to one piece of ground, a small piece of ground. He knew where it was because he'd been there with me before. I asked him how he was getting on. 'Oh not very well at all,' he said. He'd been long away at sea so he asked me to give him some cigarettes and sugar. I says to him, 'Are you going to shoot your gear tomorrow?' 'Oh,' he says, 'I don't know.' 'Well,' I says, 'You were here first, it's your choice.' He decided to shoot [the lines] in one direction and I went off to shoot on the other side of the ground. At the end of the day, we'd double the amount of fish he had. So, next day, I said we should change places. And what do you think happened? It's luck, I can't think of anything else. When I asked him on the phone how he was getting on, I thought I couldn't tell him what we had. Eventually he just packed up and went away home. When you get a run of bad luck like that, there's just nothing you can do that's right. I felt sorry for him.

The decoration on the bow of the *Hope* (BCK 59) photographed in Buckie, with a reference to the New Testament.

A sense of religion was also very strong in most of the old communities and the Scottish fisher people held steadfastly to their faith. The nineteenth century was generally a time of strong religion – the break from the Church of Scotland to form the Free Church in 1843 affected all sections of society – but the fisher people were often particularly noted for their observance of the Sabbath and attendance at worship. Around the coast, the Sabbath was generally looked on as a day of rest for fish as well as men and no fishing was carried out, although there were exceptions to this: Aberdeen during the herring boom in the late 1870s had no scruples about landing and handling catches on a Sunday,[47] and Sunday fishing also occurred in Kintyre and the south-west.[48] A great wave of religious fervour passed through the fishing towns in 1859-60. This Revival, as it was termed, began in America and reached Scotland via Northern Ireland. James Turner, a Peterhead cooper, was a prominent preacher in this outburst of evangelical zeal and claimed to have converted over eight thousand people in the north-east .[49] Some groups of worshippers remain to this day from this time, forming local congregations of Brethren. There was another Revival in 1921, when evangelical meetings packed halls around the Moray Firth.[50] The Salvation Army became a respected, prominent institution in many fishing towns, along with the more specifically directed Royal National Mission to Deep-Sea Fishermen, founded in 1881.

For a long time the church in each parish had exacted from local fishermen a tithe or teind of one-tenth of their catch. By the nineteenth century this practice had been almost universally abandoned – almost, because in Eyemouth in the mid-1800s a dispute flared up over this very issue. The Eyemouth fishermen were doing very well at this time – in 1840 their annual catch was valued at £40,000 and a new minister in the parish, backed by his presbytery, asked for the church's share. The fishermen refused. Led by Willie Spears, known as 'Kingfisher', they signed a covenant and burned effigies of the minister and the laird. Troops were sent to the town to prevent rioting. In a dawn raid in 1861, police tried to arrest Spears but fishwives saw them in time and, after a four-hour battle with bricks and cobbles, the police withdrew.

To prevent bloodshed, Spears gave himself up and spent some weeks in jail
before contributions to his defence fund from fishing communities as far away
as Cornwall gathered to pay off his fine and tithe arrears. The dispute was
eventually settled by payment of £2000 to extinguish the tithe.[51]

The herring fishing in the early years of the nineteenth century was
marked by a considerable consumption of whisky – a bottle each day was
part of the contract between some skippers and curers – and it is perhaps
not surprising that an abstinence movement became bound up with
religion as the century went on. Many fisher communities had their
societies to fight the 'demon' drink. The Nairn Seamen's Total Abstinence
Society was formed in 1879 and until 1912 organised a march through the
town at New Year, the time when it was judged most drink was consumed.

The religious tradition, revitalised by the Revivals, still continues. It
coloured my childhood and was a major influence in the lives of most of the
older fishermen I have known. Frank Bruce also remembers his people in the
north-east as being very religious: 'Every Christmas or New Year we had a
concert in the village and we also had a temperance walk – it still goes on but
it's not called that now. Anyway, there was this concert and it was always
sacred songs they sang until after the War, the first one would have been in
1946, it wasn't sacred songs, it was Scottish songs that the choir sang. That
was the first time they varied from sacred songs. I've seen maybe a bit of
poetry being composed but it was religious poetry. They frowned on anything
that wasn't religious. On a Sunday we wouldn't be able to read comics. Folk
songs were dangerous. I remember saying to my father that Rabbie Burns was
a great man and he would say, "Oh, I don't know about that." We were Free
Kirk. There were other sects as well. The Baptist Church is strong. We were
brought up in that tradition and it has an effect on you, not necessarily a
negative one. It definitely has its positive side. Society needs a policeman –
without it you have chaos. I can remember on a Sunday in the village it was
dead quiet – the whole village was at peace. You'll never get that today.'

In October 1938, the Scottish women at the herring gutting in Lowestoft
went on strike and refused to handle fish caught by boats that had gone to
sea on Sunday, about 800 of them staying off work for two days.[52] English
fishermen, as they put to sea on a Sunday afternoon, would sometimes taunt
their Scots colleagues with cries of 'What's wrong, Scottie? Not goin' out
today?' but this did nothing to break the rigid observance of the Sabbath.[53]
It was not that all the Scottish fishermen were paragons but they were by and
large an upright lot and keen on their own ways. Their honesty in their
dealings with each other was hardly ever questioned.

The fishing crews used a range of methods to ensure a fair division of
the catch. In Golspie, for example, there were two ways of doing this. In the
first, the crew, usually four men, would make four equal piles of their catch,
turn their backs and ask a neutral passer-by to call out 'Co leis seo?' (Whose
is this?) while pointing at one of the piles, to which a crew member would
respond, and this calling was repeated until each man had claimed a pile.

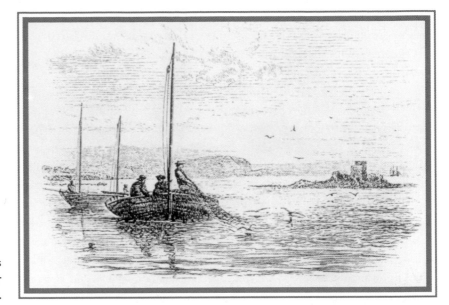

Firth of Forth boats hauling whitebait near Queensferry in the 1860s.

The second method, a refinement of the first, involved the use of tokens, in which the passer-by took the tokens of the crew members and put one on each of the piles. The ownership of the tokens – a stick, a cap, a stone, a knife, any small unique object – would be known only to the crew, and different ones were used at each share-out so that no man could come to be known by his token.[54] The use of sticks as tokens was widespread and has a long history, the Scots word for this special stick being 'cavel' or 'kevill', and the whole selection process being known as casting the cavels.

Where a catch was considered to be held in common by the crew, sharing the proceeds would be done after the fish had been sold. In our house there was a weekly 'squaring up' when my father, uncle and the third member of the crew worked out the proceeds of the week's catch and paid themselves. The sum left over after deductions for fuel and other operating expenses was divided into four: one share for each man and one for the boat. In other places the cash income was divided according to the numbers of nets or lines each man had contributed to the enterprise, and squaring up might be delayed until the end of the season. In the Shetland smack fishery, the linesmen cut the barbels from the cod they hauled in and kept them in a jar of salted water as a tally of their share of the total catch. In the 1920s, on the Golspie steam drifters, what remained after the deduction of operating costs, which included the fixed wages of the engineer, stoker and cook on these larger vessels, was divided into three parts: two parts went to the owner of the drifter as shares for boat and gear, the third part was divided again into equal shares for all the members of the crew, the skipper getting the same as the men.

Gordon Fraser said that the Buckie men he sailed with were not really religious but they were the type that would give you their last ha'penny: 'When we settled up, the skipper came down with five wage packets, put them on the table and called to each man to take his packet of choice, to show that all the shares were equal.'

CHAPTER TWO

SAIL AND STORM

You'll see the stern going one way and the bow the other

Much of the history of the design and construction of fishing boats has been lost and will never be known. The fish bones found in the prehistoric middens excavated by archaeologists show that the people who left us these intriguing piles of refuse were able to fish offshore. They were also able to cross the sea to inhabit the northern islands. What kind of vessel did they use? The hide boat is a possibility. A replica hide boat, based on a rock drawing at Kalnes in Norway, was built in 1971 by Professor Sverre Marstrander and Paul Johnstone from eight cow hides over a frame of alder and lime and proved to be seaworthy in at least inshore waters.[1] The replica hide vessel *Brendan*, built by Tim Severin in 1976, was strong enough to cross the North Atlantic via the Faroes and Iceland.

Generally, however, the ancestor of Scottish fishing craft has been looked for among the traditions of boat-building in northern Europe, particularly Scandinavia but also in all the lands around the North Sea. The Norse heritage seems clear enough in all the old forms of Scottish fishing boat – in the clinkered planks or strakes, in the double-ended design of the hull with similar stem and stern, and in the method of building whereby the keel and the lower strakes are put in place before the strengthening ribs. There are records of Norwegian boats being imported to Shetland in past centuries, for example, in 1566-7 when seventeen boats were carried from Bergen, in 1620-1 when another seventeen arrived,[2] and in the mid-1740s when a Shetland cargo vessel brought home from Suoysound in Norway eight six-oared boats and twenty-four four-oared boats as well as timber and tar.[3] Again, in the account of the island of Unst in the *Old Statistical Account*, written in 1791, the authors state: 'The boats are put together here, but the boards are brought, ready shaped and dressed, from Norway' – in effect, the boats arrived as kits[4]. There can be no doubt that during their long lives some of these boats would have found their way south to Orkney and mainland Scotland to reinforce indigenous building traditions and influence boat-building around a long coast.

The Fair Isle yole has been proposed as an archetype, for example by

Anson. These were slim vessels, 20 to 22 ft in length overall over a 15-ft keel, with a beam of 5½ ft and a maximum draught of 3 ft. Oars and a single mast with a square sail provided propulsion and the skiffs could be easily drawn out of the water. A Ness yole was very similar, and both types of vessel were widely used in inshore line fishing. Although the Shetland import records refer to four- and six-oared boats, Andrew Williamson thinks that these were really yoles and that the boats known now as fourareens and sixerns developed from their yole progenitors as the need for vessels capable of working further offshore and carrying bigger loads came to be met in the eighteenth century.

Sixerns anchored at Fedeland, Shetland. The huts where the men stayed ashore during the season can be seen in the background.

The design of traditional boats developed in response to local conditions, a subject Eric McKee has explored with much technical detail in his classic work, *Working Boats of Britain*. Requirements could vary from one locality to another but, generally, the boats had to be economical to build to match the fishermen's resources and, in the days before many harbours existed, light enough to allow hauling and launching on the shore yet strong enough to withstand what the wind and tide could throw at them. The frequency of gales and the unsheltered nature of most of the east coast created a particularly harsh school of boat-handling; on the west coast and among the islands, the long sea lochs and voes provided sheltered stretches of water but these were limited in extent and the boats had to be built to withstand the open sea.

The Shetland sixerns represented the peak of development along one

line of evolution[5]. They were in the main 30 ft long and 8½ ft in the beam.
Despite the name, some sixerns had eight oars, with the aft pair being
worked by one man, but the main propulsion was supplied by the single
sail. The hull space was divided into a series of compartments or 'rooms' by
slatted partitions: at the stern was the 'shott-hole' where the skipper-
helmsman sat and then, working forrad, came the 'shott' or 'run' where
ballast and fish were stowed; the 'owse-room' for bailing; the 'mid-room',
in effect the working area where the lines were shot and hauled; the 'fore-
room' with more ballast and the site of the fire kettle; and the 'head-room'
and 'bow space' where sails and gear could be stowed.

The sixern became the basis of an important line fishery in Shetland
waters which lasted from the early 1700s until the beginning of the
twentieth century. At its height in the early 1800s, nearly 500 sixerns and
3000 men were working in what was called the *haaf* fishing, from the old
Norse word for sea. Relying on the superb seagoing qualities of the sixern,
the crews fished in deep water often out of sight of their home islands in
all but the clearest weather, using five or six miles of line to hook cod, ling
and halibut. Navigation in the sixerns was carried on by the skipper
according to his skill, hard-won experience and knowledge handed down
to him: a glimpse of the sun at a particular time of day could provide a
rough bearing for *da manna* 'the land', soundings could be taken, the flight
of seabirds observed. Towing an oar astern could help in steering a straight
course. In thick weather, very common in northern waters in the summer,
foghorns made from the horns of cattle were blown to warn of a boat's
presence. The most common navigational aid in the sixerns as elsewhere in
Scotland was the use of landmarks – hilltops, kirk spires, the openings
between islets, even houses – in a simple form of triangulation; these were
known as marks, meithes or meezes, depending on the dialect.

I sat in a sixern for the first time in 1996 in the harbour at Baltasound
on Unst. She was the *Far Haaf*, a replica vessel built by Duncan Sandison who
runs the Unst Boat Haven, a museum devoted to traditional Shetland fishing
craft and where a number of examples can be seen. The *Far Haaf* is tarred
black on the outside and varnished on the inside, except at the bow and
stern where blue paint adds a gaudy splash; traditionally the fishermen
spent enough to allow the use of one pound of paint for this. She bobbed
in the calm water of the harbour but her size seemed frighteningly small,
her shape too fragile for the North Atlantic. Sitting on the thwart, only a
man's legs and waist were sheltered from the wind and, although the high
prow looked ready to rise over any comber that came at her, it must have
taken a special courage to go out regularly in such boats.

The sixern hull was strong, light and supple: 'hitting a big lump,' said
Andrew Williamson, 'you'll see the stern going one way and the bow the
other, and then she'll straighten herself up and away.' The sixerns could
reach high speeds with the wind. Planing out could easily happen until the
boat became, in the Shetland expression, 'sea loose', when the noise of the

air turbulence under the keel made it sound as if she was sailing over shingle. Good skippers steered their sixerns at 7 − 8 knots and there are records of homeward journeys from 30 miles off being completed in under four hours. In the great storm of 1881, a sixern kept an average speed of 9¼ knots running into Ronas Voe. The strength of the sixern lay in her ability to run before the sea and an experienced, cool-headed skipper at the tiller, in a heavy following sea, could run her along a wave trough with the wind abeam until he spotted a lower section of wave crest and turn away there; if the boat was swamped, the crew could haul the sheet, turn and pitch out the excess water over the lee gunwale, before slacking the sheet and resuming the course. (A good catch of fish with broad halibut stowed on top could act almost as a deck and shed much water.) Such handling all took split-second timing and experience but, as it was said to me, 'a sixern skipper's first mistake was almost certainly his last'. Many sixerns were lost but this may have been due as much to hypothermia slowing the reactions of the soaking men as to flaws in the vessels themselves, as in an 1887 storm when James Arthur died from exposure after sailing a 13-ft yole home to Bressay.

Andrew Williamson recounted to me what he had heard from an old skipper in Fetlar describing how he ran for safety in the disastrous storm of 1881.

> The safety was in running. Get her away before the sea, keep her away from the sea, keep her as dry as possible, and if you had to take a lump drop her shoulder and pitch it off her and bail her out, and off you go. We ran all the way down during the night from Fetlar to the north end of Bressay and by that time the weather was broken. I turned her round and I says, 'Boys, take a smoke o your pipe if ye hae any matches and then we'll heid for home.' When the skipper got back, he was asked how he had got on with his new boat. 'Oh,' he says, 'I wis ower pleised wi her. Mind du, fan we wis crossin the tide strings aff o the Vongs, I heard her complainin a bit.

The stories of the sgoth (pronounced 'skaw') fishery in the north of Lewis echo those of the sixerns and the yoles. The Lewismen used *geola* (yoles) for inshore fishing but the sgoth was a larger, sturdier vessel built for cod and ling fishing in deeper water. Up to 33 ft long on a 21-ft keel and 11 ft in the beam, with a curving rake in the stem and a straight raked sternpost, they all emerged from the open-air boatyard of the one Macleod family at Port of Ness. John Murdo Macleod, the fourth generation of the family, has constructed the replica sgoth *An Sulaire*, which is now sailed out of Stornoway by an enthusiastic group of volunteers. Two men could build one in eight weeks at a cost, excluding sails and rigging, of £35. The sgoth was traditionally varnished on the outside with a concoction made up from paraffin and resin, and tarred inside; and there were always three thwarts.

At their peak in the last decades of the ninteenth century, the sgoth fleet numbered thirty but by 1910 this had dropped to four.[6] The sgoth fishermen used long lines to catch cod and ling over the winter months from fishing banks extending from north-east of the Butt of Lewis to opposite Stoer Point on the east side of the Minch. The catches were salted and dried in the open air, and marketed through Stornoway merchants. Many of the fishermen lived in the townships of Tolsta to the north of Stornoway, where stretches of sandy beach allowed the boats to be hauled up.[7]

A sgoth weighed about six tons with another ton of ballast and launching and hauling them was backbreaking work for the six or seven men in the crew, even with the help of *lunnan*, wooden rollers or 'leens'. The long lines were baited and set for maybe 48 hours, careful bearings being

The replica sgoth *An Sulaire*.

taken of the position of the anchor stones so that the lines could be retrieved with grapnels. Each sgoth carried a fire kettle, a three-legged iron pot with burning peat inside. The sgoth was also used by the people of Port of Ness on their annual visits to the island of Sulisgeir to harvest gannets and in skilful hands a sgoth could make this 40-mile voyage in as little as four hours.

Other variants on the basic yole or yawl pattern were used in Orkney and Caithness. These were beamier than the Shetland models and the Stroma yoles, built for the fierce waters of the Pentland Firth, could be beamy indeed – the largest type could have a beam of 9½ ft on a keel of 24 ft. The rounded shape allowed the carrying of varied cargoes, including livestock, and in the turbulent streams of the Firth they were stable and sat firmly in the water, with a deep keel to take a good grip of the sea. Around the turn of the nineteenth century it was customary for the builders to calculate their cost at £1 per foot of keel. The Stroma yoles can reach nine knots running on an open reach in a Force 7, and six knots was regarded as a normal rate of progress.[8]

The fifie was the most common type of vessel along the entire east coast of the Scottish mainland in the early nineteenth century. The name indicates that Fife was the original home of the design, and in some places the smaller fifies were known as firthies, perhaps a reference to the Firth of Forth. The fifie measured from 25 ft to 30 ft in length but grew considerably in size throughout the later decades of the century as crews ventured further from land in pursuit of larger catches of herring until some touched 75 ft and were registered at 25 tons. With a vertical or only slightly raked bow and stern, they preserved traces of their Norse heritage in the clinkered

Stroma in the Pentland Firth, with all the local yoles drawn up at the haven. The picture shows the beamy design of these yoles characteristic of boats used in the Pentland Firth.

planking, although later carvel-built vessels became common.

A storm in the Moray Firth in August 1848 wreaked havoc among the fifies working at the herring fishing. Over 800 boats put to sea from Wick shortly after high water on the afternoon of Friday 18th and, as the summer dusk fell, stood out some ten miles to sea and shot their drift nets. By midnight it was evident that the weather was changing for the worse – the wind increased and the sea turned rough – and many skippers decided there and then to haul their nets and make for shelter. These, the lucky or the wise, safely made it back to harbour by high water at 1.30 a.m. Others, about thirty boats, ran for Sinclair's Bay and the lee of Noss Head. By 3 a.m., the south-easterly was whipping the sea into a storm and drenching rain was obscuring visibility. By now the tide was ebbing and only five feet of water remained at the entrance to Wick harbour. This was made worse by the large breakers

rolling in before the wind to smash on the stonework of the piers. The boats
which attempted to squeeze through the jaws of the harbour were thrown up
against the quays or swamped in the boiling water. 'It was an appalling scene,'
wrote James Calder more than a decade later, 'deepened into tenfold intensity
by the distress and agony of those who had relatives in the tiny craft that were
dimly seen at times tossing on the crests of the foaming billows, and making
for the shore, which was surrounded with a tremendous surf. Destruction
was imminent and no power of man could avert it.' Forty-one boats were
destroyed; 37 men drowned. At Helmsdale, 30 miles to the south, another 24
boats sank, taking 13 men with them; 51 went down at Peterhead, with the
loss of 31 lives; and eight more at Stonehaven, with 19 men aboard. In all,
along the east coast, that storm accounted for 124 fishing craft and 100 men,
who left 47 widows and 161 children.[9]

Captain John Washington RN was commissioned by the House of
Commons to conduct an inquiry into the disaster; and on 12 October he
began to take evidence in Wick Town Hall from eyewitnesses. Describing the
event as 'a calamity without precedent in the annals of the British fisheries',
Washington used his report to put forward proposals to make the fishery
safer.[10] His two main points were that there was a want of good harbours
accessible at all states of the tide and that the design of the boats was
deficient. He also pointed out that many landsmen, inexperienced in boat
handling, were among the crews hired for the fishing and, in perhaps a
typical Victorian touch, that there was too much drinking among the
fishermen. He took it upon himself to collect boat designs from various parts
of Britain and to submit them all to James Peake, naval architect at the
Woolwich Dockyard, for professional comment. Peake was critical of the
type of boat in use in Wick, which is described in the Report as 34 ft 6 in.
long, 13 ft in beam and with a draught of 4 ft 9 in., and thought that it
would make too much leeway, had low capacity and was unsafe to beach. He
made similar comments about the boats in use in Peterhead, Newhaven and
Aberdeen. Peake produced his own design: the overall dimensions were
little different but the proposed boat had a higher cargo capacity, a better
ability to take the beach and, most importantly, a short foredeck to give
greater protection to the crew. Washington was very keen on introducing
foredecking in the fifie which, until then, had been an open boat and hoped
that the fishermen's dislike of a foredeck would 'soon wear out'. The
fishermen, however, were used to open boats and objected that a foredeck
would be an extra expense and its existence would impede the handling of
their nets and slow the landing of their catches. However, about one half of
the herring fifies working out of Fraserburgh already had foredecks. The tide
of opinion gradually swung in their favour and part-decked boats were being
built at Buckie in 1855, and at Eyemouth in 1856.[11]

As fifies grew larger the amount of decking increased. The type reached
the peak of its development in the early 1900s. The *True Vine*, built by Innes
of St Monans for David Mair of Nairn in 1905, was among the largest, with

The fifie *Isabella Fortuna*, Arbroath (AH 153), a nineteenth-century herring drifter, now undergoing restoration by the Wick Society. She has been given the registration number WK 499, originally the number of the fifie *Alexandra*, to commemorate the record-making sail of Jim Baikie from Wick to Yarmouth in 1903.

a keel of 71 ft, an overall length of 97 ft, a beam of 21 ft 6 in., and a draught of 8 ft.[12] Her decked hull was divided into four compartments: a cabin in the stern provided four bunks for the crew, a coal stove and a table, and also housed a copper boiler to power the steam winch on the deck above. Forrad of the cabin was the warp room where the drift net warps were stowed and in the bow was the net store. The main centre section of the hull was the 'fish room' where the catch was handled and stored. The *True Vine* needed a crew of eight.

The *Reaper*, a fifie built in 1901 in Sandhaven and registered first in Fraserburgh as FR 958 and later, in 1908, in Lerwick as LK 707, is now part of the Scottish Fisheries Museum collection in Anstruther. She gives an impression of massive strength: the overall length is almost 59 ft, the beam is nearly 17 ft and her gross tonnage is 49.15. The mainmast towers 47 ft from the deck, with a shorter mizzen of 39 ft aft and set slightly to port, as was the custom to allow room for the crutch or 'mitch' on to which the mainmast was lowered while lying at the drift nets. The *Reaper* is also typical of sailing drifters in having a very low gunwale to ease the job of hauling

of sailing drifters in having a very low gunwale to ease the job of hauling

of sailing drifters in having a very low gunwale to ease the job of hauling in nets. Other surviving fifies include the *Collann* in the Helmsdale Timespan Centre and the *Isabella Fortuna*, recently acquired by the Wick Society and now undergoing restoration.

Coull Deas of Cellardyke sails the *Reaper* and is full of praise for her sailing qualities. She has the standard dipping lugsail rig, of which more below. The best quarter for sailing is with the wind slightly abaft the beam and in a steady sea, with seven tons of ballast to counter the weight of the mast, she can reach quite a speed. Coull sailed her from Anstruther to Whitby in the summer of 1997 in 14¾ hours, logging an average speed of 11 knots. She is a dry boat and does not heel much. A disadvantage is that shifting the lugsail when tacking is a heavy, slow job needing a large crew.

Another traditional model of fishing boat used in the Moray Firth was the scaffie or scaith.[13] They were 40 to 45 ft in length overall, with a keel length of 25 to 36 ft, a beam of 13 to 17 ft, and a depth of hold of 7 to 9 ft. The bow was almost vertical but the sternpost had a pronounced rake. A 40-ft scaffie cost £40 in the mid-1800s, with another £20 for spars and sails, and was worked by a crew of five men. Washington's 1848 Report describes the boats in use in Buckie as having 'a great rake given to the stern and stem posts', an objectionable feature in his view as it made the boats unsteady before the wind; he appears to be describing a variant of scaffie. Anson says that they sometimes carried three masts. Scaffies were in wide use until the late 1800s when they were replaced by the larger zulus and fifies.

For the inshore fishing in the Firth of Forth, a smaller variant of the scaffie was designed in 1860. It was called the 'baldie', named, perhaps in affectionate regard, for Giuseppe Garibaldi who was leading his famous campaign for the unification of Italy at the time. The baldie measured 15–24 ft in length and most of them were carvel-built, open boats with a shallow depth of 3 ft 6 in. Although they could be handled with oars, they used a single lugsail on a raked mast stepped well forward. Baldies were known as skiffs on the Moray Firth.[14] Elsewhere in the south of Scotland other designs were used and, just as Norse methods left their mark on northern design, boat building traditions on the English coast probably spread to influence their northern neighbours. One type, called a whammel, was used in inshore fishing in the Solway Firth and at least some of them had tanks open to the sea in which the catch could be brought live to shore.[15] The nobby or nabby was common around the Irish Sea in the early 1800s when they were usually built with square or transom sterns; the transom type was replaced by double-ended vessels later in the century.[16] The Clyde nabby was a 32–34 ft open boat with a lugsail rig. Variants of the coble, with its pointed bow, square stern and often a graceful tumblehome curve in the quarters, were found in south-east Scotland and used for inshore fishing; the coble further north was associated particularly with salmon fishing from stake nets.

In 1878, in Lossiemouth, William 'Dad' Campbell came up with a new design that became famous as the zulu. There is a story that the design resulted from a disagreement between Campbell and his wife over what each thought ideal, he being pro-scaffie and she pro-fifie. The zulu hull, so named because the Zulu Wars in South Africa were much in the news at the time, combined the straight stem of the fifie with the raked stern of the scaffie. The actual origins of the zulu design may be much more prosaic, a boat-builder's response to technical problems: the raked stern was easier to build than a fifie's and it was also perhaps easier to use a straight stem than the curved one of the scaffie.[17] With a sense of humour, Campbell called his new boat *Nonesuch* and the type was rapidly copied around the Moray Firth, growing larger during the 1890s, up to 80 or 90 ft overall on a keel some 20 ft shorter. Zulus carried large sail areas, on masts up to 70 ft, and they were fast sailers, regularly making 10 knots, as they hurried herring catches to market.

The Loch Fyne skiff, adapted for the ringnetting of herring in the comparatively sheltered waters of the Firth of Clyde, made its appearance in the early 1880s. Until that period, open skiffs had been used, gradually increasing in length over the years from about 20–30 ft. The west coast boats had slightly rounded stems and deeply raked sterns, similar in overall shape to scaffies. Foredecks had also been introduced and were incorporated into the new skiffs, the first two of which were built in Girvan in 1882 and named appropriately *Alpha* and *Beta*. Both had keels of 25 ft. Over the following years boats built to the new design were turned out by various yards around the Clyde. Their size increased until by 1914 they were up to 40 ft long.[18]

Almost all the sailing fishing boats around the Scottish coast had a lugsail rig. The yard of the sail was attached to the mast with a ring, the 'traveller', positioned one-third of the distance from the forward end. The sail was hauled up or down by a halyard which ran through a sheave on the top of the mast and also served as a stay when the sail was in position. The lack of standing rigging left a clear deckspace and run of gunwale for working nets. Rows of reefing points on the sail allowed it to be shortened in strong winds. The forward end of the sail was made fast to the bow or placed further out on a movable bowsprit. The sheet led aft from the clew of the sail through blocks. Smaller boats carried only one mast but the larger ones had two, with a dipping lugsail on the main and a standing lug on the mizen. The bowsprit would allow the setting of a jibsail in the right conditions, and a stern sprit could also be run out aft to accommodate a large spread of canvas. When changing tack, the yard and sail of the dipping lug were lowered to the deck and manhandled around the mast before being raised in its new position. On the smaller standing lug, the yard was left in position up the mast and the sail allowed to flap against the mast. The larger fifies and zulus had massive, heavy rigs and handling them required great strength as well as skill. A few vessels were worked with a smack rig – boom sail and foresails – which allowed more precise handling in enclosed waters; an example of this was the *Daring*, a Shetland boat that fished in the voes around the islands.

The building of all these traditional types of craft went ahead in scores of small yards, some of which were forerunners of the building yards still working today but many of which were small local businesses that flourished and closed as the builders themselves lived and died. There are many examples buried in local records: for instance, two Mackay brothers at Ard Neackie on Loch Eriboll turned out yoles on the Orkney pattern that were popular with the inshore fishermen of Lewis in the early years of the twentieth century; and David Banks was a famous yole-builder on Stroma in the Pentland Firth. Every fishing district seems to have had its resident boat carpenter. Two locally built boats are preserved at the Gairloch Heritage Museum: the *Queen Mary*, built in 1910 on Loch Torridon, and the *Ribhinn Bhoidheach*, built at Port Henderson on the south side of Gairloch in 1914. Launched on the day of the coronation of King George V and her namesake,

Herring drifter *Smiling Morn* at Gairloch, c.1910.

the *Queen Mary* is 31 ft 6 in. overall and has a beam of 11 ft; the keel length is 22 ft, and the steeply raked sternpost has been attributed to the influence of the zulu design although it was also characteristic of the older scaffie. The *Ribhinn Bhoidheach* is a much smaller vessel, under 15 ft in length, and she was worked by two men from Melvaig where there was no harbour and she had to be hauled up the beach after each voyage. Both boats were rigged with lugsails but were later fitted with engines, as was the trend around the time of the First World War.

The easiest name to paint

A number of customs surround the naming of fishing boats and, although the decision is finally a personal one, community values also operate and a number of name categories are evident. Biblical names were and are common in areas with a strength of religious feeling. James Slater

of Banff has made a special study of these and has published a list of over
400, although he admits that some of the naming may have been done
without any realisation of the religious significance[19]. However, this would
still leave a considerable number deliberately chosen to express Christian
faith. Murdo Maclennan's father in Lewis called his drifter *Ebenezer*, which
signifies the help of God, and this name has been given to many boats over
the years. Other names quote from Scripture — *Quiet Waters, Guide Us, Celestial
Dawn, Rose of Sharon, Genesis* — but saint names are relatively rare, perhaps an
indication of the Presbyterian feelings of many fishermen. Slater lists many
saint names but I came across only two, in Eyemouth and Pittenweem,
while travelling around the coast; many boats would have been at sea
during my visit of course. *Olsen's Fisherman's Nautical Almanack* for 1997 lists
only seven Scottish fishing vessels over 10 m with saint names.

A second category of names may be loosely termed as expressing
'virtues' or 'desirable qualities' — *Prowess, Gratitude, Faithful* — or positions of
status such as *Ambassador*. Gaelic names are relatively rare but *Sealgair Mara*,
'Hunter of the Sea', is an apt and popular one. The Golspie boats in the early
1900s kept the English names they already had, if they were acquired from
the Moray Firth ports, but occasionally a new boat would be built to local
order and given a name of local significance.[20] Family names are common,
either as surnames (*Taits* FR 229) or more commonly as first names: there
are many *Boy* ... and *Girl* ... combinations, and sometimes more original
names such as *Helenus*. In Shetland, boats were very often named after
female relatives or, as the islands supplied many men to the merchant
service, after a ship on which the owner may have served. Sentiment was
not always the only factor at work: if a boat was called after a person
prominent in the local community, it was only fit that that individual would
buy the vessel her first suit of sails. Certain poetic concepts recur in names
incorporating *Dawn* or *Ocean*, and classical references are found in *Argonaut*
and *Quo Vadis*. There was a fashion in the East Neuk of Fife and some other
harbours for giving boats Latin names: Alex Watson's family-owned boat at
Cellardyke was the *Internos* ('between us') and another example is the *Spes
Melior* ('better hope').

Many fishermen would keep names associated with their family history
in the fishing. John Thomson in Lossiemouth called his three boats *Caledonia*
(very much a family name, his grandfather had a *Caledonia*), *Horizon* and *St
Kilda*. He chose *Horizon* because he thought it a beautiful abstract name — 'as
far as you can see, and what's beyond'. *St Kilda* arose because he was fishing
mainly in that area but there was a traditional connection here, too, as his
great-grandfather, Alexander Thomson, had had a boat with the same name
and had fished for herring out of Barra a century ago. In Macduff, William
West named the *Atlas* after the firm that supplied her electronics.

Madge Mitchell's uncle in Portmahomack called his boat *Rose* because,
he said, perhaps jokingly, 'it was the easiest name to paint.'

General deepening and improving

Many of the small harbours that now grace the fishertouns were not built until the nineteenth century but the south-west coast and the east coast, at least as far north as the Moray Firth, were supplied with several harbours before then. Ports such as Dunbar in East Lothian had grown up to serve the country's trade with Europe. Improvement to Dunbar harbour came during the rule of Oliver Cromwell in the late 1650s – in 1661 it is recorded that 20,000 people came to the town to take part in the herring fishing – and a further new basin was added in 1842.[21] The harbours of the East Neuk have their roots in the same period: the oldest part of Crail harbour, the East Pier, dates from about 1610 but some of her neighbours predate her: Pittenweem (1540s), Anstruther (1579) and Elie (1582). St Andrews had a harbour in the sixteenth century[22]. Eyemouth's first pier was built in 1747. In East Lothian there were also harbours at North Berwick, Cockenzie and Morison's Haven.[23] In the south-west, the main trading ports until the 16th century were Dumbarton, Irvine, Ayr, Wigton and Kirkcudbright[24] – herring figure among the lists of exports. On the Solway Firth there were also harbours of some kind at Annan and Glencaple, and others were added later: at Port William in the 1790s, Port Logan between 1818-32 and Portpatrick between 1821-36.[25] There seem to have been no proper harbours further to the north. Inveraray had 'no pier worthy of the name' before 1809.[26] Oban was designated as a fishing station in 1786 but distance from the markets may have been the main factor in precluding much development until the railway reached the small town in 1880. Mallaig acquired the first stage of its harbour when the West Highland line was pushed through from Fort William in 1901.

In the north-east, Lord Pitsligo began the building of Pitsligo harbour in about 1679 but at this time Fraserburgh was reckoned to have the best harbour in the region, with 10 ft of water during neap tides. Fraserburgh harbour dates from 1546 as part of the development of the town by the Fraser lairds of Philorth from the original earlier village of Faithlie. The town has the distinction of having Scotland's oldest modern lighthouse, established in 1787. The building of a harbour at Aberdeen had begun in the early seventeenth century and, to the north, Peterhead's original harbour, known in the early days as Port Henry pier, was first built in the 1590s shortly after the town was granted Royal Burgh status. Portsoy harbour was built in the late 1500s and the town had a lively trade; the old harbour as existing now dates from the 1600s. Banff traded with the Hanseatic League in the twelfth century and the port's customs accounts have records from the fourteenth century; the harbour was built in the 1770s and a fishing community grew up in the suburb of Scotstown. Lossiemouth harbour began as a pier constructed in the rivermouth and completed in 1703; the old fishertoun grew up on the left bank of the river, divided from the town by the Spynie Canal, and the present harbour had its beginnings only in 1837 when the local laird, Brander of Pitgaveny, instigated the building of the new town of Branderburgh to the north at Stotfield Point.[27] Before the port of Lossiemouth, Elgin was served by the port of Spynie but that became cut off from the sea by shingle and sand brought down by the river Lossie. Gardenstown was founded in 1720 by Alexander Garden of Troup, although it is generally known locally as Gamrie after the bay on its doorstep. Cromarty had a long history as a trading port for Easter Ross. The towns in the northern islands, despite their long association with the sea, had to wait until the Age of Improvement for constructed harbours – Stornoway in 1785, Kirkwall in 1811, Scalloway in the 1830s – and the oldest seatown is Stromness, where the harbour began its long history in 1701.

Painting by P. McLeod of Wick harbour during the savage storm in August 1848 that destroyed many boats in the Moray Firth herring fleet.

Fishing communities existed at these harbours but at the close of the eighteenth century it was probably still true to say that a large percentage of Scotland's fishermen worked from shores where the beaching and hauling of their boats was the normal practice. At the start of the nineteenth century, there were about seventy fishing communities along the coast between Montrose and the rivermouth of the Spey alone. At this time, however, there began an upsurge in the building of new harbours, an era of construction encouraged by the rapid growth of the east-coast herring fishing and financed partly by the private initiatives of lairds and partly by public funds or such bodies as the British Fisheries Society. Portknockie in the lee of Greencastle Hill,was established in the late 1700s as a fishing harbour open at all states of the tide; and Portgordon was founded and named after the fourth Duke of Gordon in 1797 as a herring port.

It is not always easy to be precise about the dates of harbour building as construction could be phased over several years; for example, the building of Keiss harbour began in 1818 but was completed not until about

1834. By 1848, when Captain Washington presented his views on the subject to the House of Commons, fishing harbours of some sort existed at, among other places, Hopeman, Lybster, Lochinver, Portmahomack, Macduff, Cullen, Lerwick, Helmsdale, Nairn, Embo, Cockburnspath, St Abbs, Reay and Granton. A tribute must be paid to those who supervised so much of this early building phase, as they include such men as James Bremner, Thomas Telford, the Stevensons, John Smeaton, George Burn and Joseph Mitchell, some of the country's most prominent civil engineers of the time.

Captain Washington, in reviewing the factors that contributed to the heavy loss of life in the August 1848 storm, was, however, critical of the harbours around the Moray Firth. 'I would yet more earnestly recommend the general deepening and improving of all the harbours along the east coast of Scotland, and the placing them under proper control,' he wrote. He was angered by the fact that, although fishermen paid harbour dues, their needs were not being met by harbour authorities. 'It would be an act of mercy', he wrote, 'to a race of hardy, industrious, frugal men, to 10,000 fishermen ... 'to increase the annual Parliamentary grant for harbours and piers from £2500, a 'scarcely credible ... small sum' to £10,000 for a few years to remedy the lack. 'It is a most serious reflection', he went on, 'that vigilance, foresight, and efficient management on the part of the harbour authorities in maintaining their several harbours and lights in a proper state, might have saved fully one-half out of the 100 fishermen who perished on this occasion.' He also predicted that the catching of white fish would increase and that fishermen should be encouraged in providing such 'a ready supply of good food' by having effective low-water harbours for their safety.

Harbour building continued during the rest of the century. Lossiemouth benefited from a new one in 1860, and the Cluny Harbour at Buckie was completed in 1880 – the area was already the centre of a thriving series of linked communities spread along the shore. The harbour at Dunbeath, later to be made famous as Dunster in Neil Gunn's epic novel of the herring fishing, *The Silver Darlings*, was built in 1850. Harbours were built at Port of Ness in about 1885, at Balintore and Hilton in 1890, and at Golspie in 1894–5. In the same period the harbours at Thurso and Scrabster were rebuilt. In 1900 Whitehills harbour was completed, although the fishing community there had been using the haven for most of the century before. A new deepwater quay and herring market opened in Lerwick in 1905.

A bit extra

Whether they enjoyed access to good harbours or not, the fishermen were superb boat-handlers. Matthew Mackaile's comment, possibly made in the late 1670s, that 'The common people' of Orkney ' ... excell all people for navigation in small boats with 4 or 6 oars, and one or two sails' could serve for all the coastal communities.[28] In the days before weather forecasting and radio, the men relied on their skill at reading the sky but often this was not good enough and almost all the fisher communities in Scotland can recall at least one disaster when the boats were caught at sea by the sudden onset of a storm. Like many others, the Fisheries Museum at Lossiemouth has a memorial room, a reverent place of varnished wood and immaculately polished brass with the quiet peace of a small chapel, a feeling enhanced by the presence of a stained glass window made by the monks of Pluscarden. On the walls plaques record the names of all the fishermen lost at sea from this community in times of war and peace. The visitor notices at once the long list of names on the plaque marked with the date 25 December 1806, when the three boats working out of Stotfield, the part of the town then home to the fisher community, were driven offshore in a sudden hurricane and never seen again: all the twenty-one fishermen were drowned, leaving seventeen widows and forty-seven children fatherless.

Every fishing district has experienced a major blow like this, the sudden onset of bad weather and all or part of a local fleet wiped out. Many of these tragedies have been forgotten, as they have passed unrecorded beyond the memory of the generations who had to live through them, but we know of some. In a storm in November 1765, three of the five boats at St Andrews were lost, taking twelve men down with them. For more recent times, the records exist. Eighteen sixerns were overwhelmed off the Shetland coast in July 1832 and 105 men were lost.[29] A bad storm hit the East Neuk in November 1875 when three St Monans and two Cellardyke boats were lost along with thirty-seven fishermen.[30] Almost six years later, on 13/14 July 1881, the Shetland sixern fleet suffered heavy losses again. This incident is now known as the Gloup Disaster. On a brae above the head of Gloup Voe on the north coast of Yell a monument commemorates the incident: a statue of a woman and child, the stone pitted by the weather, looks down through the jaws of the inlet to the open sea and a plaque records that nine sixerns and one smaller boat were lost, taking fifty-eight men to their deaths. Many boats did, however, survive the run to shelter on that day and a crewman on one of them recalled his experience some fifty years later.[31] Charles Johnson of Toam, in North Roe on the Mainland, was serving in his first season at the *haaf* fishing, one of a crew of seven, and they were working the lines about 30 miles out when the storm struck them:

> We had come a short way through our second line when we heard
> and saw the weather coming. It struck us about on the bow, and being
> heavy aft, of course she payed off. The sea began to rain over us. The
> two men stopped shutting [shooting the line] … [we] put on oilskins
> [and] started to haul back. The skipper turned to a man who had been
> a skipper and asked him what he had to say about this. He replied,

'Making for the land now we will come there in the darkness'. These men was cool, and spoke the matter over. [The decision was taken to run for the Mainland, and the race with the weather began. The lines still out were cut and the skipper put the sixern before the wind, as the crew prepared to handle the sail and bail. To reach the Mainland near Ronasvoe the skipper had to steer across the wind, which was north by east.] The skipper … took notice of the wind with the compass – the wind had to be his guide. They did not expect the wind to shift after the first bat. There would be wild steering in any case when the water was going over the boat and flooding the glass of the compass, and no suitable place for it in front of the man steering … She was not taking much water – just sprays and wash anof [enough] to keep the shovel going in the owse-room. I notice he run the seas in the weakest parts, what we called the tails … Only once did I notice him having to run a sea in the centre. This sea rose very high astern. They pressed her with the sail when the surge came around her, and although the sail was laid down she run in it for a bit (like a field of snow) and took water over both sides. It was not good to look at, but it was only a look. She could not have stood much of that. She took the water from the mast aft to the owse-room … not a lot, but we were standing on the boddom to the boot-tops in the owse-room … The three men who were managing the boat did not pass any remarks to us nor to one another; they appeared to be quite contented and fairly understood what they were doing. I had been brought up with boating since I was a child, but this of course was a bit extra.

Johnson's 'bit extra' – almost swamped in a north-easterly in a sixern – underlines the laconic courage with which these men faced their predicament. There was no panic, there was no place for panic, just a quiet, methodical attention to what they had to do to keep going. Nearer the shore, they were almost swamped again:

He had just well got up when a sea made … They gave her the sail, or more sail. He did not run that sea, it was too close on us; he just kept her going; the last tail struck her from the mast and aft. She lay down to this – that's the sail. She had no high side to receive a big knock. It's the only time she's laying down to it since we started. She was submerged where the sea came; I lost sight of the man in the owse-room and the skipper, and as it passed over her he rather kept her away, and the sail was eased.

The sixern came in to Ronas Voe and, when the exhausted men had tied up, the skipper looked at his watch. It was 1.30 a.m. at the end of the brief Shetland night. They had taken four hours to run in and they had brought home 26 hundredweight of fish.

Twenty-two Shetland men were lost in another incident in December 1900 when four boats were caught by a north-westerly when they were line fishing at Mossbank in Delting. Five sailing drifters with forty men on their way home from Yarmouth to the Moray Firth went down in a gale in November 1893.[32] The heaviest loss of life occurred in the Eyemouth disaster of 14 October 1881. On this occasion, remembered as Black Friday in Berwickshire, the local fleet put to sea on a morning that was calm and sunny, despite the barometers reading extremely low, at Burnmouth reported to be '27, the lowest … remembered to have been seen here'. The boats were about an hour's sail offshore, fishing with lines, when the wind got up from the north and the sky turned black. Many were overwhelmed in the rush to find shelter, under the eyes of their families who crowded to the shore to assist in any way they could, as reported in the *Berwickshire News*:

> The force of the hurricane had startled the inhabitants and a general move was made to the pier, the sea wall and the top of the adjoining cliffs, to endeavour to discover the whereabouts of the fleet. In consequence of the blinding rain which accompanied the wind, the gloom which prevailed in the atmosphere, and the driving clouds of spray from the crests of the breakers, nothing could be seen five hundred yards from land. Intense anxiety prevailed in these circumstances for the safety of the boats, and the gloomiest forebodings were entertained.[33]

The incoming boats had to negotiate the Hurcars, rocks guarding the entrance to Eyemouth harbour, and fight through the broiling surf. Many failed to make it and were capsized, swamped or smashed to bits in the attempt. The lifeboat, most of whose crew were at sea already in the fishing boats, could not be launched, and the rocket lines were not effective against the wind but some of the heroic efforts made by many of the onlookers to save men from the breaking waves were successful. In all, from Eyemouth, Burnmouth, Cove and St Abbs, 189 men were drowned.

The advent of weather forecasting, engines and better rescue services mean that large-scale disasters are consigned to the past, but fishing remains one of the most dangerous livelihoods to follow, and Lady Nairne's line in 'Caller Herrin' about the price of fish being 'the lives o' men' still has its resonance. Accidents with gear, bad weather, engine breakdown – these cause a steady attrition every year. Fishing boats are overwhelmed by the sea sometimes with no warning. In 1991, John MacKay of the Seafish Industry Authority claimed that a fisherman is killed every eight days; in 1995, sixteen fishermen lost their lives, in 1996 the figure rose to twenty.[34]

CHAPTER THREE

LINES AND HOOKS

Sa gret plente is of fische

The beginning of the Scottish fishing industry lies in the harvesting of the coast. Many shell middens have been found: they vary in size – one on Oronsay rises to over three metres in height – but they show that for many generations these sites must have been frequented by bands of hunters, some of them having been dated to around 7000 BC. As well as the shells of limpets, winkles and whelks, there are otoliths, the small earbones from fish, and fish hooks and barbed pieces of antler that may have been used as harpoons. The surviving fish bones show that saithe or coley was an important catch; and this will surprise no one who is familiar with coastal fish. The east coast shell middens – in the Forth valley, at Inveravon and Polmonthill – contain oysters, mussels, cockles and other shellfish remains; and the bones of whales have been found near Stirling.[1] The exploitation of

Fishermen with bags of winkles (whelks) at Keiss harbour, Caithness, photographed possibly in the 1920s. The winkles were collected in rockpools and sent by train to Billingsgate.

the intertidal zone continues to this day, although now its importance has diminished to that of pastime and families no longer rely on what they can find between the tide marks for survival. It is not so long, however, since this was the case. In seasons of dearth or famine poorer families resorted to the beach to dig for cockles and spoots, knock limpets and cut ware from the rocks, or try for shoals of coley in creeks or pools. In 1782 and 1783, it is recorded that people harvested cockles in the Dornoch Firth to alleviate the scarcity of food, and the poor people in the parish of Tongue, Sutherland, 'had scarcely any other subsistence but the cockles and mussels' they could gather in the bay.[2] The humblest food of all was the limpet (*Patella*). The stone tools found in Mesolithic middens include what are believed to be limpet hammers, used thousands of years ago to knock the creatures from their beds. The common periwinkle (*Littorina*), usually called a whelk in Scots, is another creature whose abundance has supplied a steady yield. The gathering of winkles for shipping in bags by train to Billingsgate was one custom that provided some families with ready cash up until the 1950s, if not more recently. The extent of this simple gathering is shown by the statistics, for example for 1967, when nearly 20,000 hundredweight of winkles, with a market value of over £42,500, were collected and sold.[3]

The littoral has also sustained some locally important fisheries. This is especially true of the Solway Firth. In the 1790s, the people of Kirkinner in Galloway are described as standing in the ebbing tide with baskets and catching 'fleuks, sole fleuks, tarbets and severall other fish'.[4] There was once a sand-eel fishery in the Dornoch Firth.[5] Andrew Symson noted in 1684 that the Galloway people found fish on shore enough to allow them to take 'little paines to seek the sea'; and in the estuary of the Nith they caught peckfuls of shrimps.[6] *Haaf*-net fishing continues to this day in the river Nith and neighbouring creeks, where the men stand up to their chests in the water, braced against the fierce current, with large nets on poles.

One of the oldest techniques of catching fish as opposed simply to gathering animals from the beach is line fishing, a method particularly suited to white fish. These are the gadoids, the members of the cod family, the prime catch of generations of fishermen. The cod itself, with its handsome marbled green and brown back and its white lateral line, figures in references to fishing since the Middle Ages. If left to live its natural span, the cod can reach the length of a grown man and weigh over eighty lbs. Such giants are rare now but I can recall the Caithness linesmen bringing them ashore in the winter months in the 1950s, swollen with lumps of nutritious roe. The ling, most common along the west coast of the British Isles, has a long body, up to two metres, with a dorsal fin running most of its length. In the accounts of the line fisheries, ling are paired with cod as the desirable catch. Haddock, by far the most popular fish eaten in Scotland, and whiting also form a partnership in our minds. The former is easily distinguished by its black lateral line and the dark spot on its flanks, traditionally the thumbprint of St Peter or even that of Christ at the feeding of the five thousand. Whiting has a dark spot, much less obvious than the haddock's, at the base of the pectoral fin. Neither haddock nor whiting reaches the size of cod or ling but their abundance more than makes up for their smaller stature.

Coley, or coalfish, from the charcoal black of its back, is only one of an almost endless list of names for this fish: depending on where you are and how old or big is the fish, you may hear cudding, cuithe, sellag, peltag, piltock, greylord, saithe, baddock, pickie, sillo, get, podler, cheeto, *saoidhean*, rolki, colmie, sye, *ucsa*, stainlock or cowmag. Although not a favourite food, the flesh being greyish when raw and not as appealing as the cream-white of other gadoids, the humble coley has saved many from starvation. It swarms in its millions in inshore waters in the summer and especially the early autumn and is easily captured by hook and line or in dip nets or traps. In the Caithness geos a dip net could bring in a boll in a few hauls and in Shetland they were caught by the bushel. On Orkney, 1000 sellags, or fingerlings, could be bought for a sixpence. The comment about Nesting, Shetland, in 1793 that coley was 'the principal part of subsistence' could have applied to any township on the northern or western seaboard.[7] From Kilmartin to Unst, its liver provided oil for lamps or for sale, from 6d a Scots pint on Barra in 1793 to a more usual 16d, as in Argyll, to pay the rent.[8]

The Scottish fishery takes several species of flatfish. Plaice, recognised by the orange spots on its back, is perhaps the best known but the list includes flounders (or flukes in Scots), megrim, brill, soles and dabs. The relatively rare turbot can grow up to a metre in size but the giant of the flatfish is the halibut. It can reach two metres and weigh around 300 kilos, and there are many stories of tussles in the landing of such fish. It inhabits deeper, more northern waters than other flatfish. Among the many sharks and rays, only the dogfish and the skate are commercially important. Shark fisheries have been started at various times but they have generally been short-lived ventures. The principal dogfish species (*Scyliorhinus*) can be good eating and is usually marketed under the euphemistic names of 'rock salmon' or 'rock eel'. In the past dogfish were often caught for their oil. The common skate (*Raja clavata*) has a mottled grey back with two yellow-black imitation eye-spots. It lives near the bottom, planing over the seabed. The wings are good eating and the central part of the body, including the head and tail, was reckoned by many to be the best bait for crabs and lobsters.

The sea is home to many strange-looking fish, among them the John Dory and the gurnard, but a prize of some kind must go to the monkfish or anglerfish. It is a bottom dweller and lies superbly camouflaged with its mottled yellow-brown skin and tubercles like warts that resemble tufts of weed. It appears all head and mouth, with an ugly expression to match, and the gape of a large specimen can accommodate small cod. It has in the past few decades acquired a high reputation among gourmets for the flavour of its tail meat but fishermen have always known monkfish taste good.

The mention of fishermen around the Scottish coast in early written sources is scarce. Several of the Acts passed in the Middle Ages refer to salmon fisheries, granting the rights in these to this monastery or that priory or lord, but sea fisheries do not receive the same attention. In around 1154 Tynemouth Priory was confirmed in its right to all fisheries and draughts of nets in the water of Tynemouth[9] and Dunfermline Abbey had the right to the whole head, except the tongue, of every whale or other large fish coming ashore on the royal lands on the north side of the Firth of Forth; whales were a valuable source of oil for altar lamps. At around the same time, the fishermen frequenting the Isle of May were ordered to pay teinds to the monks at the priory there and to fish only with their permission. In 1178, the May priory was granted the right to receive 4d from fishing boats putting in at the ports of Pittenweem and Anstruther[10] and sea fishing rights were granted to the Benedictine monks of Coldingham in 1298.[11] European fishermen frequented the Scottish coast – in the case of the Dutch, from 1164[12] – and these Flemish, German and Dutch boats were considered as something of a nuisance at times, as well as being an embarrassment to those who could see local resources going to line foreign pockets. Laws were passed in an effort to promote the domestic industry, for example, James IV ordered that coastal burghs should build two-ton vessels for fishing and that idle persons should be pressed into that service.[13]

In 1527, Hector Boece praised the wealth of the Scottish seas: 'sa gret plente is of fische in all partis of our seis, specially towart the north, that the samin is sufficient ineuch to nuris all our peple, howbeit thair wer na frutis growand on oure land … France, Flanderis, Zeland, Holland, and mekill of Almany [Germany] cumis with sindry flotis sekand fische yeirlie in our seis.' The European fleets caught or bought enough fish to sustain people in all other lands, wrote Boece, and during Lent passed Scottish fish to the Mediterranean with great profit.[14] It seems likely that at least a few Scottish fishermen or merchants would not have missed this opportunity for trade and, although they may have been slow to develop commercial fisheries, they were active in exploiting the sea for local use. Boece himself noted, for example, the rich fishing of cockles, mussels, oysters, herring and conger eels in Galloway, the herring shoals of Loch Fyne, the 'gret plente' of white fish in the Firth of Forth and, with regard to Orkney, he observed that: 'Ilk man providis for sa mekle fische in the simer as may sustene his hous agane the winter.' Fish seem to have played a dominant role in the diet.

Donald Munro was the first to write a description of the Hebrides – in 1549 – and he makes many references to the fishing there. White fish were the main catch but he also mentions seal-hunting with dogs on Islay, herring in the lochs around Skye and Lewis, and the cockles of Barra. Of Lewis, he makes it plain that all ages and both sexes were wont to try for the pot: '[In a cove] ther uses whytteins to be slain with huikes, verey maney haddocks, and men with their wands sitting upon the craiges of that cove, and lades and women also'.[15] Gaelic place-names also provide some evidence that certain spots were associated with the sea's produce: there are two Shieldaigs, originally the Norse *sild-vik*, meaning 'herring bay', in Wester Ross, only a few miles apart, and such names as *Creagan nan cudaigean* ('rocks of the coleys') and *Camas a'Mhaoraich* ('shellfish bay').

'The saithe fishery was one of the oldest in Shetland, using lines,' said Andrew Williamson. 'The yole may have evolved in response to the saithe fishery. Down around Dunrossness there are ling bones in the archaeological sites. Creel fishing never amounted to much [in Shetland] until after the Second World War. The local boats in Yell caught lobsters but there was very little consumption of crabs and lobsters locally in the past. There was

Three Ferryden fishermen working with lines. Left to right: John 'Jeckie' Coull, Charlie Nicoll, Geordie Pert.

so much fish in Shetland to pick from that the folk settled on a few species, such as cod, for which there are about a thousand ways of cooking. Mackerel were not eaten – they were regarded as "unChristian fish" because of the mistaken belief that they ate corpses. Gurnards were not eaten because they were troublesome to clean, although it's easy enough to strip off the skin and all the thorns by plunging the fish in boiling water for five seconds. Dogfish were not eaten, although spurdogs [*Squalus acanthias*] were eaten in some places – and in Orkney they were split and dried.'

The international trade in fish was dominated in northern Europe for a long time by the Hanseatic League. This institution, in some ways a forerunner of the present European Union, was founded in the thirteenth century among German towns to protect their trade, but the reach of the League extended over the Baltic and most of Europe. Centres were established in many ports, including Bergen, Novgorod and Bruges, and trade routes spidered over a vast area. In 1297, after his victory at Stirling Bridge, William Wallace was able to write to German merchants in Hamburg and Lübeck to tell them that Scottish ports were open again for trade, and we can be sure that fish was a prominent export.

The League declined as nation states asserted their power and new maritime routes developed, and by the mid-sixteenth century the Dutch had won the bulk of the Baltic trade for themselves; but a small surviving part of the Hanseatic empire can be visited in the village of Symbister on the island of Whalsay. It is a stone warehouse, a boð or booth, and it is built right on the edge of the sea so that one wall seems to grow from the quay. It is thought to have been erected by German merchants early in the seventeenth century when the Hanse traded in Shetland for dried ling and cod. The street running up from the booth was once known as Bremer

Old fisherman redding a line. Baskets of bait stand in the background and the man is arranging the line in the scull before him.

Strasse. The building is not large – I paced one of the two floors and found it to be six strides by ten – but it was designed exactly for its purpose. Boats could come alongside and discharge their cargoes by windlass through a door in the sidewall. Standing in the cool interior, you can almost smell the stacks of dried fish.

In the early 1600s, cod and ling were taken with hooks and lines in 'small boats called Yalls'[16] in which the fishermen sailed or rowed to about 10 miles offshore. They caught fifty or sixty fish in a night. 'The fishery of Shetland is foundation both of their trade and wealth,' wrote Martin Martin in 1695, 'and though it be of late become less than before, yet the inhabitants by their industry and application, make a greater profit of it than formerly … '. Shetland had indeed been a cosmopolitan crossroads of the seas: the German merchants had arrived in mid-May and bartered linen, muslin, beer, brandy and bread for stockings, mutton, hens and, primarily, dried fish; and in June the Dutch herring fleet had come, as many as 2000 boats in good years. By the 1670s, however, the situation had changed: '… all kinds of fishing is greatly decayed here' wrote John Marr. 'In old times there was a considerable Trade kept here but now is greatly decayed … at this day only a few Hamburghers and Bremers use a small trafficking in it.'[17]

The activities of the German merchants in Shetland went into a quick decline after the Treaty of Union in 1707 and the introduction of the Salt Tax in 1712.[18] One result was great poverty in Shetland. The lairds began to act as fish merchants as that was the only way their tenants could earn the rent money. A period of great exploitation began, described in detail in Alistair Goodlad's *Shetland Fishing Saga*, and lasted until a new regime of entrepreneurs made a better job of handling the fish business.

A young man's job

Around almost all the Scottish coast at the end of the eighteenth century, line fishing was the standard method of catching white fish. It generally took one of two forms: 'sma' lines' or small lines for haddock, whiting and other inshore fish, and 'great lines' for cod and ling in deeper water. Although the fisherfolk on the Scottish mainland did not enjoy the freedom of trade of the Shetlanders, a freedom that was irksome to authority, they were as adept at exploiting the seas at hand. In 1683, Alexander Garden of Troup, the founder of Gardenstown, wrote a brief description of the fishing on the north coast of Buchan:

> The sea affords white fishes here in abundance, which are Keeling [large cod], Skaitt, Turbitt and Codfish, this they call their great fish, whereof they begin the fishing about the later end of Februar, making use of other Fishes for bait and especially haddocks, and continue it till the Dogfish come in which at the furthest is about Lambas and remove at Hallow day, or the first of Novr at farthest … We have also haddocks, whitings … Seath, Mackreel and Flook … the Seath fish is catched at the foot of rocks close by the shoar and is only found upon this coast May June and July.[19]

What was true of the Buchan coast also applied elsewhere: in the 1720s, exports from Thurso included 40,000 dried cod[20] and Durness was described at the same time as having 'plenty of cod and other white fish'.[21]

The minister of Buckie described in 1792 two classes of boat that corresponded with the two methods of line fishing: a larger type of vessel, capable of carrying 10 tons of cargo, and a smaller type, of four tons. The large boats had a crew of six men, each one working a line armed with up to 120 hooks set seven fathoms apart, and in February, March and April they fished for cod and ling as much as '16 leagues' out in the Moray Firth. In May they went further, in search of skate. The smaller type of boat had five men, working lighter lines, with up to 900 hooks set one fathom apart, taking cod, ling and tusk in the spring and haddock in the autumn and winter. July was reckoned the best time for halibut, and close on the back of them came mackerel. In Buckie as in many villages a boy sailed with each crew and fished with a line half the standard length, serving an apprenticeship of the sea. The handling of the catch varied according to the species. Large white fish were salted in pits on the beach at Buckie and then dried on the rocks. Skate were dried without salt, halibut were used fresh, and haddock and whiting could be preserved by drying and smoking. Liver oil was extracted from ling and skate.[22]

In the old days fish could be preserved or cured only by smoking, drying or salting them. White fish could be split, cleaned and dried in the sun, with some salt. The smoking of white fish was widely carried on. In

Splitting a cod probably for smoking in the premises of Allan & Dey Ltd, Aberdeen.

Golspie, every fisherman had a kiln in the back garden. Sawdust was freely available from the local sawmill to provide the fuel but damp fir cones were also used. Every household had its own 'secret' recipe to produce the best result but generally haddock were split and soaked in brine before smoking. The Golspie families also kept pigs that were fattened on fish offal; if the pig was for home consumption it was taken off the fish diet about six weeks before slaughter but pigs to be sold were not so delicately provisioned to avoid a taint of fish in the pork. The name 'speldings' or, in Gaelic, *spealltagan*, was widely given to smoked haddock and a few places such as Nairn became noted for the quality of their cured fish. Findon is famous for its 'Finnan' haddies, originally smoked over peat fires, and Arbroath for its 'smokies'. James Boswell bought speldings made from whiting in the Firth of Forth for Samuel Johnson who did not like them.[23]

The marketing of cured fish was the basis of commercial fishing until recent times. The scale of these operations in the Viking and early Middle Ages have been revealed by archaeological investigation at sites in Orkney and Caithness.[24] The commercial development of line fishing had reached considerable proportions by the end of the eighteenth century. Along the Moray Firth and the east coast, it was the practice for many decades for the men to make special trips south to the towns around the Firth of Forth at the end of the line fishing season, usually the end of June, to sell their cured cod and ling. It was estimated in 1791 that half the catch of the Slains

Woman making Arbroath smokies in a smoking kiln in the ground.

fishermen was sold in Dundee, Perth and the ports around the Firth of Forth.[25] This was done usually at the end of June and, in the 1790s, a cargo of dried fish could sell for £70, giving each member of the crew a cash income of up to £12. The minister of Gamrie in 1790 thought that white fishing, although 'remarkably poor' in the last few years, had been earning some fishermen £250 a year.[26] Thanks to some enterprising local merchants, Peterhead had built up its fishery business by the 1790s and was sending 400–600 barrels of salted white fish to London every year. Nine boats, crewed by forty men, worked out of the Roanheads area of the town. A few went to Barra Head in the summers and came home with 12 or 14 tons of dried cod and ling, and two boats had even tried to start an Iceland fishery, persevering in the attempt to hook cod in these cold, distant waters for several years before giving up.[27]

In the Hebrides at this time, Stornoway had an 'excellent harbour' and a thriving fishery trade, based on the efforts of the Lewis fishermen. Forty-two boats in the parish of Barvas worked at handlines, taking dogfish, cod and ling, and were selling over 8800 pints of liver oil from dogfish to the Stornoway merchants in the mid-1790s, for up to 8d per pint. The men of Ness harvested seabirds from Rona and Sulisgeir and sold feathers for 10 shillings per stone. The parish of Lochs, where 'the people from their youth are accustomed to a seafaring life', had seventy fishing boats and caught 24 tons of cod and ling each year. Uig parish, on the west side of Lewis, had seventy-three boats; and Mr Mackenzie of Seaforth kept two storehouses with salt for use in curing cod. Stornoway was exporting annually between 60 and 120 tons of dried fish, as well as several hundred barrels of 'train oil'.[28]

Elsewhere in the Hebrides, the line fishery was not so advanced. The *Old Statistical Account* contributor on South Uist noted a great variety of fish but 'no fisheries'. Some of the people, however, were trying their hand at harpooning basking sharks in the Minch, attracted by the knowledge that a large specimen could produce eight barrels of clear oil from its liver. Only one heritor, Colin Macdonald of Boisdale, had tried to develop a line fishery. However, some 'adventurers from Peterhead', presumably the same crews mentioned above, fished from March to July and were observed to be 'pretty successful'.[29]

The Barra men were fishing cod and ling and were sailing with their catch to the Glasgow markets, getting up to £6 for every 100 fish.[30] Tiree and Coll also had an extensive line fishery, and the Barra boats were attracted there and, according to one observer, were more successful than the locals through their greater experience. It was also noted that 'adventurers' from Ireland and the east of Scotland were enjoying success at the lines, with one sloop having caught 16,000 fish in two months. In 1792, a 'company' from Ayr had joined the Barra boats. The catch at this time was 100–240 fish per day.[31]

In the 1770s, according to accounts of Islay, 'four gentleman adventurers from Liverpool fitted out three smacks with wells and caught great quantities of cod and ling at the Head Lands, which supplied the Liverpool markets abundantly; but the bad conduct of the persons employed obliged them to give it up'.[32] Mr McNeill of Gigha had a bit more luck than the four Liverpool gentlemen shortly after this when, in 1788, he began to subsidise the exploitation of the fishing bank north of that island. Eight boats, with crews of four men, were pulling up to around 4000 fish for the market each year by 1792. Here again, however, there were obstacles: the boats were thought to be too small for long lining in the stormy March easterlies and, a complaint voiced almost everywhere around the Scottish coast, the duties on salt were severely inhibiting the growth of fisheries.[33] In the waters around Arran, long lining for the Glasgow market was also being actively followed at this time.[34]

In August 1788, a Shetland shipmaster called John Slatter was becalmed about 35 miles west-south-west of Foula and to while away the time his crew let down a line. To their surprise they caught 250 cod in a few hours. The spot became known as Slatter's Ground but was apparently neglected until almost thirty years later, in 1817, another native skipper, John Petrie in a sloop called *Alert*, tried it and took 900 cod in 30 hours. Petrie and his son tried to keep the knowledge of the fishing ground to themselves. Another skipper, John Thomson of the schooner *Don Cossac*, found it for himself in the following year and landed so much fish that his movements at sea were closely observed. The fertile ground was renamed the Regent Bank and thereafter became famous as a resort for the Shetland smack fishery which flourished for much of the nineteenth century.[35] The term smack was applied to any sailing vessel of a reasonable size: most were sloops but fast cutters and dandies were also used, and in the latter years of the fishery big two-masted ketches, up to 70 ft, had appeared. The first vessel to be acquired in Shetland solely for cod fishing was, as far as we know, the sloop *Ann*, built in Shields in 1816, lengthened in Newcastle two years later so that she could come within the dimensions required under the current bounty regulations, and bought by her Shetland owners in 1820. The 19-ton *Ann* was just over 39 ft long. The smack fishery developed separately from the *haaf* fishery, based on the sixern, and the inshore haddock line fishing. The sixern was too slight for the cod fishing: she could not carry enough, as, to be profitable, cod had to be caught by the thousand, whereas the sixern could make a living from the more valuable ling, profitable by the hundred.[36]

For the smack fishery the crew numbered up to fifteen. They used 50-fathom hemp lines with two large hooks. Two cod took considerable effort to haul and skin could easily be stripped from a fisherman's fingers. The men were paid according to the number of fish they each caught; they kept tally by cutting the barbel from the fish's chin and collecting these small appendages in a jar of salted water sitting beside them as they worked. Herring was used for bait and the smacks usually carried a few drift nets to keep themselves supplied. Horse mussels ('yoags') were also used as bait, and these were dredged by old men from the voes around the islands and stored in salt barrels for the smack fishers. In the early days, the over-exploitation of inshore mussel beds led to complaints from other, poorer fishermen who used them for their own inshore haddock fishing.

Other cod banks around Shetland were found and exploited. In 1819, there were twenty-four smacks in operation and between them they took 342 tons of dried fish.[37] The season on the Regent Bank extended from the end of April until July and in the first few years it was normal to catch up to 2000 cod in two days. By 1819, the take fell dramatically to just 200 for a week's work and in 1820 Arthur Edmonston wrote that 'it may be said to have failed altogether, for scarcely a single fish could be met with on the same ground off which thousands were taken last year'. Edmonston ascribed the disappearance of the cod from the Regent Bank to a change in the distribution of the fish's own food supply.

Shetland was fortunately surrounded by fertile cod grounds and the smack fishery continued for the rest of the century. By the 1840s and 1850s the cod boats were big enough to venture to the Faroes and then to Iceland, and they were probably also the first commercial fishing boats to work at Rockall. According to Andrew Williamson:

> At the end of March or early in April, the smacks would go to the Faroes
> and if the grounds there were not yielding much they would sail down

to Rockall, or maybe try banks between, and if there were not many cod at Rockall they would go back to the Faroes and try there again – they did not think too much of sailing a few hundred miles. By the end of the summer, they would land their catches in Shetland, replenish their stores and set off to fish the coast of Iceland. Some smacks circumnavigated Iceland several times and a few even ventured as far as Spitsbergen, the Davis Straits and possibly the Grand Banks off Newfoundland. The cod were cured in salt. Spain was the main market. A few of the smacks, which were also recognised as merchant vessels, sailed with their own catches as far as Italy or the Black Sea, and on the way home brought cargoes of salt from Spain.

Andrew Williamson's uncle worked at the cod lines and passed on this account of his experiences:

We'd come up to the fishing grounds, drop the sail, use a drogue to stop drifting, clear the decks of the sails and gear, set up pond boards, and start hauling cod. There was no let up if the cod were biting. We kept working until we were absolutely exhausted, eating cold mutton on slices of bread, keeping a kettle going to make strong coffee with a slug of rum in it. The skipper would be keeping an eye on the ship and he could tell from the mast and the motion when the incoming weight of cod on the deck might cause concern for the stability. Then he would say, 'Right, boys, in lines and set up the splitting boards.' We set up two benches on the deck. The skipper and the mate would do the splitting as the crew gutted and passed the fish to them. The livers were often kept but the head and guts were dumped. The fish were split open with a big knife and this had to be done very carefully, to keep up the market value of the fish. Then they were thrown into saltwater washing vats where the boys [every smack carried three or four lads in the crew] scrubbed out every last trace of blood and gut lining. The fish were put in a pile to drip and then they were passed to two hands below to be laid head to tail in banks with salt thrown on them. This carried on until the decks were clear. Then, if we were able, we would start fishing again. If not, we might make sail for some place like Thorshaven where we would anchor and sleep. If we stayed at the sea, we would sleep in shifts while the rest of the crew kept fishing. There was no let up. It was a murderous job – a young man's job.

The smack fishery began to decline in the late 1800s. The last smack with a Shetland crew, the *William Martin*, went out in 1904 but the operation failed to pay.[38] Smack fishing continued with Faroese crews – the Shetlanders had taught the trade to the Faroese in the first place – but the Shetland men turned to the more lucrative herring fishing. Owning and outfitting a smack was an expensive business, and the trade was in the hands of merchants and bankers. A share in a drifter, on the other hand, was within the financial grasp of the fishermen, and all around the coast, the herring fishing was looked on as the most lucrative harvest of the sea.

Baiting's okay, it's getting the bait

As a suburb of Aberdeen, Torry was destined to grow in the 1880s into a great trawler port but a century before this it was a village which, with its neighbour Cove, was home to line fishing boats and a number of yoles. In 1791 there were ten of the former, 23 ft long, 9 ft in the beam, twin-masted and with a crew of six, taking haddock in January, flatfish in prime condition on the sandy offshore grounds in spring, haddock, whiting and turbot in summer and, from November on through the winter, cod. They fished with sma' lines – 720 hooks on each, fixed a yard apart by snoods of horsehair – but used a stronger dog-line in August to catch dogfish from whose livers they extracted oil for sale; twenty livers produced a pint of oil which fetched up to one shilling. They also fished with great lines in the summer: strong lines with sixty hooks on fathom-long snoods set $4^1/_2$ fathoms apart were set down to catch ling, halibut, skate and keeling as much as 15 leagues offshore. The lines were baited with limpets, sand eels, lugworm, mussels and offal; and it was the job of the fisherman's children to gather this every day.[39]

The coastal line fishing was often subsidised by the local laird, whose tenants the fisherfolk were, but the specific terms of the contractual agreements between the fishertoun and the big house varied from place to place. The cost of one of the larger boats, with its rigging and gear, was about £24 in the late 1700s and, in Buckie, the laird provided security for the boat's crew on the condition they served in her for seven years and paid their rent, which typically might have been £5 3s 3d and six dried cod or ling. The smaller boats belonged to the fishermen themselves and they paid no boat rent.[40] Another arrangement applied at Stotfield, whose five boats supplied Elgin with fresh fish: the annual rent for each boat was £5 and the laird furnished a new vessel and gear every seven years at a cost of up to £20.[41] The Findon fishermen paid £3 rent for an acre of ground with their house and garden, 'liberty of fuel' [peat] and harbour rights, while their neighbours in Portlethen paid less rent for smaller plots of ground. In the five fishertouns in Tarbat, Easter Ross, the lairds furnished a new boat every seven years in exchange for a fifth of the catch annually, usually in 1792 rendered in its cash equivalent, £4 for a larger boat and £3 for a smaller one.[42] In the 1840s, the 'old arrangement' was still practised in Fordyce whereby a crewman paid rent to the laird in return for a share in a new boat every seven years[43] but in other places, such as Boyndie, the fishermen were commuting this arrangement to simple annual cash rents.[44]

In Cullen, in the 1840s, seven boats, each with eight or nine men, deployed deep-sea lines on grounds 20–60 miles offshore, spending several days at sea in a season extending from February to the end of May. In June they turned to catching haddock closer inshore and, over the winter months, after the summer herring fishing, the Cullen men turned to using four-man yoles to fish for haddock up to six miles out. This pattern of line fishing combined with drifting for herring was found all along the coast.[45] At Whitehills, a few miles to the east of Cullen, sixteen boats fished for haddock and the local minister estimated that they averaged 'not less than twelve dozen haddocks per boat each day, which will amount to about 23,000 dozen haddocks per annum, besides about 10,000 cod, ling and skate'. He went on to reckon 'in a moderate calculation' that the haddock brought in

John Main, Shoreheads, Stonehaven, redding a sma'line. John Main was George Leiper's grandfather.

10d per dozen and the other fish from 4d to 5d each.[46] The small lines on Lewis were 60 fathoms long, with 240 hooks, and sand eel, limpets and pieces of herring or mackerel were used for bait. An extensive line fishery was carried on in Kirkwall bay in the late nineteenth century; the fisher families lived at the Shore in the town and the catches, after being landed at piers at Carness and Pickie, were spread over drying greens.[47] Between 30–40 boats fished lines from Buckie in the 1860s. Each boat with its lines and hooks was worth about £100 and was owned on an equal-share basis by its crew of eight or nine men. The boats ventured 40-50 miles offshore in search of cod and ling, on trips lasting up to 20 hours.[48]

Donald MacDonald described to me the line fishing practised from Golspie in the late 1800s and into the first half of the twentieth century:

It was basically done from yoles. Some of them were half-decked and there are still a few of them around. They're 80 to 100 years old now. In Golspie we used lines with 300 to 500 hooks with 18 inches between each hook. They were baited at the back of the house before we went to sea. You had to clean off the old bait, put the new bait on and lay the lines in layers in a basket. If you could afford them, you could use newspapers to keep the layers of lines, each layer with ten to twenty hooks, separate, or you could use bent [marram grass]. The baskets were homemade – from willow, hazel or dog-rose briar. In Gaelic the line basket was called a *sguil* or, in Scots, a 'scoo' or scull. It took hours to bait a line. We were very fortunate in having a ready supply of bait – we got lugworm along the shore and in Loch Fleet there were acres of lug, as well as mussels and cockles in abundance at Little Ferry. Children were expected to be expert in opening mussels and cockles with a knife by the age of ten or eleven. At the sea we shot the lines at night and looked them on the following morning. The number of lines per boat depended on what the crew could afford to buy; the skipper might have three lines, and the rest one line each. The line fishing here at Golspie was excellent. The minister in the 1790s called the men lazy because the fish were so plentiful.

Each man might bring home about one hundredweight of fish for a day's work, of which half would be gutted and reserved for smoking and half passed to the women for selling fresh on their rounds.[49]

The Golspie men built rings of stones in handy positions offshore and planted mussels there for future use. The ring was called a *carn* and each one was identified by a float of a distinctive colour. Cargoes of mussels were brought monthly in summer from Meikle Ferry in the Dornoch Firth to replenish the carns; the estate owner with mussel beds would be paid about £1 for a cargo of mussels. The line fishermen of Embo, a few miles to the south of Golspie, preferred cockles as bait and they gathered them daily from around Little Ferry: although cockles had to be dug for, they were reputed to stay on the hook better.

Inshore line fishing had the advantage of fitting in well with other activities, of vital importance to the many communities where exploiting the sea was combined with crofting. In Shetland the use of the sea and the land was combined in such a typical pattern, as William Anderson of Whalsay described it to me:

About November they started rigging out for the haddock lines. That went on from possibly the end of November until the spring. The haddock boats were about 35 ft long – they varied a bit too – not much more than 40 ft. During the winter they were manned by four men, and each man had a share of lines – three each, twelve per boat. The family would clear and bait the lines ashore – if the family couldn't do it, they got some other people to do it. The mending of the herring nets used in the summer went along with the line fishing. A lot of them stopped the haddock lines to prepare for the voar – the tilling of the ground in the spring, planting tatties, sowing corn, repairing dykes, and so on. That was the way of life, the year's cycle. But there's little of that now. No crops. It's all altered – the land's all laid down as grazing for sheep, with a few patches of tatties here and there.

On Whalsay, the line bait was invariably mussels and cut mackerel, alternating on the hooks. The mussels were fetched from some of the voes, for example Mid Yell and Collafirth, in the early part of the year, but most of the mussels were bought from places such as Newhaven. The people had places along the shore where a stone square was made and the mussels were planted there in the tidal zone.

'It was up early in the morning, about five or six o'clock,' said William Anderson. 'You had to fetch in the mussels and shell them. For three lines you needed quite a few. Each line had 450 hooks, and every second one was a mussel. It took time but my mother was always the one here who shelled the mussels and she was fairly fast at it. She was also at the herring gutting – she had speed with the knife.'

'Two years of fishing for haddock with lines, with a break in May going herring fishing for two or three weeks, then back to catching haddock again from my home port were my introduction to the life of a fisherman,' wrote William Stewart of Lossiemouth , who died in November 1993 at the age of eighty-nine. 'I was barely sixteen when my father took ill and was unable to go to sea again. My elderly uncle took over as skipper of the yawl and we carried on haddock fishing.' Mr Stewart became skipper of the yawl himself not long after this and during the early years of his long career at sea he frequently resorted to lines whenever other forms of fishing were not available. The mussels for bait were obtained from the firths between Inverness and Dornoch, and the female members of the family were always involved in the tedious chores of shelling, cleaning and baiting. 'At that time [early 1920s] seine-net fishing was in its infancy and earnings were meagre, sometimes nil. The haddock line boats were doing little better but with low expenses to meet there was always a little money to take home. Lack of haddock in those days was no problem and from every hamlet or harbour up and down the east coast of Scotland, fishermen went line fishing till 1939.'[50]

Dodie Gunn fished with lines in the Pentland Firth, out of the little haven at John o'Groats, in the 1930s:

The sailing time to Dunnet Head was one hour exactly, with the first of the ebb. We fished there the whole of the ebb and came back with the flood. We never used bait, we worked the ripper. We used to work great lines too, and used herring for bait. We might get a halibut, two

or three, or we might get none. Going through the Men o' Mey [a
tidal roost in the Firth] didn't bother us, we knew how to negotiate
it. You can easy keep clear of it. For the handline we'd be out for the
whole day – six in the morning and back at five or six at night. We
split the fish and dried them, and got four bob a stone when they
were dried. We dried them at the house. Sometimes we sold them
fresh. Latterly we got a small pick-up and took them into Wick. There
was always just the two of us, my brother and myself.

The ripper was a form of line fishing that used a shining lure, cast from
lead, with embedded hooks instead of bait. It was operated by jigging it up
and down in the water and was sometimes called a 'murderer', a name
indicative of its fierce efficiency in the right hands. A similar instrument
could be used to take herring; in this, the hooks were set apart from each
other on the ends of a metal bar called a 'sprool'.

On the Ayrshire coast, up to 1920 the pattern of fishing hardly altered,
with ring net in the season and line fishing in the winter. As Angus
McCrindle explained:

> The line fishing was done from the home port of Maidens with the
> wives clearing and baiting the hooks and stowing the lines in a baikie
> [scull], with grass between the layers of hooks. This practice was
> prevalent up until the boats began to have engines fitted, in Maidens
> probably in about 1910 or 1912. My mother had a photo of herself
> baiting lines at Weary Neuk in about 1905. There was great-line
> fishing for cod in the spring of the year at Brown Head [Arran] and
> south-west of the Craig. The hooks were stuck into a cork lashed
> around the top of a basket and, when they were shot, they were lifted
> out and baited with herring, a specialist job for someone with nimble
> fingers, if he wanted to keep them that way. All the lines had to be
> hauled by hand and the men's palms used to be like leather in those
> days. After a lifetime of hauling ropes and lines, my father could not
> straighten his fingers and it was only after a few years' retirement that
> the hard ridges on them disappeared. He used to say that he finished
> up with hands like a gentleman.

When Andrew Mearns began his fishing at Ferryden, his first job was line
fishing with lugworm:

> My father was a seine-net man, and then we had lobster pots as well
> and in the winter lining with lug for bait. We got the lug in the
> Montrose basin, behind the station. The last time I went for lug was a
> long time ago. I was okay as long as I was digging away but, when I
> stood up, my back … well, I said that's the finish, I'm not going back.
> Baiting's okay, it's getting the bait. We used mussels but that didn't last

long, because you need people to sheel the mussels, and the women here who could do that were in their seventies. My mother couldn't do it, she could mend herring nets, because her father was a herring man, and my wife, although she learned to bait the lug lines, never worked the mussels. It's a trade, the mussels. If you see it, it's magic, just the movement of the hands and the knife all the time – 60-70 score and double that for one line.

Dredging the river to deepen harbour access at Montrose removed the mussel beds the Ferryden fishermen used to exploit. To get enough lug for a day's fishing required about two hours of digging in the cloying mud of the Basin:

We did everything ourselves, we used to bait the lines as well, we used to clear the lines, it was murder as a job. You can only get the bait at low tide, and you had to fit in your fishing with when you could get the bait. I kept that up for five or six years. You can't cut lug – that's another thing, and we used to bait some times with the rigger worm [Nereis] and you can break them up, a big one would do maybe three hooks – you can bait lug only one to each hook. The mussel lines, worked from 6 miles to 20 miles off, had 2 ft between each hook maybe, but on the lug lines we took a hook out so that the hooks were further apart – we did that because you just couldn't catch all that lug, you would have been killed with the work – so we worked maybe twenty-five score hooks on one line. The lug lines were for cod, the hooks were slightly bigger than the sma' line hooks – No 17 as opposed to No 19.

The sma' lines were for haddies. We got flatfish but not a lot. We used to get prawns as well. I remember an old man – he was in his nineties when he died about twenty year ago – saying that when they were crossing the prawn grounds they used to knock the prawns off the lines because they were of no value. With the mussel lines, you looked for the hardest bottom, put your lines out, lay about an hour, pulled them in and came in. Then you redd the lines and put them along to the women, who had the mussels all sheeled, and they baited them for the next day. Baiting the lug line took about a couple of hours, depending on how quick you were. You would go out before dark, lay the line with an anchor on each end and leave it all night. We also had weights because you didn't put the line out straight, you zigzagged back and fore. If you were on sand, the line would move. There would be maybe six or ten boats in the area at one time, and there were some terrible messes when you'd get three or four lots of lines coming up together. So that was it, you put the line out, providing that the tide was suitable, and in the morning went out and pulled it up. If the tide was at lunchtime, you had to get the lug the day before.

The Ferryden fishermen also used sea anemones as bait, known as 'clypes'
in the local form of Scots. According to Andrew Mearns:

> A fair-sized clype could be good for ten baits. We started using them
> when the cod fishing started, in October or November, but they were
> no good after the New Year. After the New Year we used lug. The good
> thing about clypes was that you could use them two or three times. At
> the lines, if you got a fish on every hook, the line wouldn't hold
> them. The mussel lines had to be strong because, working on a hard
> bottom, you very often came fast. If you broke the line, you went to
> the other end to haul, but if it broke again you put over your
> creepers, grapnels, to catch it again. The mussel lines were always in
> good condition. When they got a little bit older you used them for
> lug lines. It was common for the lines to break. You also had to be
> careful where you put your lines when you'd finished. They had to be
> properly dried and put in a dry store. At Ferryden a lot of water
> comes down out of the fields and quite a few houses were damp. The
> dampness could go for stored lines. What you did to test it was to put
> it over your back and pull, not too strong.

Line fishing persisted for a long time all around the coast as a main method
of fishing in certain seasons and as a stand-by when times were not so
good. Not much of it is done inshore on any scale now.

CHAPTER FOUR

SILVER DARLINGS

A game of hazard

Herring is the one fish that perhaps above all others has signified to Scottish fishermen the wealth of the sea. It is not a large fish, growing to about a maximum of two feet. The population of herring in shoals can reach enormous numbers – one possible derivation of the word is from an old German term for 'host' or 'army' – and the species has a complex population distribution, with different races frequenting different parts of the coast and breeding at different times. The changing migratory behaviour of the different populations probably explains some of the sudden appearances and disappearances recorded in history. The herring is also a prolific breeder, and larger females have been found to produce 48,500 eggs.[1] The movement of the shoals follows a daily rhythm. The plankton on which the herring feed rises to the surface of the sea as the sunlight wanes. The herring follow them and the normal method of catching them in driftnets took place at night.

Unlike the species lumped together as white fish, herring has its body oils spread throughout its flesh. This gives it its distinctive flavour and high nutritional value, and also means that it has to be preserved in particular ways. Traditionally there were two ways of doing this: 'red' herring were made by smoking whole, salted fish above wood fires for four to six weeks in specially built smokehouses; 'white' herring were preserved by gutting them and packing them tightly in barrels between layers of salt.

Herring has played an important role in Scotland's fisheries for many centuries. Don Pedro de Ayala, the Spanish ambassador to the Scottish court, noted in 1491 that quantities of herring were exported to Italy, France, Flanders and England.[2] It was the Dutch, however, who seem first to have exploited the vast shoals in Scottish waters on a large commercial scale. There is an old saying that Amsterdam was built on herring bones. A Flanders man, William Beuckel of Biervliet, is credited with the invention in 1397 of the method of gutting and packing herring in salt that has remained a standard for many centuries, although he may have refined and perfected an already existing technique. There is a tradition that in the ninth century herring were being caught and salted on the east coast of Scotland by Scots and exported to Holland but that this trade was nipped in the bud by the royal burghs who ruled that local townspeople had to be supplied at a fixed price before export could be allowed; the tradition goes on to maintain that some Scottish fishermen, resenting this interference, moved to Holland and in this way alerted the Dutch to the potential of Scottish waters.[3]

Dutch fleets came over every year in large numbers. The practice may have begun in the twelfth century and the fleet probably reached its peak in about 1640.[4] The fishing was carried out by busses, substantial three-masted boats of 70–100 tons, precursors of the modern factory ship, but the fleet also contained armed escorts and sleek *vent-jagers* (hunters of the wind), for quick passages home with valuable barrels of newly salted herring. Yoles acted as tenders to the busses and the need for these handy, small craft boosted the Shetland boat-building industry. Strict fishery rules were observed, for example no nets were put in the water before midsummer, the Feast of St John the Baptist. In 1633, Captain John Smith described a fleet of 1500 busses at Shetland and reckoned the value of the Dutch catch to be over £300,000.[5] Other estimates of the value of the Dutch fishery place it as high as £1 million a year and employing 500,000 people, one fifth of the population of the Netherlands, and even as much as £3 million in the reign of Charles II.[6] Smith called for a ban on the foreign fishermen and for the development of a home fleet. The size of the fleet has been described as being as many as 2000 but it is now thought that the maximum number was probably 500.[7]

Captain Smith was far from alone in resenting the presence of so many foreign fishermen. Various attempts were made to curb or at least draw some benefit from them. In 1609, James VI tried to impose a tax on the fishery but this was not successful. In 1636 Charles I sent a fleet north to issue fishing licences to the Dutch but the naval vessels arrived late and, most of the Dutch busses having left for home, issued only about 200 licences.[8] Another approach, to prove equally unsuccessful, was to start a native fishery. In a foreshadowing of the plans of Lord Leverhulme for the Hebrides after the First World War, James V, as early as about 1550, tried unsuccessfully to 'plant' Fife fishermen, already experienced in catching herring in the Firth of Forth, in the Hebrides, where the Dutch were also active.[9] James VI tried again to start a fishery in Lewis by moving Fife fishermen to the island but this came to naught within a few years through local opposition.[10] In what must have been a private initiative, Lord Seaforth tried to bring Dutch fishermen to the Western Isles in 1623 but this too failed.[11] Charles I formed an Association for the Fishing in 1632 and settled on Lewis as a likely focus for the new industry. The fishers established themselves at Stornoway in May 1633 and set about catching herring, ling and cod. The incomers used herring busses, large vessels of around 70 tons, but they found that the local men were better equipped in their small boats to carry on the fishing. It also turned out that the Dutch were ignoring the British government's attempts to keep them out and were aided in their defiance by the island landlords. A government commission looked into the problems in the Hebrides in 1634; the landlords said they were following the old practice of extracting dues from visiting fishing boats in the form of ale and meal, fees for anchorage, and a share of the herring catch, and claimed that they had reduced these charges in favour of the Association vessels. It was clear, however, that the newcomers were resented: the fishermen were hindered, English ships driven ashore in bad weather were pillaged, and gear was stolen from boats fishing in the lochs. The Council of Scotland was forced to warn the islanders not to harass the Association crews and caution the landlords that they would be held responsible for the misdeeds of their tenants.[12] It seems that Seaforth, the principal laird in Lewis, bore a grudge against Charles I for taking over land for the fishing station. In 1637 the Association resolved to abandon the Lewis fishery and cut their losses, already considerable through, among other factors, subscribers failing to keep up payments and the actions of Dunkirk privateers in seizing herring busses. The outbreak of the Civil War soon after this diverted thoughts away from fishery development.

The Dutch fleets suffered greatly in the wars between England and Holland in 1652 and 1665-78[13] and never really recovered. The size of the fleet fluctuated but slowly dwindled as the eighteenth century passed: there were still 200 busses in Bressay Sound in 1774 but their numbers had now been equalled by fleets from other nations: Denmark, Flanders, Prussia, France and, belatedly, Scotland and England. There were complaints in the 1790s about Dutch boats coming 'so near [to Fraserburgh] as to preclude the inhabitants from usual stations'.[14]

The herring were abundant along the whole west coast: in the 1630s, Holy Loch, Lochgoil, Inveraray and Loch Fyne are mentioned along with many other places in this regard.[15] They were being caught in all the north-west sea-lochs in the 1720s.[16] Martin Martin described the fishing in Lochmaddy in the seventeenth century: 'This loch hath been famous for the great quantity of herrings yearly taken in it within these fifty years last past. The natives told me, that in the memory of some yet alive, there had been 400 sail loaded in it with herrings at one season; but it is not now frequented for fishing, though the herrings do still abound in it …' Martin thought it strange that there was not a herring net to be found now on North Uist but felt that they could soon be provided if the people received some encouragement. On the east coast, too, the herring swarmed:

> At Dumbar [sic] and on the coast thereabout yearly after Lambmas an
> Herring fishing, which are sold to the countrey people, and many
> made in white and red herrings sent over seas, especially to France for
> wines. There are houses for the making of the red herring. Many fisher-
> touns on the sea-coast, whereby many fishes of all sorts are taken for
> the use of the Inhabitants and neighbouring Shires especially Edr.[17]

The west coast fishery, in and around the Firth of Clyde and the sea-lochs of Kintyre, was at this time the most developed. Cured herring, to the amount of 20,400 barrels, were exported from the Clyde to La Rochelle in 1674.[18] In relation to Greenock, where one of the royal fishing companies had a base, and its neighbouring towns, it was written:

> The Fishing of Herrings on all accounts hath for many years been the most noted of any in Scotland or about it ... There have been reckoned 2500 Lost [last] which comes to 3750 Tun of Herrings made and salted and exported in a year, beside vast quantities which are consumed within the Countrey ... daily food of all the shires adjacent, especially in Harvest time; the Fishers themselves may some years be reckoned to consume 1400 Tun by their own eating.[19]

The migration of the herring in summer up the Firth of Clyde along the east coast of the Mull of Kintyre was such that '... in calm Weather they will swell and move the very Ocean ...' – an exaggeration, but one that illustrates the excitement felt by witnesses. The fish moved by Greenock and could be taken in yairs at Dumbarton; 600 boats worked at the fishery.[20]

Throughout the 1700s, the herring fishery was encouraged by bounty schemes. A major drawback, however, complained about again and again, was the Salt Tax, first introduced in 1712. This essential preservative carried a Customs duty from that date and fishcurers who needed it in larger quantities could obtain it only from a limited series of outlets where the Customs and Excise could regulate its issue; the curers also had to account for their use of it. The excise duty on foreign salt was 10 shillings per bushel in the 1770s and each barrel of pickled herring needed over this amount; imports of salt to Scotland at this time reached over 900,000 bushels.[21] Scottish salt was made by evaporation of sea water but the product was unsuitable for large-scale preservation of fish. There were few Customs depots on the west coast of Scotland where salt could be obtained and they were not generally convenient to the fishing grounds. Without the development of an efficient curing process, the herring catch was sold for fresh consumption. The herring season in the area lasted from July until almost Christmas. In the parish of Glassary in 1792, the local tenants by Loch Fyne crewed thirty boats, with four men in each, and, wrote the local minister, 'from what I can learn every one on an average clears from £20 to £25 Sterling free of all charges.' Men in the parish of Kilfinan on the east shore of Loch Fyne were earning up to £24 from their share in the fishing and some were bringing in up to £1 16s a month and a free barrel or half-barrel of salt fish by working aboard the busses further north.[22]

A net with herring appears on the arms of the town of Inveraray, where sometimes in the late 1700s as many as 500 boats resorted and which exported in the best seasons some 20,000 barrels of cured fish.[23] All the parishes in the area had a stake in the herring. In 1790, over 500 men worked in 120 boats in Loch Goil and Loch Long and, in a little over four months, netted a profit of £5000, of which £1200 was reckoned to stay within the parish of Lochgoilhead and Kilmorich;[24] it was noted, however, that such success did not attend every year and that 'there are some seasons in which this fish entirely disappears'. The Revd Dr John Smith, in Campbeltown, described the fishery as 'a game of hazard'.[25] There was also a vigorous herring fishery on the east coast, in the Firth of Forth: the minister at North Queensferry counted 80–100 boats daily at the nets outside Inverkeithing Bay, and busses were coming through the Forth & Clyde Canal from Glasgow to share in the bonanza.[26] On the Fife side, in Dalgety parish, the herring were considered 'a very beneficial article of food … and are sold at an easy rate, being frequently 6d the hundred of six score'.[27] About 6000 barrels were cured for export in 1793–4.[28] Herring were noted as being abundant in the Solway Firth in some years but no large effort was made to catch them.[29]

In an attempt to encourage the fishery on Mull, the Duke of Argyll brought some fishing families from Shetland to settle at Ross to teach the locals how to cure the catch[30] but the plan came to naught, through the inconvenience of the Salt Tax (the nearest Customs House was at Oban) and the fishing being less productive than expected. The islanders of Bute and Arran enjoyed the shoals swimming around their homes. In the 1690s, the tenants of Rothesay paid their rent from the profits of the herring fishing and had at their disposal eighty 'large boats'.[31] A century later, in Kingarth they were said to fish only for herring and to ignore the white fish which were left to be taken by 'north country strolling fishermen', presumably from Buchan.[32] At Rothesay, 'Many, both young and old, are … employed in spinning and in making and mending nets'; the town had almost 100 boats, each crewed by four men.[33] When the herring appeared on the Kilbride coast in July, off the harbours of Lamlash and Lochranza, 'the inhabitants bestow the most unwearied application to the fishing till the end of November' and it was estimated that the herring brought in £1000 a year.[34] The Clyde herring busses sailed up the west coast of the Highlands and augmented the often considerable numbers of local boats. In Glenelg, in 1793, the minister noted that 30,000 barrels had been caught annually for some years past in Loch Hourn but that the salt laws inhibited the locals who 'at present … are content with fishing a barrel or two to help the maintenance of their families'.[35] In the late summer, vessels from the 'borders of England' came north to Loch Duich to buy herring, and in Lochalsh the locals were selling fresh herring to busses for one or two shillings per barrel,[36] a nice pre-echo of the way the East European klondikers would operate in the 1980s. Stornoway was a centre of the herring fishery in the 1790s. About thirty-five vessels of 20–80 tons were fishing there with bounty support in 1796 and, although in the most recent years, the catches had diminished, the town was exporting several thousand barrels of fish each year, with a peak of nearly 11,000 barrels in 1793.[37] In

the 1760s, there had been an 'immense' herring fishery in Loch Roag and
in the 1790s over ninety vessels fished there, buying the catch from local
people at nine to 12 shillings per cran.[38]

In inshore waters there were local fisheries for sprats, a relative of the
herring and known more often by the Scots word 'garvie'. Garvies were
caught in traps or cruives set at low tide, for example on the coast at Culross
and other sites in the upper Firth of Forth.[39] The fishing of herring in the
inner Moray Firth was limited compared to the riches on the west coast:
eight boats fished from Ardersier in 1790 but sold their catch to busses.
Avoch fishermen sailed north to Caithness or around to Loch Broom to catch
herring but also took some in their home waters: 5000–6000 barrels had

Whaligoe on the east Caithness
coast. Boats landed herring at the
small platform below the cliffs
and women carried fish in baskets
up the flight of over 360 steps.

been cured there in 1786–7 but the annual appearance of the shoals was
unpredictable. When the fish were plentiful, boats came over from Nairn and
adjoining parishes to exploit the bounty and sixty or eighty boats could be
counted on the grounds at one time. In 1792–3, however, the herring were
'uncommonly scarce' and the succeeding year was described as 'indifferent'.
Local merchants who had invested in the herring fishery were bankrupted.
A company, that of Robert Fall of Dunbar, encouraged the Avoch men but this
firm failed and the Northumberland or Beadnel Company stepped in, with
the result that in 1791 three Avoch crews went south to try their nets off the
Northumberland coast.[40] Cromarty was also suffering from a decline in the
herring fishing at this time: the shoals were thin in the Cromarty Firth and
the fishermen's boats were too small to make much of a go in the Moray
Firth – the minister also noted the 'extreme timidity' of the men, an unchar-
acteristic comment about fishermen at any time.[41]

A white horse!

In 1750, the British government decided to encourage fishermen to take part in the Shetland fishery and bounties were offered to the buss owners. At first the bounty was a subsidy of 30 shillings per ton, but this was raised in 1757 to 50 shillings. To qualify for the bounty, the vessel had to fulfil a number of stringent requirements and had to be examined by a Customs officer at the start of the season to ensure it was properly equipped. All the busses bound for the Shetland fishery had to rendezvous at Bressay Sound on or before 11 June. Fishing started on the 13th. A similar rendezvous was established at Campbeltown on 1 September for the Clyde fishing, in the latter half of the eighteenth century, the centre of the Scottish herring fishery. Of the national total of 441,145 barrels of cured white herring exported between 1771 and 1787, 86 per cent came from the Clyde area and 51 per cent passed through Greenock. The area in which the bulk of the fish were taken shifted throughout the century: Loch Fyne was a centre before 1750 but later the busses fished mainly further north on the west coast.[42]

The Act of Parliament setting up the bounty system also brought into being the Society of Free British Fishery, designed to oversee the development of the herring fishery. Although the Society did build busses, it ran into financial difficulties and, amid a welter of criticism over how it had conducted its business, folded after twenty-one years. The herring fishing in the Firth of Forth had declined after 1725. The Fife ports were hit by this. Eyemouth also suffered but Dunbar managed to stay in the game and had taken over the new red herring industry. To the north, the development of the herring fishery on the east coast was not very great at this time – Aberdeen and Thurso exported – but it was as if the east coast fishermen were gathering their breath for the great development that was about to burst forth.

In the late 1700s, the development of the northern fisheries was a matter of public debate among politicians, economists and academics. Foremost among the latter was the retired Edinburgh bookseller, John Knox, who made sixteen tours of the north and wrote an influential book in which he argued for investment in fishing villages. A House of Commons Committee was formed to consider the subject. It sent Knox off on an official tour in 1784, a journey that produced enthusiastic reports of the abundance of herring in Highland sea-lochs. In March 1786, Knox gave an invited lecture to members of the Highland Society in London. The Society had been in existence for eight years and in that time its members, all Highland gentlemen keen to develop the economic and cultural life of their native braes, had raised capital for several projects. Knox enthusiastically presented a plan for the creation of some forty villages around the northern coast from Arran to Dornoch, each to act as a nucleus for a budding fishing industry. The houses would be let or sold to fishermen and other tradespeople who wished to settle in them. Knox reckoned that each village would cost about £2000.

The House of Commons Committee on the Fisheries published its report about two months after Knox's lecture had stirred up interest. Parliament had already passed an Act in 1785 to remove some of the restrictions surrounding the bounty system in existence since 1750; in a second Act, in 1786, new bounties were created. The original bounty, of thirty shillings per ton, had been aimed at the herring busses and had been designed to encourage these large vessels to remain at sea for the three months of the herring season (and in the process act as a useful training ground for potential recruits to the Royal Navy); under the 1786 Act, a reduced bounty of twenty shillings per ton was retained for the busses and a new bounty of four shillings per barrel of cured herring was introduced, designed to encourage the small herring boats. Parliament also looked with favour on Knox's idea of planned villages and the Highland Society began to collect subscriptions to finance the development. A new organisation was formed: the British Society for Extending the Fisheries and Improving the Sea Coasts of This Kingdom. In time it became known as the British Fisheries Society. The office bearers were elected at a meeting on 10 August 1786: the Duke of Argyll became the governor, the Earl of Breadalbane the deputy governor, and among the thirteen directors were Members of Parliament, Highland landowners and Lowland lairds, many of whom would be commemorated later in the street names of Wick.

The Society set to work to raise money and met with an enthusiastic response both in Britain and among expatriate Scots in the colonies. Then it turned its attention to the building of settlements. The first land bought for this purpose was at Tobermory in 1787. Ullapool was acquired in February 1788 and Lochbay on Skye in December 1790. Tobermory was destined to become a trading port rather than a fishing town. At Lochbay the settlers became crofters rather than full-time fishermen. Ullapool thrived for a time but the herring shoals on the north-west coast thinned after 1797, the last good year for the Loch Broom settlement and, although the fish later returned, by then the focus of the fishery had shifted to the east coast. Ullapool suffered through some lean years: in 1823, the only herring caught in Loch Broom were trapped in the yair, intended to catch salmon, of the Revd Dr Thomas Ross. At this time, some of the Ullapool fishermen began to sail around to Caithness where the fishing was booming, the first recorded boat to make the trip being the *Peggy*, skippered by John Cameron.[43] Clyde herring busses were still visiting the area and in 1832 the indefatigable Revd Dr Ross was reported to have earned £150 from his yair by selling herring to them. Two hundred angry Ullapool fishermen, who claimed that the fishing had been a 'total failure' since 1815, smashed the minister's yair and others in the vicinity.

The Salt Tax was one of the first problems tackled by the British Fisheries Society: permission was obtained from the Treasury to erect a salt warehouse and Customs House at Tobermory and to upgrade the one on Isle Martin near Ullapool. Before this, the only Customs House in the north-west had been at Stornoway. The difficulties with salt did not take into account the fact that herring shoals could appear suddenly in lochs remote from the Customs posts, creating an urgent need for salt and no way of meeting it. The market for fresh herring in the Highlands was very limited. Also there were few curers big enough to keep salt in locked warehouses, as demanded by the law. At last, in 1801, a Parliamentary committee reconsidered the Salt Tax but, despite the urging of the British Fisheries Society and other interests for abolition, this did not happen until 1825.

Wick bay in the early days of the herring boom. Picture by William Daniell, 1816-17.

The standard technique for catching herring was the drift net, a relatively simple technology that in essence remained unchanged until the 1960s. The drift net is shot so that it hangs like a curtain in the sea, with a line of floats attached to the upper edge and weights to the lower. In the early nineteenth century the nets were home-made from linen or hemp and a drifter would shoot perhaps twelve of these, joined to form a wall of net in the water. In the night when the herring shoals followed their plankton food to the surface they brushed into the hanging folds. As boats grew bigger the number of nets in the drift increased. By 1860 a drifter might carry twenty-four nets, each 120 ft long and 20 ft deep; the 'wall' of the drift would extend about half a mile from the boat lying to at one end with its mizen up to help keep position. The mesh size was slightly over 1 inch. A hemp net weighed by this time about 25 lb, so the whole drift would weigh some 600 lb; when it was wet and filled with a herring shoal the load the men had to haul into the boat represented a back-breaking task that could take several hours to complete. In the 1860s cotton nets were introduced, a major advance, as the cotton was lighter to handle and fished better. The cotton nets grew longer – in 1878 they are described as 180 ft in length, about 30 ft deep, and with a smaller mesh, but such a net weighed dry only about 14 lb.[44] Cotton was more easily torn than hemp but

the fishermen were prepared to put up with the increased amount of mending. The length of net increased until by the late 1800s a drift was often two miles long. The life of the fabric was lengthened by soaking the net in an extract of oak or birch bark but, after 1840, an extract of the trunks of *Acacia* trees was used. This was called cutch and was imported from India in hard, dark blocks which the fishermen boiled up to make a tar-like soup in which nets were steeped. In deference to the older practice, the process was still called 'barking' the nets. The Forth fishermen preferred to treat their nets with alum, as it produced a white fabric reckoned to be less visible in the water.[45]

Wick harbour in 1865, with herring boats lined up along the waterfront and herring barrels stacked on the quays.

With the simple device of the drift net, the east coast herring fishing became for many communities the fount of all wealth. The British Fisheries Society played an instrumental role in the development and, after the disappointments on the west coast – the Society was to sell Lochbay in 1838, Tobermory in 1844 and Ullapool in 1848 – found their great success at last at Wick. The Society commissioned the engineer Thomas Telford to survey the north-east coast in 1790. Telford travelled from Duncansby to Portmahomack and identified possible sites – he found small fisheries operating from some of the creeks but concluded that the Society would do best to improve the natural harbour at Wick which, he felt, showed promise of greater things. In March 1803, the Society bought 390 acres of land on the south side of the Wick river. Seven families lived there. Telford had

The herring fleet in Castlebay, Barra, in the 1840s.

reported to the Treasury in 1802 on the need to build a new harbour at Wick and, in 1806, Parliament granted £7500 to the Society towards the costs of building, a sum that brought the Society's fund for Wick up to £9500 and allowed work to start. The new settlement was named Pulteneytown. By 1808, the harbour was taking shape, built under the direction of George Burn, according to Telford's plans. By 1809, 20-30 busses were using the harbour. Telford also planned the layout of streets of the new town, and the division of the land into plots. It was strictly laid down that no fisherman could own more than a small plot, to prevent the development of agriculture in preference to fishing; and to encourage fishers and coopers to settle they were offered plots free from rent for the first three years. By 1810, about sixty plots had been taken for dwelling houses. Plots for curing yards were also taken and Pulteneytown grew quickly. But as Dunlop says: 'The truth was that the Society ... had comparatively little to do with the sudden popularity of their new settlement. The real cause was the continued success of the fishery.'

In the years after 1815 the herring fishery spread quickly along the east coast and the ports on the south side of the Moray Firth became by 1836, in the words of an observer in Banff, 'flourishing and extensive' and, despite the withdrawal of the bounty (in 1834), 'still carried on with great spirit'.[46] He observed that 30,000 barrels of cured herring were being exported in a good season from the coast between Gardenstown and Portsoy. At Whitehills, a herring boat ready for sea was reckoned to cost £66 and a fleet of drift nets, good enough to last for six years, could be had for £75. The fifty boats working from Macduff were landing 100 barrels of herring each in the 1840s and the thirty-four Gardenstown boats were doing better still, catching 150 barrels each in the season.

Some of the wonder of the fishery is communicated in a series of five letters Hugh Miller, destined to become one of the country's leading journalists, wrote for the *Inverness Courier* in 1829. He was a careful observer and noted, for example, the chirping sound as the shoal of herring was pulled inboard, caused by the release of air from thousands of swim bladders. Using evocative language that would have been heard from the lips of few fishermen, Miller's rich descriptive prose would, nevertheless, surely have been appreciated by the men he described:

> In the latter end of August 1819, I went out to the fishing then prosecuted on Guilliam [a fishing ground east of the Sutors of Cromarty] in a Cromarty boat ... Our boat, as the tides were not powerful, drifted slowly over the bank. The buoys stretched out from the bows in an unbroken line. There was no sign of fish, and the boatmen, after spreading the sail over the beams, laid themselves down on it. The scene was at the time so new to me and, though of a somewhat melancholy cast, so pleasing that I stayed up. A singular appearance attracted my notice. 'How,' said I to one of the boatmen, who a moment before had made me an offer of his greatcoat, 'do you account for that calm silvery spot on the water, which moves at such a rate in the line of our drift?' He started up. A moment after he called on the others to rise, and then replied: 'That moving speck of calm water covers a shoal of herrings ... ' It moved onward with increased velocity. It came in contact with the line of the drift, and three of the buoys immediately sunk ... The three first [nets], from the phosphoric light of the water, appeared as if bursting into flames of a pale green colour. The fourth was still brighter, and glittered through the waves

while it was yet several fathoms away, reminding me of an intensely bright sheet of the aurora borealis. As it approached the side, the pale green of the phosphoric matter appeared as if mingled with large flakes of snow. It contained a body of fish. 'A white horse! A white horse!' exclaimed one of the men at the cork baulk; 'lend us a haul' … In somewhat less than half an hour we had all the nets on board and rather more than twelve barrels of herring.

Herring fishing at Cromarty ceased in about 1839[47] but at most of the other ports around the Moray Firth the great fishery continued. In the account of Wick in the *New Statistical Account of Scotland*, the author was able to assert that the effort of the 150 men engaged in line fishing was 'of very trifling importance indeed' when compared to the herring fishing. The number of boats that congregated on Wick in the herring season became so great that in 1824 the British Fisheries Society began to build a seaward extension of the harbour and, when the government's bounties were withdrawn, the fishery had no need of support. In 1840, there were 428 local boats and a further 337 from other places. The crews numbered 3828; there were 265 coopers keeping up the supply of barrels and a small army of about 2500, mostly women, worked as gutters and labourers. There were four rope-works, one shipyard and twelve boatyards, an iron foundry, four sawmills and one distillery and brewery among the burgeoning industries; and all the women seemed to be spinning yarn and weaving herring nets. An annual average of 88,500 barrels of fish had been caught in the twenty years from 1820 to 1840.

The herrin' it is the fish for me

The fishery arose every year around the coast like a great chorus and it may have been about this time that these lines of a song began to be sung, the verses accumulating in question-and-answer fashion until the thumping final one:

> Oh fit'll I dae wi the herrin's tail?
> I'll mak it a ship wi a beautiful sail.
> Herrin's tail, ship wi a sail,
> Herrin's belly, lassie ca'ed Nelly,
> Herrin's back, laddie ca'ed Jack,
> Herrin's fins, needles an pins,
> Herrin's heids, loaves o breid,
> An aa sorts o things.
> O all the fish that live in the sea
> The herrin' it is the fish for me
> Sing falla la lido, falla la lido
> Falla la li the day oh.

The song may have originated in the north of England but this version is in Scots. It may be a very old song indeed, with echoes of magic ritual in its evocative lines, but perhaps more than anything it expresses the wonder and gratitude for the wealth flowing from the shoals of the silver darlings.

'The herring fishery has in a very rapid manner increased the population ... and the pecuniary resources of many of the parishioners,' wrote the parish minister of Wick rather sourly, 'but whether it has added to the happiness and comfort of the people at large, may well be questioned.' Wickedness had increased as much as wealth, thought the minister, adding 'No care was taken of the 10,000 young strangers of both sexes who were crowded together with the inhabitants within the narrow limits of Wick during the six principal weeks of the fishing, exposed to drink and numerous other temptations.'[48]

It was the custom of the fishermen to seal a contract with a curer in whisky and various figures have been offered as to the amount of whisky drunk in a day at the height of the herring season – they are all large, running from 500 gallons upwards. 'To the credit of the fishermen at Embo,' wrote the Dornoch minister in 1834, 'it should be observed that, with a few exceptions, they are sober and industrious, and some of them pious.'[49]

To share in the flow of wealth, men began to fish from every creek and small harbour. Whaligoe seems an improbable haven, a tiny shelf of land at the foot of a long stair down a sheer cliff, but it had its little herring fleet – according to Captain Washington's Report, twenty-one boats, crewed by ninety men, in 1840 – and there were other equally unlikely locations, the 'little quarry-holes' Bertram observed in 1865. The herring provided some work also for the fishermen along the north coast of Sutherland, in the county where the Clearances had so recently resulted in the forced eviction of many people from the interior to the coast. From Assynt those with larger boats sailed to Caithness to join in the fishing in August but a large number found good fishing closer to home in the sea-lochs of Glendhu and Glencoul where, in 1839, 200 men worked with twenty-four 'large' and eighty-nine 'small' boats.[50] Throughout the nineteenth century, a feature of the herring fishing on the east coast was the large number of Highlanders who migrated there to find work. This did not please everyone, especially the minister of Tongue who wrote of his flock in 1840 that 'It is manifest that intercourse with the ungodly when south and at the herring fishing in Caithness, together with the desecration of the Lord's day by travellers from other places (a sin till lately happily unknown) are very injurious to their morals and religious sentiments'[51] – an ironic comment in light of the high degree of piety generally shown by Scottish fisher people.

The annual migration from the west coast to the Caithness herring fishing brought much-needed cash into the impoverished crofting townships. The Napier Commission, when it reported on the state of the Highlands in 1884, stated 'By far the greater number of the crofters and cottars ... are wholly or largely dependent for their subsistence on their earnings as fishermen'. There was also interchange of cultural ideas. It was noted in Edderachillis that, although 'the elderly people dress in cloth of their own manufacture', 'Such as repair to the south and Caithness herring-fishing adopt, to a considerable extent, the lowland dress and habits'.[52] The east-coasters were struck by the dignity of the Highlanders and commented on how well they attended public worship. A less happy incident occurred one Saturday evening in Wick in August 1859: a Lewis boy and a Wick lad got into a fight over an orange and, the locals taking side according to language, joined in with the result that the stalls in Market Square were wrecked. The police arrested a Lewisman but his compatriots regarded this as the height of injustice and besieged the Court House to rescue him. Iain Sutherland tells the whole story in his pamphlet *The War of the Orange;*[53] the incident is still remembered in the islands and someone mentioned it to me, although in this version the offending fruit had become an apple!

In Orkney, a Stromness Herring Fishing Company was formed in 1819 and opened curing bases in Hoxa and Herston but lasted only about four years,[54] and it was not until the latter half of the nineteenth century that Stromness became noted as a herring station – it had thirty-eight curing yards in 1898 but a decade later none, and later attempts to revive the industry in the 1920s met with no success. South Ronaldsay was also a centre of curing for a while – it had 245 boats in 1838[55] – but Stronsay had the greatest and most lasting success. Centred on the village of Whitehall, the herring fleet numbered around 400 by the 1840s.[56] Herring fishing also took place on the north coast of Sutherland, from Farr, Durness and Tongue,[57] but this did not reach the scale of the operation based at Helmsdale, where the numbers of barrels of cured fish rose from about 2000 per year in 1815 to over 46,000 in 1839.[58]

On the south side of the Moray Firth every harbour had a few boats at the herring. The larger ports and even some of the villages had whole fleets: Buckie had 245 in the 1840s, Macduff had fifty, Gardenstown thirty-four, Cullen thirty.[59] When the fishing was slack, as happened in some years such as 1834 and 1836, the men from the south side of the Firth hired themselves to the curers in the larger centres at Wick, Fraserburgh and Peterhead. The herring fishery evolved as a great annual event. In 1848, when the August storm attracted government attention, Captain John Washington reckoned that about 3500 boats were active along the east coast of the mainland, crewed by an estimated 17,000–18,000 men.[60] To this should be added the number of shore jobs as gutters, packers, coopers, chandlers, carters, shopkeepers, boat-builders, sail-makers – all dependent on the herring. The barrels themselves were made by an army of coopers from spruce staves imported from Scandinavia and their sizes were fixed by law at 26⅔ Imperial gallons; there were also half-barrels and quarter-barrels or firkins. The coopers served a four-year apprenticeship; a skilled man might make seventy barrels in a week's work.[61] Great attention was paid to the quality of the cured fish to protect the reputation of the export trade.

The herring were sorted and graded according to a seven-point scale before inspectors from the Fishery Board checked the barrels and allowed them to be sealed and branded. The seven categories of herring ranged from 'large full', fish equal to or over 11¼ in. with milt or roe in place, to 'mattie', young maturing fish 9 in. long.[62]

In the 1830s, in the Firth of Clyde, men began to use driftnets in a new way. Instead of shooting the curtain of net and passively waiting for a shoal to blunder into it, they dragged the net through the water and entrapped any herring they encountered. 'The first ring net as we know it was made by sewing drift nets together to make a trawl, and drawing it to anchors or beaches,' explained Angus McCrindle. 'Later the two-boat method was adopted.' Ring nets were in use in Norway in the 1760s for the taking of herring[63] and a similar technique was in common use in parts of Scotland to drag for salmon. This type of fishing was often called trawling but it came to be distinguished, especially in relation to herring, by the more specific term of ringnetting.[64] It may have first been done in 1833 or 1835 at Tarbert. Very soon nets were being woven specifically for trawling. The fishery officer at Inveraray reported them being used in December 1836 at Otter Spit on the east shore of Loch Fyne. The mesh in these nets adhered to the regulation one inch but, as ringnetting proved to be very successful at catching herring, suspicions arose that smaller meshes were being illegally used. Ringnetting was to develop into a sophisticated method, a forerunner of the efficient – some would say deadly – purse seine that made its appearance in Scottish waters in the 1960s. By the 1950s, a ring net measured over 300 yds long and extended to a depth of 45 yds in the open sea. The boats worked in pairs called partners or neighbours. One boat shot the net and then the partner picked up one end before the two vessels towed the net and turned towards each other to entrap the shoal of fish. As the boats came together, the crew jumped from the partner to the shooting boat and helped to haul, the partner meanwhile keeping a steady pull on the towrope to stop the other from drifting over the net.[65] The ringers came to feel themselves to be a cut above the driftnet men who, in Tom Ralston's words, 'simply shot the nets and hoped for the best'.[66]

Ringnetting in experienced hands was so efficient that, in the early days, it was the source of much unrest. Driftnet fishermen objected strongly to the ringnet, as its use spread in the 1840s, and they feared that the method would deplete the shoals. Most of the lairds in Kintyre supported the driftnetters in condemning ringnetting. Only John Campbell of Stonefield, on whose estate most of the Tarbert fishermen lived, supported ringnetting and got up a petition to the Fishery Board in December 1848 in its favour. In 1849 two petitions against it were submitted to the Board and a further petition signed by eleven Glasgow fishcurers followed. The ringnet fishermen were accused of destroying herring spawn and fry, interfering with the operation of driftnets and taking the catch from among them, and dumping dead fish after a heavy catch. Fears were expressed for the future of the Loch Fyne stocks. Adherents of ringnetting said the method was cheaper – a skiff cost about £10, and a net £10–£12, compared with £35–£40 for a driftnet boat and £30–£35 for set of driftnets – but earnings were greater: £20–£200 per boat in 1848, compared with maximum of £140 for drifters.

In July 1851 ringnetting was condemned as illegal by Act of Parliament. However, it was not expected that fishermen would observe the law, and in the summer of 1852, the Fishery Board cutter *Princess Royal* and HMS *Porcupine* were sent to Loch Fyne to enforce the Act. Ringnetting was curtailed but not entirely suppressed. Ringnetters were reported to be fishing secretly and making off with their catches but leaving large numbers of dead fish on shore. The dispute went on and in the following year, in June 1853, a

Painting of the Montrose fishing fleet c.1886 by William Findlay.

fisherman was shot and wounded one night by a patrol from HMS *Porcupine*. Some officials came to realise, however, that ringnetting could not be suppressed and the law was succeeding only in making otherwise law-abiding men criminals. By 1858, 119 trawlers were at work in Loch Fyne. The use of the net spread to the upper reaches of the loch, north of Otter Spit. Fights broke out between Tarbert ringers and Inveraray drifters. There were more outbreaks of violence, more petitions, for and against, and heated public debates. The Royal Navy patrols and Fishery Board officers seized nets and boats but could not prevent the determined inhabitants of Tarbert from carrying on the ringnetting. Nasty encounters took place between the two sides, reaching a tragic climax on a June night in 1861 when a fisherman, Peter McDougall of Ardrishaig, was shot in the head and killed on the skiff *Weatherside* by men from HMS *Jackal*. After this, there was a decrease in trawling and Tarbert suffered economically. Royal Commissions in 1863 and 1865 declared that the anti-trawling laws had been passed to protect existing business interests among the curers and the driftenetters and that trawling had increased the supply of cheap, wholesome fish to the country at large.

The suppression of trawling had not resulted in increased yields from drift-netting. The continuing tension and occasional violence around the shores of the Firth of Clyde were also having their wearing effect and, finally, Parliament bowed to the inevitable and in July 1867 made ringnetting legal.

There was a sizeable fishery in the Firth of Forth for garvies, as already mentioned, and for herring. The work was seasonal, with a winter fishing in January to March and a summer fishing off the East Neuk, called the Lammas Drave, in August and September.[67] In the late 1830s, herring boats from St Monans, Pittenweem and Cellardyke began to sail north to Wick to take part in the fishing there. West-coast fishermen introduced the ringnet to the Forth in 1884[68] amid some controversy over its use but the method was adopted and became a standard technique for the local fishermen. Jim Wilson described to me how some Forth boats worked the ringnet solo, using a pig-iron anchor to hold the boat from drifting in over the circle of net while the catch was being taken aboard. Sprats were caught inshore and the net could be shot even in the old Leith docks or in Granton harbour itself, but generally they worked upstream as far as Alloa and seawards to St Abb's Head or round to St Andrews. Mixed shoals of sprats and small or 'halflin' herring were separated after they were aboard by riddling; nets of different mesh were placed inside each other and the catch was sorted by hand, a task that could take six men some hours to complete.

Nothing that man is likely to do is likely to diminish the general stock of herrings

The herring fishing fuelled a large export trade in cured fish. In the early years the barrels of salt herring were sent to the West Indies as food for the slave population, and a considerable proportion was also exported to Ireland. After 1815 and the end of the Napoleonic Wars the continental market in Europe gradually assumed prominence and became the dominant one. The burghers of Germany demanded herring of high quality and great pains were taken to ensure they received them. Although there were fluctuations from year to year, the overall size of the cure trended upwards as the years went by – from 300,000 barrels in the 1830s to 1,300,000 or so in the 1880s.

The fishermen also began to go further afield and to work outside the initially narrow summer season to maintain the catch. In the 1840s east coast boats moved through the Pentland Firth to fish in the Minch in the early summer, in May and June. Stornoway was the focus of this fishery at first but curing stations were set up at other sites in the Hebrides: along the east coast of Lewis and Harris, on Scalpay, at Lochmaddy, in South Uist, and at Castlebay on Barra. The Hebrides fishing reached its peak in the 1880s with some 1400 boats at work, 80 per cent of which came from the east coast.[69] With help from public funds, Liz Duvill's great-grandfather bought Dry Island at Badachro near Gairloch in 1884 and established a curing station, one of three in the vicinity. Fife boats began to venture south to catch herring off the east coast of England in the 1860s, and from the 1890s boats from the Moray Firth began to follow them; the winter herring fishing based on the East Anglian ports of Yarmouth and Lowestoft became an established part of the fishing season. The fishing fleets in Wick and other places also began to fish for their herring closer to home in the winter months. The Shetland herring fishing began to develop in the 1880s and quickly grew as boats flocked north from the Moray Firth to exploit these 'new' shoals. As in the Hebrides, a network of curing stations sprouted among the northern islands, with the most northerly at Baltasound on Unst. The final pattern of the fishing was now established. The east-coast season started in the far north in the summer and moved southward to end late in the year off East Anglia. This pattern lasted right through the transition from sail to steam, through good years and bad, until the 1950s with very little variation.

Aberdeen did not play a significant part in the east coast herring fishing until the 1870s. Until then it saw mostly line fishing by the men from Footdee and Torry and a considerable salmon fishery on the twin rivers of the Dee and the Don. In 1869 only sixty-nine drifters were working out of the town but in that year work began on diverting the course of the Dee to make improvements to the harbour. A large area of land was reclaimed from the rivermouth south of the area called the Inches, where the Albert Basin is now, and let to curers for yards. In the following year, the number of boats had grown to ninety-six, still low compared to the fleets of over 500 landing in Peterhead and Fraserburgh and lower than the 200 or more working from Stonehaven. However, the Aberdeen fleet of drifters bloomed and quickly reached over 400, staying at that level for most of the decade. The number of people employed reached the 5000 mark and Aberdeen became the fourth, in some years the third, largest herring port in Scotland.[70]

This was in keeping with a trend that had been apparent for many years. As the fishing grew and bigger boats appeared, the capacity of many of the smaller harbours to accommodate them was outstripped. Peterhead had become the second largest herring port, after Wick, by the 1850s. In 1836, 260 boats had fished from the town but this figure had risen to over 400 by the 1850s. There was extensive harbour development throughout the nineteenth century and the town was able to accommodate the newer, larger fifies. Fraserburgh also saw extensive improvements and, between 1861 and 1876, displaced Wick from its place as first herring port. New harbours were completed at Anstruther and Buckie in 1877, the former funded by the government and the latter built by private capital put up by John Gordon of Cluny.

The boom years could not go on for ever. Fears were being voiced about the effect of the continuing and expanding assault on the stocks of herring but these were dismissed in a cheerily optimistic way by Frank Buckland and his colleagues in 1878.[71] The men were charged to inspect the fishing and report to the House of Commons. 'Nothing that man has yet done, and nothing that man is likely to do,' they wrote, 'has diminished, or is likely to diminish, the general stock of herrings in the sea.' There was no need to impose any restrictions on the fishing effort, they said. With a Victorian love of big numbers, they calculated that the Scottish fleet was catching 800 million herring in a year but that this was only a fraction of the amount consumed by predators; they reckoned that cod and ling were eating 29,400 million herring – thirty-seven times the Scottish catch – and that gannets were swallowing a further 1110 million annually. For no apparent reason other than enthusiasm, they calculated that the driftnets of the fleet could form a continuous line for nearly 12,000 miles, three times the distance from Liverpool to New York, and cover an area of 70 square miles. Confidently they felt it probable that this vast extent of net was having no diminishing effect on the herring population but might be scaring fish from narrower, inshore waters.

Herring landings at smaller ports such as Lybster, Helmsdale, Buckie and Burghead on the Moray Firth, in the Firth of Forth, on the Berwickshire coast, in the western sea lochs and in the Hebrides had all declined dramatically in the late 1860s and early 1870s. Buckland and his colleagues ascribed the decline partly to a want of good harbour accommodation: the efficient boats were working from big harbours and only smaller, inefficient boats were left in the smaller places, resulting in smaller catches there. They had to admit, however, that this could not account for the whole of the decline and that 'herrings visit the districts in fewer numbers than formerly'.

The near-collapse of the herring stock still lay many decades in the future and before that happened the economics of the curing industry reached its own crisis. Over-production and a rapid drop in price for cured fish occurred in 1884, a year when the quality of the herring themselves was mixed. Curers' losses were as high as £1 per barrel in some instances. Debts could be carried over from year to year but the large catches in the next two years exacerbated the downturn. Banks withdrew support and the slump affected the ancillary trades of boat-building and net-making as well as the incomes of the fishermen themselves. Some curers went out of business and others began to buy fish at the quay by auction rather than take catches according to previously agreed fixed prices. The fishing effort decreased. The industry was, however, to recover from this setback in the early to mid-1890s and continue to expand until the eve of the First World War.

CHAPTER FIVE

FROM SAIL TO ENGINE

An efficient fishing machine

The herring boom brought about changes in the old fishing communities. The number of men and women drawing a living directly from the sea increased, and many of them travelled extensively as the season passed to work first from one base and then another. Towns such as Lerwick and Wick were home at least for a few weeks to people from other parts of the country. Hundreds of hired hands came from crofts throughout the Highlands to work on the drifters or in the curing yards, and many of them learned enough and were inspired enough to acquire a boat and nets of their own. Then, as the industry became concentrated on the larger ports, the villages had to adapt. Some settlements flourished only briefly and then died back to quiet hamlets with only a few local boats making a living from the lines or the creels. And other changes were taking place which also had their far-reaching effects.

In 1788, Patrick Miller of Dalswinton, a few miles north of Dumfries, had tried out steam-powered boats on the loch near his home; he had a paddle steamer called the *Experiment* built in Leith and chugged for some miles up the Forth in it. Other trials of steam were made, on both sides of the Atlantic: Robert Fulton's literally named *Steamboat* ran up the Hudson River in 1807 and Henry Bell's *Comet* first sailed on the Clyde in 1812. The *Comet's* engine generated 3 horsepower and pushed her at a speed of 7 knots. She was soon sailing regularly from Glasgow to Tarbert and on through the Crinan Canal to Oban, Port Appin and Fort William. In 1833 the *Royal William* became the first ship to cross the Atlantic all the way by steam. Steamer traffic was common in the Firth of Clyde by the mid-1800s. It was to be a long time, however, before steam was harnessed for fishing. Paddle wheels had no place aboard a vessel with nets to haul and, in any case, the expenses of construction and fuel would have been beyond the purse of any fisherman.

Industrial processes were being applied to other areas of interest to the fisherman. Machines for making nets were patented in Britain as early as 1778 and William Paterson of Musselburgh invented his famous net loom in 1826. Net-making remained, however, a cottage activity for a long time

and many a man or woman skilled with the needle could earn some money
during the winter months by weaving a net by the fireside. Indeed, long
after netting could be bought readily off the shelf, fishermen continued to
make and mend their own gear, partly for economy and partly because
factory-made netting had to be rigged up anyway before it could be used.

Before factory-made gear became readily available, fishermen made use
of whatever resources were at hand. For example, animal skins were widely
used to make buoys. In the Seatown area of Lossiemouth in the early
nineteenth century, dogs were still being bred for this purpose, a practice
that gave rise to the nickname of 'doggers' for the fishermen of the area.[1]

Steam made its first impact on fishing not on driftnetting but on
trawling. The technique was not a new method when it began to make its
presence felt in the mid-1800s but its use had been on a limited scale until
then. Trawling for herring, in the form of ringnetting, was of course already
established in the Clyde area. Now it was to be applied to the taking of
white fish. Unlike line fishing and driftnetting, it was an active rather than
a passive way of catching. In line fishing, if the cod and ling fail to bite, they
are not caught, and if the herring shoals do not swim in the direction of the
drifts they likewise escape – but trawling is different. The net is dragged like
an open mouth after the fish and swallows them. It is not difficult to
conceive of such a method, and the word itself is derived, like so many
fishing terms, from old Dutch *traghelen*, to drag. In inshore waters, trawling
a net was easy, as the operators could stand on firm ground and lend their
shoulders to the pull. In the open sea the development of the technique had
to wait for vessels able to exert a strong pull through the water.

In the early days, the trawl was used mostly in southern English waters
by boats working out of such ports as Hull and Barking. Its use had
penetratred as far north as Sunderland and Berwick by the mid-1800s but
Bertram could still observe in 1865 that 'in Scotland there are no resident
trawlers'. In this he may have been mistaken. In April 1850 there had been
a 'riot' in St Monans because two trawlers had been working in the Treath
or Fluke Hole, and there were sporadic workings with the beam trawl in
later years, such as in 1861 when men from St Monans itself were using it;
it was reported that the trawl was destroying herring spawn and that
fishermen were selling spawn to farmers as manure for 1 shilling per
cartload![2] The Buckland Commission reported in 1878 that the Anstruther
and Pittenweem fishermen had discontinued the trawl after these early
experiments but that the St Monans men kept it up until the Fishery Board
banned it for three years from 1862.[3] No advantage was seen in this ban
and it was later withdrawn.

Bertram described the typical trawler of his day as a vessel of about 35
tons burthen with a crew of seven. The trawl-rope was 120 fathoms long and
6 in. in circumference. At this time trawling meant beam trawling – the
beam was a heavy spar of elm, 38 ft long and 2 ft in circumference in the
middle but tapered towards each end where vertical legs, 3 ft high, called

trawl heads or trawl irons, jutted downward to hold the beam off the sea bottom. The trawl warps were attached to oval rings at the ends of the beam, and the bag net, 100 ft long, trailed behind the beam, attached to it and the ground-rope. Trawlers worked these nets on muddy or sandy bottoms, generally 20–30 fathoms deep (although Hull trawlers were working the much deeper Silver Pits 90 miles off the Humber), dragging them at 2 or 2½ knots. Sailing trawlers were, of course, entirely dependent on the wind for the direction and power of their dragging. The method was yielding 12–14 baskets of fish a day which were brought to market packed in ice.

Trawling was widely regarded as causing damage to the grounds, damage Bertram felt was greatly exaggerated. The method's critics, he says, have described 'this instrument of the fishery as terrible in its effects, leaving … deep furrows in the bottom of the sea, and crushing alike the fry and the spawn'. The trawl, however, could be worked only on clean ground and Bertram thought its effects on spawn were exaggerated as herring laid their eggs on rocky ground. (It was to be some years before biologists realised that white fish laid pelagic eggs, also safely out of the way of a working trawl.) Bertram felt that the trawl net could not be dispensed with, and most of the white fish in the wholesale markets in England were caught by the method. Nevertheless there was much opposition to its use. Its opponents claimed that trawling was leaving some fishing grounds bare of fish, large proportions of the catch were too crushed to bring to market and were being dumped at sea, and spawn, the seed-corn of the stocks, was being dragged up from the seabed by the ton. The method had its supporters who argued that only a small proportion of fish were damaged beyond saleability, that spawn was not taken up, and that catches were not falling off.

In 1872 David Walker of Johnshaven tried beam trawling under sail in more open water.[4] Buckhaven became a centre for beam trawling. The method really became important, however, when steam engines provided a new and far more powerful means of propulsion than the wind. Britain's first steam trawler, the *Thistle*, was launched in Dartmouth in Devon in 1867 from George Bidder's yard[5] and was followed a year later by the *Florence*. At 49 ft and 48 ft respectively, they both proved too small and in 1870 the larger *Bertha*, 66 ft, was launched; she sailed to the Tyne and had her steam engine fitted by George Robert Stevenson. Capable of 11 knots and with a steam winch, the *Bertha* proved to be an efficient 'fishing machine' but there was one drawback: the towing warp to the trawl frequently fell foul of the propeller and was often cut. Her successor, the *Edith*, launched by Bidder in 1872, was fitted with a lifting propeller and, another innovation, a steam capstan.[6] In 1877, a Mr Purdy converted a Sunderland steam tug called the *Messenger* to a trawler and, as is often the case with an experiment, the sailing skippers laughed but probably thought again when she cleared £710 profit on her first trip.[7]

Iain Sutherland tells how Scotland's first screw-driven steam fishing boat was launched in Wick from Robert Steven's yard in March 1869: the

the first one later, in Aberdeen in 1871.[9] In Aberdeen some unsuccessful
attempts to fish with steam were made in the 1860s. More success was
achieved elsewhere – line fishing boats from Leith were powered by 1878
and trawlers from South Shields were towing in the Firth of Forth for seven
or eight boxes a day in the same year.[10] In October 1878, a steam trawler
from Blyth, called the *Integrity*, collided with a ferry in the Firth of Forth and
sank. A steam propeller vessel, the *Alpha*, was built in Thurso in 1879; after
the herring season she beam-trawled in Orkney waters but mechanical
problems and damage to the fishing gear made the operation less than
successful.

The drift net fishermen saw the new technique as a threat. It was
alleged that the warps came up from the seabed sticky with herring spawn.
Up and down the coast, meetings were called to protest the upstart trawlers
and feelings ran very high. In some places, trawler crews were molested.
Boys in Wick in May 1884 stoned a trawler crew while they were mending
their nets.[11] Trawling had, however, arrived to stay. Early in 1882 two English
trawlers steamed into Aberdeen from the North Sea to land their catches.
Some local businessmen were impressed enough by this method of fishing
to buy a steam tug from Dublin called the *Toiler* and fit her out for trawling.
She is said to have cost £1550 and she may also have been the first Aberdeen
vessel to use the newer method of otter trawling, where two large wooden
'doors' were towed before the net so that the pressure of the water on them
held the mouth of the net open. Otter trawling was not to become widely
adopted until the 1890s. The *Toiler* made £200 in her first month and at the
end of the year bonuses of £520 were shared out to the crew.[12] The
Aberdonians were convinced that trawling was worth sticking with. Two
new ones, the *North Star* and the *Gypsy*, both 100 ft long, were built and
launched in 1883 and the granite city was on her way to becoming
Scotland's top trawler port, less than a decade after she had taken to herring
fishing on any scale. By 1892, thirty-eight trawlers were registered in
Aberdeen, by 1900 there were 148[13] and, by 1912, 230.[14]

The conflicts between trawlermen and other fishermen reached such a
level that, in 1883, the government set up a Commission to investigate the
nature of the dispute. Under its chairman, the Earl of Dalhousie, the
Secretary of State for Scotland, the Commission not only travelled around
the country and drew evidence from scores of witnesses in fishing
communities as far north as Golspie but also went to sea to see the trawls
in action. The latter experiments were carried out under the supervision of
Professor William McIntosh of St Andrews, a pioneer in marine biology
studies. The Commission reported in March 1885 and one outcome was the
amending in 1885 of the 1883 Sea Fisheries Act to give the Fishery Board
for Scotland the right to pass by-laws to regulate the fishing in home waters.
The International Convention in The Hague in 1883 had established the
three-mile limit as the standard extent of territorial water around all the

coasts of western Europe (the Scandinavians settled for a four-mile limit) but this had at first applied only to foreign vessels. British fishing boats could fish right up to the shore anywhere around the British coast. In April 1886, Dalhousie signed by-laws to exclude beam trawlers from the Firth of Forth, St Andrews Bay, the Firth of Tay and a stretch of coast between the Cruden Scars Rocks and Girdleness lighthouse. The exclusion zones were added to over the years until in August 1896 the whole Moray Firth between Buchanness and Duncansby Head was placed off-limits to trawlers.

This still left large areas in which the trawlermen could work and disputes continued to flare up. Ross-shire County Council passed a unanimous motion on 31 January 1894 in which the councillors called on the government to protect the line fishermen of the Highlands from the 'depredations' of trawlers working within the three-mile limit, and asked for a ban on trawling in the Minch.[15] Meanwhile the Admiralty had despatched a gunboat, the *Foxhound*, to patrol Hebridean waters but before long there were complaints that the *Foxhound* was spending too much time in Stornoway harbour while trawlers were pillaging the Lewis sea-lochs. The irate fishermen also pointed out that, while steam trawlers could reach 12–13 knots, the *Foxhound's* top speed was only 8 knots. The Ross-shire MP provoked laughter in the House of Commons when he claimed that the officers of the *Jackal*, a gunboat patrolling on the east coast, were attending every tennis tournament, garden party and fête in Easter Ross when, presumably, they ought to have been out chasing trawlers.

The trawlers did not, however, enjoy total freedom in flouting the law. The *Nellie* from North Shields was arrested in December 1893 for fishing about one mile from Golsta Head in the Minch; the skipper was offered a £50 fine or thirty days in prison, and he chose the latter.[16] Another North Shields trawler, the *Stephenson*, was taken in dramatic fashion on 30 June 1894 in Shetland waters by the gunboat, the *Cockchafer*: 'The chase, in course of which the trawler was repeatedly fired upon, was a long and exciting one, and owing to the prevalence of fog the gunboat nearly lost its prize but ultimately the trawler was caught and taken to Lerwick, where the master Matthew Telford was lodged in the county jail.'[17]

By 1900, trawling had become more important in Aberdeen than herring fishing, only four years after the city's best year for the latter. Granton and its neighbour, Leith, were also established as trawler ports by this time and a small fleet operated from Dundee. Aberdeen remained, however, the premier trawler port in Scotland. In 1900 of the 232 Scottish trawlers, 148 were Aberdonian. At this time it is also interesting to note that there were seventy trawlers operating under sail in the Firth of Clyde and the Solway Firth.[18] The cities, with their large fish markets and efficient rail connections to the large urban centres in the country, were to remain the centres for trawling until the series of far-reaching changes that overtook the industry from the 1960s onwards.

As well as making trawling possible, steam benefited the herring fishery. The steam drifter chuffed on to the scene. An early one would appear to have been the *Content* which arrived in Wick from Yarmouth in July 1899.[19] From photographs of her, the steam engine sits amidships, just behind the boom of the smack-rigged main mast, and a hutch-like wheelhouse stands just forward of the mizen-mast. Peter Anson identifies the *Rob Roy*, built in Aberdeen in 1882 and registered in Leith, as being typical of the early steam drifters:[20] she was 56 ft long and 12 ft in beam, with ketch-rigged masts and a funnel rising just behind the fish hold.

Matthew Tanner pinpoints another vessel, the *Perseverance*, as an early drifter; she was built in Leith in 1886 for an English owner and her design represented even more the transition to the new source of power.[21] She had no wheel-house and a full set of lugsails on two masts with the tall smokestack from the engine reaching up between them to pour out its smoke high above the deck.

The *Content* (WK 54) in Wick.

The design of the steam drifter settled quickly into a familiar form. The sails, now redundant apart from the mizen which still helped the boat lie to at the end of the drift net, were removed and the main-mast acquired its principal function as a crane for lifting ashore the catch. The hulls were still built of wood but the shape was changing to produce the counter stern. The wheel-house was erected as part of a larger superstructure comprising a deck-house and the roof of the engine-room, now set aft. The steam winch was positioned at the break of the foredeck. The thin, high funnels were nicknamed 'Woodbines' from their resemblance to the cigarettes the fishermen smoked. Steam trawlers had a similar overall shape to the drifters except that the trawling winch was positioned in front of the wheel-house.

Most early steam drifters were built with wooden hulls in Yarmouth and Lowestoft[22] but these proved to need considerable strengthening for the more northern waters. There was a great upsurge in the building of steam drifters

Drifters in Fraserburgh in 1900.

at many ports, for example around the Moray Firth, where adaptations to local conditions were introduced. Ron Stewart has published a study of boat-building in Moray and pinpoints many yards turning out steam drifters – in Portgordon and Buckie from 1903, in Cullen and Portknockie from 1906, in Portessie from 1907.[23] Nairn acquired her first steam drifter, *Magnificent I*, in 1904. These vessels ranged in length generally between 75 ft and 90 ft. The first Shetland vessel to be equipped with steam was a line fishing boat, the *Owners' Delight*, built in 1911, and she had sails as well.[24]

Many of the yards switched to building steam drifters from the construction of zulus and the hull form of the newer vessels retained much of the stout build of the sailing drifter. The sailing drifter took a long time to disappear. For one thing, they were much cheaper to build and run: a zulu might cost £800 against the £3000 required for a steam drifter of similar size, and the wind was free whereas coal was consumed in the new engines by the ton, not to mention the need to ship and pay a fireman to look after the boiler. Also many of the older fishermen knew how to handle their vessels under sail and, in the early days, could outdo the steamers for speed in the right conditions. In 1903, a Wick skipper called Jim Baikie took his fifie, the *Alexandra*, under sail from his northern home port to Yarmouth, quay to quay, in just over forty-two hours; the distance is about 460 miles and he must have averaged about 10 knots.[25] In 1914, sailing boats still comprised 72 per cent of the Scottish fishing fleet.[26] Gradually, however, the reliability of steam, probably coupled with the enthusiasm of the younger men for the new technology, won the day. But there were still over 5000 sailing craft at the fishing after the First World War, or 62 per cent of the total fleet.[27] By 1925 the proportion had dropped to 54 per cent, and the *Fishing News* observed that 'the process of elimination will probably continue; it is now mainly on the West Coast and in the Shetlands that the sailing boats are to be found'.[28] On the eve of the Second World War, there were still over

Dry Island, Badachro, near Gairloch showing the herring curing station, staffed by Stornoway workers, and the local drifter *Dream* in 1894.

1800 sailing boats, almost all under 30 ft in length, at work;[29] finally, in 1967 the number dropped to none.[30]

Steel hulls made their appearance very soon in the history of the steam fishing boat but the wooden hull was slow to disappear. The last wooden steam drifters to be built were the *John Herd* (FR 149) and the *Lizzie West* (BF 213), launched from Herd & Mackenzie's yard in Buckie in 1930. When her fishing career finished, the *Lizzie West* was given a retirement role as a place where nets could be barked, until her boiler blew up and she was scrapped in the early 1970s.[31] The last steam drifter with a steel hull, the *Wilson Line* (KY 322), was built in 1932 in Hall's yard in Aberdeen for an Anstruther skipper, David Watson. Skipper J. Muir of Cellardyke continued to fish with a steam drifter, the *Coriedalis* (KY 21), until 1956.

Hardly had steam begun to displace sail as a means of propulsion than it too was challenged by the oil-fired internal combustion engine. Early experiments with motor power were carried out in the Baltic – a Danish fishing boat was motorised in 1895 – and a Royal Navy officer was sent to inspect them in 1905, and a new fifie was equipped with a 25 hp Dan motor from Copenhagen. The motor engines had the advantage of being easily fitted into the existing fifie hulls, the propeller shaft being driven through the sturdy, vertical sternpost; on other vessels, where the sternpost was too small or weak, the shaft was put through to one side. The Gardner Company in Manchester had developed a paraffin marine engine in 1894. The birth of the second great fishing-boat engine, the Kelvin, followed in 1906 when Walter Bergius installed a 12 hp car engine in a rowing boat on the Clyde and, impressed by the speed, began to manufacture marine engines. The Bergius Launch & Engine Company was established in Dobbie's Loan in Glasgow.

A Wick boat called the *Crystal River* had an engine installed in 1906.[32] An Eyemouth fifie, the *Maggie Jane's* (BK 146) was fitted with a 55 hp Gardner paraffin engine in 1907[33] and, in the same year, Robert Robertson of Campbeltown, a ringnet skipper who was to become famed for innovative development, installed a 7–9 hp Kelvin in his skiff, the *Brothers*. Motor engines were soon being fitted in boats up and down the coast. In Maidens boats' engines began to be fitted in about 1907–08. They were 7–9 hp and later 15–20 hp – all Kelvin petrol/paraffin engines. These early models generally cost between £70 and £100 and the different types offered a choice of features such as reverse gear or feathering propellers. Fuel costs were low or at least within what a fisherman could afford: a 7 hp engine could run on a half-gallon of paraffin, which cost about 3d, for an hour or so, and push a small boat at speeds up to 6 or 7 knots.[34] An Eyemouth skipper in 1910 was described as being happy with the fuel bill for his 50 hp engine – for about 2 shillings an hour, he could maintain 8 knots.[35] My grandfather in Keiss had a Kelvin put into his yole in 1915 and by that time in Scotland the number of motor boats equalled those with steam power – Anson says there were 910 of each.[36] In 1919, the MacDonalds in Golspie fitted their boat *I'll Try* with a 6–7hp Kelvin and, by then, the number of motor boats had risen to 1844, representing 23 per cent of the registered Scottish fleet, and steam was found in 324 trawlers and 872 drifters.[37]

Motor engines were installed largely in boats of the 18-30 ft range, at least in the early years, and the impact was great on the lives of what the officials called the 'smaller' fishermen, as can be readily imagined. In the early 1920s the fishing press was filled with advertisements for many types of engine – a 10–22hp engine could be had for not much over £200 – and the talk on the quays must have been all about the different makes and their advantages and disadvantages. The fishermen were freed from the tyranny of canvas and, although a few may have lamented the passing of sail, it was unlikely that many tears were shed for the old days.

Creels and oysters

In its review of the herring fishing during the first quarter of the twentieth century, the *Fishing News* noted that a feature of the period was 'the reduction in the number of curing stations and a concentration of operations in the larger ports'.[38] Such stations as Lybster, Helmsdale, Stromness and Baltasound had become 'either derelict or of negligible importance'. In 1903 there had been 111 curing stations on the west side of Shetland, supported by 1500 boats and 8000 fishermen, but these had gone by 1914. The fishing in Loch Fyne had declined after 1904 and did not really recover until the early 1920s. As herring fishing became concentrated on bigger ports, the fishermen in many of the smaller harbours turned to catching other species, and in Keiss, as in many other villages, this became most notably the catching of crabs and lobsters with creels. The appearance of a herring shoal, however, could still produce an irresistible chance. Thus it was on the night of 31 July and 1 August 1944 when my father, my uncle Sanny Miller and a neighbour, Jim Mowat, put out in the *Lupin* with drift nets aboard. At six o'clock on a fine evening they set four drift nets, 80 fathoms long, across the tide flowing southwards towards Noss Head and anchored them. Twelve hours later, in the early morning, they hauled in seven cran of herring and sent them to Wick to be sold. This is said to have been the last herring landed in Keiss, a reminder to the village of how it came into existence in the first place.

In 1855 the village was home to forty-nine boats, thirty-five of them firthies over 30 ft, and the herring fishing supported over 400 people, including 180 fishermen, seven coopers, several hundred gutters, vendors and netmakers, and twenty-one curers. There was also a boat-building yard. There were still fifty-eight boats in 1881 but by 1928 the size of the fleet had fallen to just ten. Shellfish landings in Keiss far outweighed herring and white fish in value by this time and, in that year, only Catterline, Crail, Dunbar, Cove, St Abbs and Burnmouth had higher shellfish landings.

The edible crab (*Cancer pagurus*), or partan, was the main catch and the fishery followed an annual pattern that reflected the crab's migratory habits. In the winter, it lives offshore, maybe five miles out where the sea is 30 fathoms deep, but in March and April it moves towards the coast where it remains until September or so when, after it has moulted and its new shell has hardened, it turns once more towards the deeper water. The fishermen set their creels when the crabs were inshore, in 5–10 fathoms, and followed them out until by December creels were being dropped at the 30-fathom line. By this time, the distance of five miles each way, the short day and the unsettled weather and sea state brought an end to the crab season, and the men resorted to line fishing for cod, ling and halibut. The catching of lobsters (*Homarus vulgaris*) was also important. The lobster is a territorial and aggressive individual, lurking in hiding holes among the rocks like a cantankerous, blue-black knight, ready to challenge intruders with its large claws. It inhabits relatively shallow water and can be taken from the shore at extreme low tides. However, as for the crab, most are taken in baited pots or creels.

Different designs of creel have been found in use. A new type was introduced in Cove in the late 1780s,[39] described as a 'basket 5 ft long, 2 ft wide, nearly a cylinder, cutting a good section off for a base, is formed of plain wood, in slits, for the bottom, and hoops for the curve, netted over. From the ends the net-work is wrought inward into a narrow entrance for the fish, bait being hung within to entice it.' Such a creel cost 10s 6d, which seems a high figure for the time, but the fishermen attributed their economic survival to it after the hardships of the near-famine in 1783.

A device called a lobster ring was also used. This was a shallow circle of net on a hoop, perhaps 2 ft in diameter, weighted to sit flat on the bottom. These were left baited on the seabed, their positions marked by a corked rope.[40] Such rings were the main means of catching lobsters in the sizeable fishery that developed on the north coast at the end of the eighteenth century. In the 1790s about sixty boats, each with two men, worked in Orkney in the spring and the autumn, and as elsewhere, sold their catch to companies operating well-smacks to bring the live animals to market in London. The minister of Walls and Flotta reckoned that 120,000 lobsters were being taken in a year. Durness was sending 6000–8000 in a summer.[41] About 4000 lobsters were being exported annually from Peterhead to London, so many that the locals were complaining of difficulty in catching them and were being hired to set traps further west in the Moray Firth, where a successful season could bring in £20 – £30.[42] Lobsters were also being exported from North Berwick to London.[43] By 1808, about 100 boats were working the lobsters in Orkney[44] and in 1833 the catch was estimated to be bringing in £2000 in a year, by which time the northern islands were annually sending out 100,000 lobsters. At this time six boats were working the coast at Durness for the southern market.[45]

Another technique was used by Newhaven fishermen on the rocky shores of the Forth inches. In the summer months, they let down vertical sections of net, 25 fathoms long and 2 fathoms high, weighted on the bottom with stones fixed in loops of line. The net had a 6-in. mesh. Bait was not generally used though sometimes dead fish might be put down to entice the lobsters and crabs out to become ensnared in the nets. A dinghy could be used to shoot these nets inshore early in the morning, and they were left for several hours before being hauled. The nets needed plenty of mending but the Newhaven men found that they yielded two to three times the catch with creels.[46]

The creel common along the Scottish coast was made by the fishermen to more or less a standard pattern and this has changed little in design over the many years it has been used. The base was a wooden frame, usually 2 ft 3 in by 18 in, with four hoops fixed to it to give a height of about 15 in, over which a net was woven. A stone from the beach served as a sinker and a little arrangement of twine in the centre held the bait. Two funnel-shaped holes, called 'monkeys' in the local Caithness speech, were woven into the sides of the creel to allow the crabs to enter but not to escape. Before 1935, the fishermen deployed their creels on what they called a standing rope system, with forty creels spaced at 15-fathom intervals along a single length of rope, but then they changed to the 'fleicher' or fleet system in which fewer creels, up to twenty-five, were set at 12-fathom intervals along a series of separate ropes. If the crab stock became exhausted in one area, the fleet was easily lifted and shot elsewhere.

The crab fishermen's favoured bait, at least in the north-east corner of Caithness, was skate 'gumps', the head and bony tail of skate bought cheaply from fish dealers in Wick as a by-product of the seine-netting. The availability of bait depended, therefore, on the success of the seiners and occasionally there were days when no bait was to be had; when this lack became serious, the crab fishermen set out to catch their own, taking cod and mackerel on hand lines. These fish were regarded as inferior to skate. The crab fishing on the east Caithness coast yielded well for many years. Throughout the 1940s, the gross income of my father's boat was around £800 per year and, from his record for 1962, a fairly typical year by his own account and his last before retirement, the crew were catching a daily average of 180 crabs for a season lasting 189 days.

Dodie Gunn worked out of John o'Groats harbour:

We went to the creels all around the coast, up at the Stacks [of Duncansby] and round to Skirsa Head and Freswick bay. Freswick bay was as far as we went on the east side, we met the Keiss men there then. We went as far west as the Men o' Mey [in the Pentland Firth]. We had about eighty creels as a rule, but sometimes 120. We had no fleichers, it was all hand creels for the lobster. There wasn't really scope for putting fleichers on. We had one or two in about 1936–7 when we went out in deeper water but it was mostly single creels for the lobster. We finished up the creels here at the end of October and did the hand line then in the winter. Dunnet Head was a good place for cod. With the strong stream tides we used to go west but the rest of the time we fished out there in the Firth. There was a lot of fish there some years.

Liz Duvill fished creels with her father, Alex Mackenzie, at Badachro in Gairloch in the mid-1950s. It was already becoming quite popular to fish for prawns but they also caught lobsters:

There were some crabs, but not very many. The price for crabs was absolutely dreadful, you got nothing for them. My father was sending his lobsters to Billingsgate in boxes at that time. He didn't have a car or a lorry, he didn't drive, and he would collect all the lobsters in big boxes with holes in them and keep them in the sea a bit far out where the fresh water from the Badachro River wouldn't affect them. When he had sufficient, he put them in a regular fishbox with lots of sawdust and took them over to Gairloch pier. Then they would go with the fish lorry to Inverness to catch the train to Billingsgate. However, they used to get stolen and you couldn't claim insurance, and often they were delayed for one reason or another and he would lose those too, with no compensation. It was a very risky, hard business. At that time there was no sale locally apart from hotels in summertime and they didn't pay well for lobsters.

Like most fishermen before the mid-1950s, Alex Mackenzie threw away prawns, unaware that very soon they would become the main prey of much of the Scottish fleet. 'We operated about 200 creels,' said Liz, 'in fleets of about fifty. Conger eel was the main bait. He used to set a line to catch them. Eels were plentiful. You used a big knife and cut them into big lumps. For prawns it was used fresh but for lobsters it was stinking rotten with a little bit of coarse salt on it.'

Creel fishing took place all around the coast but crabs and lobsters were not the only kinds of shellfish that have had a prominent place in the exploitation of the sea. In the east-coast firths there were extensive oyster beds and the dredging of oysters was a major industry in the Forth. 'Caller ou' from Newhaven were famous and millions were exported to London where they were a staple food of the poor.[47] The Firth of Forth was divided into areas where the right to exploit the scalps, the oyster beds, was jealously guarded and fought over. The Admiralty High Court held an inquiry in 1791 into the allotting of oyster rights in an effort to restore some order. The Society of Free Fishermen of Newhaven had access to scalps around Inchkeith and boats from other villages, from Prestonpans, Cockenzie or Fisherrow, were sometimes arrested for intruding. The Society also had the right to fish on the Duke of Buccleuch's grounds immediately off Newhaven and west as far as Cramond Island. A description of the oyster fishing in Prestonpans in the 1790s says that ten boats, each with five men, were dragging up 400–500 a day each from depths between 4–15 fathoms. Twenty years before, however, forty boats had been at work and were then each taking 6000 in a day.[48] The writer adds the interesting comment that 'When they [the fishers] drive the dredge they begin the oyster song, which they sing till the dredge is hauled up.' Oysters were also dredged off the Petty coast, in the Moray Firth to the east of Inverness, but in 1790 were described as being 'entirely gone' except for a small spot, with the implication that this was due to over-exploitation.[49] Scarcity through over-dragging to supply the city markets was recorded in several places in the 1790s.[50] Cockles and mussels were also harvested for food and in St Andrews were being sold in 1794 for 2d a peck.[51]

Not a great use of made of bivalves in Scotland now as food. There is some cultivation of oysters and experiments in this are carried out, but the main markets are in France and Spain rather than at home. Some mussel cultivation is done and there is also gathering of cockles, mainly for local use. Creel fishing is still, however, extremely important in many places, and the number of boats for which this is the main method of working number around 1500.[52] Around one-tenth of this total are vessels over 10m in length, capable of fishing farther offshore and travelling faster than their forebears. It is usual now for a crab boat to work 400–500 creels.

CHAPTER SIX

BETWEEN THE WARS

A sea fit for heroes

On the eve of the First World War the number of fishermen in Scotland was recorded as 32,678, with 52,448 dependants and 8534 vessels.[1] The total would never be as high again. In September 1914, when the War broke out, the Royal Navy began to requisition fishing boats. About 300 were taken into service in the first month; by April 1915, almost the entire British trawler fleet of 1500 vessels and a similar number of steam drifters had been commandeered or voluntarily offered for national service.[2] Thousands of men from the fishing communities served in the armed forces – the Navy in particular benefited from their experience – or on the drafted fishing boats. The drifters and trawlers worked as boom boats at naval bases, as tenders, armed escorts, minesweepers or minelayers, anti-submarine and patrol vessels. In the great anchorages such as Scapa Flow, they steamed about, bringing men and supplies to and from the dreadnoughts, and worked the anti-submarine booms and nets laid across the entrances. Many were issued with small guns and the fishermen had to learn new skills. Home waters were not necessarily safe. U-boats attacked fishing boats and sank them, usually after allowing the crew to escape. Trawlers shepherded merchant vessels up and down coastal seas – the Dover Patrol was nicknamed the 'Suicide Club' from the frequency with which it was attacked. By the time the First World War ended, 675 fishing boats had become casualties and 1127 fishermen had lost their lives through enemy action.[3]

Most served in home waters but a squadron of drifters worked, for example, in the Mediterranean. On the morning of 15 May 1917, a line of these were watching anti-submarine nets in the Straits of Otranto at the mouth of the Adriatic when they were attacked by three Austrian cruisers. The fishermen refused to obey the signal to abandon ship. Skipper Joseph Watt of Gardenstown in the *Gowan Lea* slipped the net, rang for full speed ahead and proceeded to attack the cruisers. The other drifters showed equal mettle. Watt and his crew manned their little three-pounder gun until a direct hit put it out of action and then, while trying to repair the damage, they turned to assist their colleagues. Some of the driftermen were wounded or killed but they refused to surrender or abandon ship, although their boats were sinking under them. By the time Royal Navy cruisers arrived and chased the enemy away, thirteen drifters were either sunk or sinking, and Skipper Watt was busily engaged in rescuing survivors. Watt was awarded the Victoria Cross, and William Farquhar of Buckie in the *Admirable*, and Robert Stephen in the *Taits* and Robert Cowe in the *Coral Haven*, both from Fraserburgh, won the Distinguished Service Cross.[4]

Some fishing continued during the War. The nation could not neglect such an important source of food. Restrictions were placed on the activity of the boats and access to fishing grounds was limited by minefields. Line fishing enjoyed a brief revival. With so many drifters on active service, the total landings of herring fell from 177,459 crans in 1914 to only 12,289 in 1916 but it rose again to 202,485 in 1918.[5] The Admiralty saw in the trawlers and drifters essential handmaidens to the warships and built several hundred of their own. This official trawler came in three classes – the 'Mersey' (138 ft), the 'Castle' (125 ft) and the 'Strath' (115 ft) class – and there were two classes of drifter: wooden and steel, both 86 ft long. Most of these vessels, known as standard drifters, were sold to fishermen after the War. The Admiralty had decided that the drifters should all be named after elements or natural phenomena – *Sea Fog*, *Sheet Lightning* and *Undertow* being a few of the perhaps less happy choices – and most of them were renamed by their new owners.

The Admiralty had the commandeered fishing boats refitted before they were returned to their pre-War owners and, in 1919, the herring fishing resumed. The Scottish drifters went down as before to Lowestoft and Yarmouth in the late autumn and did well: the fish stocks had had a rest from pursuit for four years and the food shortages after the War ensured a good price for the catches. In the following year, however, although catches were again good, prices slumped. The government intervened in response to calls for help and fixed a price for the summer, with the result that the drifters did well in home waters but badly when they later steamed south to East Anglia. It turned out to be the worst year since the 1880s. Stocks of unsold herring were accumulating in curers' yards around the country. The winter fishing was unsuccessful as well and in the spring of 1921 unemployment was the immediate prospect for many hands in the herring industry. The years immediately after the War were filled with social unrest. By the end of 1920 the economy slumped and unemployment rose. In many parts of Scotland, men saw their only hope in emigration. The fishing communities suffered along with everyone else. The fishermen had to deal with a severe setback when the lucrative pre-War market in Russia was lost to them. A miners' strike in April 1921 deprived many ports of the necessary coal stocks. The hopes for 'a fit country for heroes to live in' lay shattered. In the autumn of 1921 a motor drifter and sixty nets could be bought for £500 in Buckie whereas less than two years previously it would have cost £2000.[6] Many fishermen ended the season in debt. Rampant inflation in the German Weimar Republic in 1922 and 1923 all but wiped out the continental market for herring. The situation gradually grew worse. In 1926, the General Strike again deprived the fishing boats of coal. It began more and more to look as if the days of the steam drifter were over. The *Fishing News* recorded that in 1926 60 per cent of the British fishing fleet had been laid up for want of coal and that fishermen's wages had dropped from 1925, with £30 now being the return from the twelve-week herring season.[7] Although Scottish landings had increased from that in 1925, their market value had decreased.

In May 1918, Lord Leverhulme, immensely wealthy from his soap manufacturing, had bought the island of Lewis. In 1919 he added Harris to his estate and set about realising his private dream of creating an integrated large-scale economic venture where before there had been mainly crofting. The sea played a vital role in this scheme. It was envisaged that aircraft would be used to spot the herring shoals around the Hebrides and would guide the fishing boats, a modern trawler fleet based in Stornoway and Obbe, now renamed Leverburgh, on to them. Ashore a cannery and an ice plant would help to feed the riches of the west coast waters to a chain of fish shops called MacFisheries. He bought out and resurrected an abandoned Norwegian whaling station at Bunaveneader in north Harris.[8] Leverhulme's great idea might have worked but, running into financial difficulties and losing the government support he had won from a reluctant Westminster, he finally decided to abandon his plans in September 1923. He got rid of his land holdings on Lewis and held on to Harris, but the dream of a sea-based commercial empire on the Long Island finally died with Leverhulme himself in May 1925.

Throughout this period, the fishing communities turned to some old stand-bys to supplement the living they were barely scraping from the silver darlings. Line fishing continued where families could still work together at the tasks of baiting and redding the gear. For example, in 1920, eighty sma' line boats worked out of Peterhead and this old style of fishing could still turn up a bonanza – one boat caught 52 hundredweight of haddock in one day on the west of Shetland – but generally it did not pay a living wage.[9] Men went to Aberdeen to find berths on the trawler or liner fleets. Cod netting, a method that had been introduced to the Moray Firth in 1906, became crucial to some boats. It took place in the winter and early spring months: cod nets had a large mesh of 6 in. and were shot to form a weighted, vertical curtain, perhaps 30 fathoms long and rising 2 fathoms from the seabed. Boats could net as few as five or as many as 100 large cod each. It was a traditional technique and it brought in catches of prime fish, but in the early 1920s it too ran into serious problems. The strictures on trawling within the Moray Firth did not apply to foreign boats; trawlers from several European countries were now fishing in the areas and they caused considerable damage to the cod nets.

Each man £1 to take home

In the midst of this bleak time, some fishermen were still determined to look to the future and prominent among them was Robert Robertson of

Campbeltown. In March 1921 he ordered a pair of boats of a new design from the St Monans firm of builders, James Miller & Son. Robertson had already been the first in his home town, in 1907, to install a motor engine in his ringnetter. Now he was to prove a pioneer for the second time. He based the design of his new boats on vessels he had seen in Norway – not the first time Scandinavian boat-building had had important consequences for Scotland – and in April and May 1922 respectively the pair, named the *Falcon* and the *Frigate Bird*, steamed into Campbeltown. With a length of slightly over 50 ft and a beam of 15 ft, they were longer and wider than the type of herring boat normal to the Clyde; they were decked throughout, had a small wheel-house aft, a steering wheel instead of a tiller, and two Gleniffer paraffin engines generating 18–22 hp. The hull had a pronounced canoe-shaped stern and a rounded bow. Robertson was taking a gamble – over £1200 was invested in the pair of boats – but, after a little time, during which the handling of the ring net from such a novel craft had to be relearned, the gamble paid off.

On the east coast, too, there were signs of hope, though at first they were hardly recognised as such. The fishermen had observed in 1921 that Danish boats were landing good catches of plaice at Grimsby. They were using a net called a seine. Although the technique was new to Scotland, it had been in use in various forms elsewhere for many years – Bertram described it as being the main means of catching mackerel in England in the 1860s. The Danish seine consisted of a net with long wings extending from either side. Long warp ropes were attached to each wing. One end of the warp was anchored. The boat then steamed away from it, paying out the warp, turned through a right angle, shot the net, turned again and steered back to the anchored end. Then the two warps were carefully drawn in against the tide, to keep the net open, until the net was near to the boat, by which time the warps had brought the wings of the net together, entrapping the flatfish that the weighted ground rope had roused from the bottom. The whole net normally spanned about 160 ft with the bag extending 60 ft in depth, and the long warps were normally 120 fathoms on each side.

Some fishermen from Lossiemouth, Buckie and Macduff were intrigued by this method. They bought one or two seines and experimented with them from their drifters. It did not take them long to become adept and soon good catches of plaice and flounders were being taken in the Moray Firth. William Stewart was involved in this and wrote about it in a brief history of the fishing in Lossiemouth:

> Fortunately for Lossie, a little experimenting on seine-netting was being carried out by two motor zulus. These boats were catching some plaice, but operations were hampered by lack of knowledge, and possibly their skippers were older men than the drifter skippers who were commencing operations with seining. In any case the

Peter Anson's drawing of
Eyemouth in 1929, with
drifters and seine netters
in the harbour.

drifters were soon mastering the art of seine-netting and landing
huge catches of plaice in Lossie. The drifter men in Buckie and
Macduff were slower off the mark and success was not so marked
with them. Many factors helped the Lossie men to success … Lossie
had always had a good market for white fish, including plaice caught
by lines, a good knowledge of the sea bottom, especially inshore by
the older fishermen, and ample landmarks ashore to mark fishing
grounds. With these and other advantages, the Lossie men managed to
survive the winter of 1921, and the success of some gave hope for the
future.[10]

As early as November 1920 yoles from Aberdeen were fishing with small
seine nets on the east coast, mostly for plaice, rousing anger among the line
and creel men working out of Johnshaven, Gourdon, Ferryden and other
villages. The disputes over the seine net echoed those over the introduction
of the trawl net some decades before, and for much the same reasons: the
inshore men saw their fishing grounds being depleted and their static gear

being damaged by the passing nets. The Fishery Board intervened and issued in April 1921 a by-law to restrict the area seiners could use, the size of their gear and of the fish they could keep. Before the by-law had come into force, however, three skippers had been charged with illegal use of the method: in May 1921 they were fined £1 each in Dundee Sheriff Court[11] and, as Iain Sutherland points out, became probably the first fishermen in Scotland to be caught for poaching.[12] Soon after, a Gourdon skipper was also caught for the same offence and fined £50 in Aberdeen. In the Moray Firth the shooting of a seine net within the three-mile limit became a common occurrence and for a time there was doubt over the legality of this: a charge against a Peterhead skipper was found not proven in October 1921 as both the Sheriff and the Procurator Fiscal in Aberdeen could not decide whether he had actually dragged his net and thus trawled.[13]

The seine net had many advantages over the driftnet. A whole net could be bought for £10 – seine nets were now being manufactured in Musselburgh – and it could be operated by four or five men. It took only about an hour to shoot and haul and, if one ground was proving barren, it was easy to move on to try somewhere else. The whole technique was cheaper and more mobile. It was not long before the skippers on the Moray Firth were experimenting further. They began to use larger seines and put a bag into the extent of net. Certain refinements and adjustments were made to increase the efficiency of the gear. They abandoned the attaching of one end to an anchor and left it freely floating attached to a buoy or dahn instead so that, when they brought both ends of the warps together, they could tow the whole net to catch the free-swimming haddock and cod, a method called fly-dragging. The different ports were developing their own ways of rigging the net, adapting it to local conditions. They were also learning more about the nature of the seabed – the seine net needs a clean bottom free from rocks and other obstructions – and where the good spots for fishing were.

Although the east coast boats turned to herring in the summer and autumn as they had done for a century or more, in the winter they devoted more and more time to seining. A few abandoned herring altogether and went after white fish the year round, steaming out to the large banks in the North Sea and landing in the larger east coast ports. As William Stewart recalled:

> While some drifters were making a living catching herring from 1920 till 1928, most were slowly falling into debt. Repairs to engines, boilers and boats were costly, and a few owners sold out, while others struggled on. By 1928 a few families had emigrated, some settled in Aberdeen and went trawling. A number of yawls still went to the haddock lines but their number had decreased to around twelve, and they were down to starvation wages also. From 1921 to 1930 the fisher folk in Lossie like their brethren all over the country were more or less on the breadline.[14]

The *Fairy Hill* became the first Wick drifter to use a seine net, in 1922. Alfred Mackay remembered her fishing on the Dogger Bank, under her skipper, William Waters:

> After the *Fairy Hill* there was the *Morven Hill*, then the *Drift Fisher* and the *Spectrum*. The *Spectrum* went to the great lines as well. Seine nets were ordered. None was made locally then. The first seine net cost £7 and some odds. First-class manila rope was £1 10 shillings a coil. There were no man-made fibres then. It was 1931 when the seine net boats started in Wick. We seined in a different way to the Danes. They shot their gear on an anchor and came back to it and heaved the net towards them. We used 'fly fishing' – there was no anchor, we just towed the gear. We covered more ground. We probably scared off more fish, and their way was more sensible. They would lie at anchor a week and shoot off in different directions according to the set of the tide. I started on the *Sprightly*, as second hand, from Macduff. We went to sea for £220, including the gear. That was in 1931. Money was scarce. The herring had been overfished and there was no price. The seine was something new and we got more money in the first two or three months at it than in a whole year at the drifters. On my last visit to Yarmouth, we came back to Wick £12 in debt. The herring were scarce and we went to the seine after that, with the option of going back to the herring next season – but that did not happen and we stayed at the seine. Between New Year and April we grossed £80.

On the Moray Firth, Lossiemouth became the first port to make a whole-hearted commitment to the new method. Overcoming his own doubts and those of several others, John Campbell had a new boat, the *Marigold* (INS 234), built in 1927 especially for seine net fishing. She was successful and a friend of his, James Macleod, then ordered another new vessel of the same type, the *Briar* (INS 420). Seine netting was becoming established quickly as an alternative to herring fishing and another new vessel, launched in the spring of 1928, symbolised the change: she was the *Cutty Sark*, built in Sandhaven and designed as a dual-purpose vessel, capable of switching easily from one method of fishing to another. At the same time the amount of fish caught by new motor-powered seiners began to equal that by their steam-powered predecessors. The Lossie seiners searched out new territory and in February 1935 two started to fish off Ardglass in Northern Ireland, where they were joined in the following year by between fifteen to twenty vessels.[15]

William Stewart was still hesitating over whether to commit himself to the seine. He writes that he had finished the previous herring season £100 in debt but was still carrying on at the haddock lines: 'I did not hold the project with much enthusiasm, my disastrous summer fishing had dented my own ego as a skipper quite a bit, and the thought that I might do just as badly in a motor-seine boat was a bit terrifying at the time.' With the backing of his wife, a fish salesman and a banker, he crossed this personal Rubicon. 'The total cost ready to go to sea was nearly £1400, my share of the boat was one-eighth, for which the bank loaned me the money, the other [shares] were owned by the salesman and two land owners.' Until his new boat was ready, he did a training course in minesweeping with the Royal Naval Reserve and worked as a deckhand on another seiner. Then the great day arrived. 'Our first day's fishing was a case of trial and error. Winch belts too tight ... Roller heads not in line ... hours wasted ... A week saw most of the faults ironed out, and we had caught as much fish as would give each man £1 to take home'.[16] William Stewart's *Rival* (INS 95) was to become one of the best-known seiners in the Moray Firth and he a much-respected skipper, dying at the age of eighty-nine in November 1993.

Throughout the 1930s the seine net became more popular but its spread to other parts of Scotland did not take place quickly. Some trials with the new net had been done in Shetland in 1926, yielding good catches of flatfish near Mousa, but the line fishing was still profitable and use of the seine was abandoned for nearly another twenty years.[17] In 1931 some boats from the East Neuk followed the example of Arbroath fishermen and tried it off the Fife coast[18] between the Bell Rock and Isle of May. In Pittenweem, the seine net was not wholly welcome and some fishermen felt it was a threat to the line fishing. The Forth fishermen, like their brethren on the west coast, were still wedded to the herring fishing. The herring fishers from the south side of the Forth, from Newhaven and its neighbouring ports, followed the same seasons. The Forth & Clyde Canal allowed the west coast fishing boats to steam through to fish in the Forth. In 1884 they introduced the ring net to the area to the annoyance of the local fishermen, but many of the latter adopted it and used it to great effect in their home waters.[19] The Forth boats also began to use the Canal to fish on the west coast, probably first doing so in 1902 after reports of excellent herring fishing off the Donegal coast,[20] and this became a regular seasonal trip. Jim Wilson in Newhaven can recall his first voyage across the Central Belt in 1937 and seeing the hull of the then unfinished and unnamed *Queen Mary* on the stocks at John Brown's Clyde yard.

Black outlook for the fishermen

Following Robert Robertson's lead with the *Falcon* and the *Frigate Bird*, several new ringnetters were built for Clyde fishermen during the 1920s and 1930s. Some of these incorporated novel design features, such as the forward wheel-house in the *Nil Desperandum* (CN 232) – although it proved to be impracticable and was later shifted aft – and new winches especially adapted for ringnetting which, in turn, allowed the deployment of larger nets in deeper water. Herring catches by the Clyde boats and the prices offered for them fluctuated from year to year but the ringnetters continued to find fish in the long sea-lochs and among the islands, and seemed to have weathered the troubled times much better than their east coast brethren. Fresh herring was sold directly from the fishing boats to steamers called 'screws', often old drifters, who operated from Ardrossan, Greenock, Fairlie and other ports handily placed for the Glasgow fish market. Some screws were owned by city fishmongers and there was great competition between them to reach the fishing boats first and buy their catches.[21]

In Girvan, Angus McCrindle told me:

Around 1925–6, semi-diesel engines were introduced. The *Golden West* (BA 52) of Maidens had a Gardner direct reverse engine installed before launching. The first full diesel engine in Maidens was installed in the *Margarita* (BA 117) in 1929, a Gardner of around 48 hp with a Gleniffer gearbox – Gardner's did not produce their own gearboxes until around 1938, as their earlier engines were originally intended for tractors and started by hand. Around 1933–4 they brought out the L3 type diesel with air start and the 5L3 was rated at 85 hp. This was a breakthrough for Gardner and they produced this type of engine up until the mid-1970s. Electric start was introduced in about 1940.

Once engines were installed and the ring net was perfected, women had an easier time of it and had no involvement in the day-to-day work. The fishermen themselves had an easier time and were away for up to a week at a time. Money was more plentiful in the late 1920s and early 1930s – fishermen were building their own houses, cars were appearing, and the women had more to spend on themselves and their families. So the ring net was the best thing that had come to our village.

The fishermen followed the herring all over the Clyde, from spring to autumn in the outer Firth and in the winter in the inner Firth. There were exceptions to this and I can remember up to about 1930 three boats used small lines in the winter and hawkers sold the fish around the district, and often the horses brought the hawkers back, worse for wear through drink. Also there were innovations in the ring net during the winter in the upper Clyde and Loch Fyne.

A new device for locating herring shoals, the feeling wire, was introduced in 1928–9 and was used successfully by Angus McCrindle's father, John Turner McCrindle, and his uncle, Tommy Sloan, at the sunk-net fishery that winter. The wire used at first was piano wire about 20 fathoms with a 3-lb lead attached and mounted on a handgrip fashioned from the end of a fishbox. One man on each boat was a specialist at this, keen to the touch, able to detect the herring brushing against the wire, and Angus considers it to have been certainly an art on its own. Through time different types of wire were used with less resistance to the water, and Brunton's of

Musselburgh were instrumental in introducing these different types of wire. Finally, a 6-lb pear-shaped lead was used to allow the boat to go a little faster while looking for fish. New winches eased the hauling of the nets. Brailers were first fitted to the *Mary Sturgeon* (BA 52) of Dunure in 1933. Johnny Simpson who had recently joined her had been fishing in Alaska and had seen this worked successfully for a number of years. The use of the brailer, a strong hoop about 3 ft in diameter with a suspended net, speeded up the emptying of the herring from the ring-net into the fish hold. The successful fishing from the Clyde ports resulted in them landing herring worth over £2.2 million between 1926 and 1939, in third place in Scotland after Lerwick and Fraserburgh.[22]

A west-coast ringnetter with a hold full of herring.

On the north-west coast the conflict between the drift net and the ring net continued in the inter-War period.[23] The ring net was gradually winning converts, with a growing fleet based in Mallaig, but for example in the early 1920s only a few of the Skye boats were using the method. The gutters on Scalpay refused to handle herring caught by the ring net; the *Comunn Iasgairean na Mara*, the Sea Fishermen's League, was formed in 1933 to defend the use of the drift net; and ring net men found it safer to land their herring in Ullapool or Mallaig rather than face hostility in Stornoway. The Fishery Board investigated the situation in 1933 and recorded complaints that ring netting was destroying immature herring and breaking up the shoals.

The herring fishing on the east coast remained generally in the doldrums throughout the 1930s. The grim 1920s had ended with a sting in the tail, when the so-called Armistice Gale on 11 November 1929 had inflicted heavy damage on the gear of the Scottish boats at the East Anglia fishing. At Buckie, the port with the largest fleet of steam drifters in 1920, the number of boats fell steadily from 404 in 1920 to 197 in 1933.[24] The Stornoway herring fleet numbered only nine in 1935, half of what it had been at the start of the century.[25] The last Lossiemouth steam drifter shot her

nets in 1936.[26] In 1934 the price for the fish was so poor, at about 10
shillings per cran, that thousands of crans were thrown overboard. In 1937,
the Stronsay herring fishing failed.[27] The export trade continued to decline.
The government appointed a Sea Fish Commission at the end of 1933 to
look into the problems of the industry. It reported in 1934 and in January
1935 the Herring Industry Bill was published, with the setting up of the
Herring Industry Board two months later.

In the season, however, the east coast ports could still be thrumming
with activity, as Alfred Mackay recalled:

> Up to about 150 drifters used Wick, you could walk across the
> harbour on them, There was such a press in the harbour that when
> boats were landing they were encouraged to sail again as soon as
> possible to let others in; and the harbourmaster employed assistants
> who threatened to cut the mooring ropes with axes if a crew did not
> shift fast enough. And they were burning up to 1500 tons of coal in a
> week. The harbour was a busy place then. The season extended from
> the end of June to September — 6 September being the official date
> for termination of the crew engagement.
>
> We shot the net before dark and then we could have a cup of tea
> and lie down for two hours, except for the watch in case of a shift in
> the wind. If the wind shifted we were all roused and the boat
> changed position, letting go the end of the drift and steaming to the
> other end, following the line of buoys. The net was shot with the bow
> to the wind and the mizen kept the boat steady. There was about two
> miles of net, twelve to fourteen coil of bush rope [also known as a
> messenger rope, the heavy rope on the bottom of the driftnet] with
> 120 fathoms in each coil. Each boat shot sixty-five to seventy nets but
> the larger boats shot eighty. If the catch was low, about a cran, it
> would be too far to steam for harbour to be worth going in, and the
> boat 'lay on', waiting for the following night to try again and perhaps
> shifting the ground to chance the hand.

By 1935 the number of fishermen in Scotland had fallen to 22,175, of
whom 5369 were crofter-fishermen. Steam drifters had fallen to 644 in
number; the totals of motor boats, at 2391, and of steam trawlers, at 373,
were rising. There were still over 2200 sailing boats but their landings
represented less than one per cent of the total.[28] The great east coast herring
boom that started in the early 1800s was dwindling painfully to a close.
Anson writes in the 1930s of the decline of fishing on the Moray Firth in
tones remarkably similar to those heard today. In 1937 there were still
19,364 fishermen in Scotland with over 35,000 dependants,[29] but it was a
hard time for many of them. Up in Buchan, Frank Bruce remembered the
1930s as a time when 'you hadn't a backside to your trousers. Clothes were
in short supply, so was food.' In Aberdeen, George Leiper recalled for me

how difficult it was to find a job in 1932; he wanted to become an instrument maker but the two firms in Aberdeen were not taking on young lads, and he decided to go to sea, against the wishes of his parents. He begged his father to allow him to go: 'He said, "I'll take you away to sea on one condition – that you go to be a skipper, you're not going to stay as a deckhand." That's all right, I'll easily be a skipper, I thought, it never worried me what it was all about. I started going to sea. I was an apprentice for a year on the *Vale of Clyde*, 122 ft in length. She was a line fishing vessel, privately owned. I was away with her for a year and then I was offered a berth by another skipper, going on full share.'

'Black outlook for the fishermen' were the words heading an editorial in the *Fishing News* on the prospects for 1938.[30] For the crofter-fishermen and

Drifters in the Firth of Forth in the 1930s.

the small-scale inshore men, the outlook was perhaps blackest of all. Dodie Gunn and his brother David fished from John o'Groats:

> It was 1930 when I started. I left the school on the Friday and started on the Monday. I was fourteen. There was just the two of us on the boat. It was force that put me to the sea. There was nothing else here. I had to like it. In the 1920s, you know, once men were eighteen or twenty years old, they all emigrated. They're all over the world. After the War, after I got married, I considered emigration but an uncle in Canada wrote 'If you can make a living at home at all, stay.' We heard about them that did well out there but we didn't here about them that didn't do so well.
>
> We bought a little single-cylinder engine for the first boatie we had, then we got the *Hope* in 1931 and my brother-in-law happened to be home on holiday here – he was a superintendent of the railways

in Uganda – and I borrowed money from him to buy an engine which cost £56. You know how hard up we were. It was quite a lot of money in 1931. There came a ship ashore on Swona [in the Pentland Firth] in August 1931 – we raided her and with the first raid we paid the engine back. That was the famous *Pennsylvania*. We took so much stuff off her, latterly we had to buy her. We paid a £100 for her, we clubbed together with the Stroma men and had fifty £2 shares. We took everything off her and held a big roup, and we all got about £100. Our new engine was 6 hp – an Ailsa Craig. We never went out without a sail in the Pentland Firth, in case we broke down, and if there came a breeze of wind we could get some extra speed.

The Keiss men packed up the crabs in 1931 – that was the year the road was tarred between John o'Groats and Wick, and most of them worked on the road for tenpence an hour. One boat carried on – and I mind they got nineteen crabs for their fishing one day. In the 1930s the lobsters were sent to Billingsgate by train. Down here on the Monday morning we packed them – at four o'clock to catch the seven o'clock train – the lorry went round all the little places collecting all the lobsters. We kept them in boxes. The six boats working out of John o'Groats were mostly part-time – they were crofters. At the beginning of the Second World War, there were only three or four boats working here – the rest were old men who had retired. The crabs came back after that and they had some good years. But on the whole there were more bad years than good years. There was just a living in it, there were no fortunes to be made.

Alfred Mackay was aboard one of the fifteen or so drifters that made the trip to Yarmouth each autumn from Wick in the 1930s:

I was there four years in succession, twice in the *Mavery*, once in the *Eminent* and on the last trip in the *Guide Me*. The cruise took eighty hours. It was a pretty tough life. Once a fortnight we dried the nets and tanned them. We used to spread out the nets in fields, working up to nine o'clock at night, and folk would be coming out of the pictures by the time we went home. There was no radio contact between the boats. Off Wick you might be out of sight of the other vessels but at Yarmouth, with about 900 drifters, boats sometimes ran foul of each other's nets. The nets would clap together. The Dutch came over and fished amongst us and, if they fouled a net, their wooden floats would cause more damage than the canvas buoys used by the Scottish and English boats. After landing in the morning we would turn in for a sleep on the boat or, depending on how far out we were working, go straight off again.

Get up and tie your fingers!

The decline of the herring drifter had consequences not only for the men who crewed them but also for the large numbers of women who followed the east coast fishing as its focus moved during the year from Shetland down to Yarmouth. The gutters, or in the evocative Gaelic phrase for them, *clann nighean an sgadain*, the clan of the herring girls,[31] were famous. The number of workers employed in the east coast herring fishing in 1912 ran to 21,749 fishermen, 2136 coopers and 10,818 gutters and packers.[32] In the decade before the First World War, the height of the herring fishing,

Anstruther harbour in the mid-1930s, crowded with steam drifters.

60–80 girls, for example, went from Nairn each season for the Shetland and Yarmouth fishing.[33] Some went further: Nellie Bochel, who gutted from 1908, aged fifteen, until 1938, went as far as Kinsale with the fleets. Other towns with large gutting crews were Fraserburgh, Wick, Castlebay, Peel, Killybegs and Ardglass, and Lowestoft. The girls began gutting when they left school, and older sisters or friends showed them what to do. Earnings could be small at first but by the second season the girls' skill was enough to bring in full wages. They worked in teams or crews of three, with two gutting the fish and the third packing them in the barrels.

The voyage to Lerwick was feared: the overnight crossing of sixteen hours from Aberdeen could make many sick, the ship was too crowded for everyone to have a bunk and many lay on deck under tarpaulins. Some women might have some whisky but many of the fisher girls came from temperance communities and refused this solace. When a curer hired a gutter he paid for her fare and transport of luggage and gave her a fee called arles to seal the contract. For Nellie Bochel her first arles was £1; one shilling had been the sum in an earlier time. Luggage was carried in a kist which could also serve as a seat in the huts where the women lived. Many took wool with them and knitted goods for shopkeepers back home. They also took caff-secks, simple mattresses made from cloth stuffed with chaff, and bedding.

In Shetland, the gutters lived in huts at Gremista to the north of Lerwick. These were one-roomed affairs with usually only a table and two large bunks, where the women could sleep three to a bed. The women started cleaning on arrival and put up cheap wallpaper, curtains and a screen across the glory-hole or indoor toilet. Curers provided coal for the fire but before the 1920s the only water supply was an outside tap. In 1929 the gutters in Shetland protested about the conditions and refused to sign on until things were made a bit better.

The women attended church on Sundays or held a meeting in the huts. The weekends were very social, with the fishermen ashore. Some courting went on, among the crowds, but there was always the risk of discovery and teasing. For many of the younger women, it must have been a great adventure and friendships formed at the gutting could last for a lifetime but for such hard work wages seem to us pitifully small. In 1911 'filling up' a barrel of herring earned 3d an hour. By 1921 it was 4d, by 1929 6d and by 1936 10d. In 1911 gutting and packing brought the three in the crew 8d per barrel. In 1929 Jean Bochel and her two companions filled 1100 barrels, earning about £15 each plus filling-up money – this was considered a successful season.

Like most of the herring girls, Margaret Smith came from a fishing family. Her father had been at the herring fishing in his younger days but later he fished for crabs and lobsters and worked the ripper for mackerel out of Crovie. Her great-great-grandfather on her mother's side had been a Maclean from the island of Muck; the herring fishing had taken him to the east coast and there he had married and stayed.

> I started going to the herring gutting when I was fourteen, just when I left the school. I left at Christmas and started the gutting in the following summer, that would have been in 1933. I started in Lerwick in May. We went from home in Crovie to Aberdeen, sitting on the top of a lorry on our trunks, and then by the *St Sunniva* to Lerwick. There was a whole lot of us, up on deck, lying on our trunks. I started with a curer called Dunbar, one of the biggest. In my gutting crew we were all schoolpals, all three of us went together. We had no practice really although we practised a bit before we got there. Some of the older women showed us what to do. We were the only young crew at that

time, all from the same class at the school. I was supposed to stay on
to go to the university but my chums were leaving to go to the
gutting and I wanted to go too.

When we got off the boat in Lerwick we were taken to the huts
and we had to set to and clean them before anything else, as they'd
been lying empty since the previous year. Barrels had been stored in
them but they weren't that bad and we scrubbed them out.
Sometimes when you arrived there was herring waiting to be gutted,
so then you had to tie your fingers and get stuck in.

[Get up and tie your fingers!' was the call that awakened many a
gutting lassie in the grey, cold northern dawn. It was a reference to

(Above) Scottish herring
lassies knitting while
walking at Lowestoft.

(Above right) A gutting
crew at Tarbert in
the 1930s.

the standard practice among the gutters of wrapping all their fingers
in strips of cloth to protect them from the sharp knife blades and the
brine.]

We worked six days a week, never on a Sunday and we didn't
usually gut on Monday – that day was used for what they called
'filling up'. The barrels of herring had stood until their layers of fish
had settled and it was necessary to fill up the space at the top. That
was the day when we'd wash our oilskins; we'd put paraffin on them
and scrub them to get rid of the fish grease. The boats did not go out
until Monday afternoon and it was Tuesday morning before they came
in with a fresh catch. Only the English boats went to sea on a Sunday
at that time.

I suppose nowadays people would think the work was hard. But
we were young and it was fun. We started at six o'clock in the
morning, sometimes only half awake. We were supposed to work
from six until nine at night but I've seen us working until one in the
morning – I've seen us working until six in the morning, all through

the night just to get the herring finished. Every curer had a number of gutters. A big one could have maybe twenty teams, a small one only six or seven. They were working there from all round the coast, but they were mostly from Peterhead and up the Moray Firth – maybe one or two crews from further down. There were a few from Lewis but I can't remember any from Caithness.

It was a skilful job. You had to be quick and you had to get the gut out clean. If you took off the head that was no use, that fish was rejected. There was a foreman and there were coopers, and they used to go along the back of the farlin [the big tub into which landed herring were poured to await gutting] and watch to see that you were selecting the herring right. You had five tubs at your back and you hadn't time to look round but you had to throw the fish into the five different tubs according to their size – small, medium, large, matties, full. You threw them around your back and the coopers measured the odd one to see you were selecting them right. You left the roe in but you took out what was called the 'long gut'. At certain times of the year you could get the gutting done with one cut but at other times you needed two cuts with the knife – two dabs, as it was called. You didn't actually lift your hand with the knife – you put the knife in and in again. The guts went into the gut cog which you emptied every so often into a gut barrel. The farmers took away the guts for fertiliser.

When the tubs were full, you shouted to the packer and she came over and helped you lift them, two at a time, to empty them into the rousing tub. Salt was added and the fish and brine were roused together. Then they were immediately packed into barrels. That was a skilled job. In the first layer the fish were laid with their heads pointing out and their tails all in the centre, and in the second layer the fish were laid with their heads pointing the other way. Salt was thrown in as you went on filling, and there was skill in knowing how much salt to add. When the barrel was full it was left standing all night and the cooper put a lid on it. On Mondays, after the contents had settled, the barrels were filled up again to make them level to the top. We had what we called top tiers, the layer of fish on top of the barrel. The best packers got the job of top tiering. I was one of them. You had to make a lovely top tier, lay out the fish so that when the lid came off the fish looked just beautiful. It wasn't always so beautiful further down. Some of the packers used to cheat and, if they were in a hurry, they would dump in the fish without packing them; that spoiled a lot of things. Again, if a packer was busy and couldn't keep up with the gutters, she would maybe slip in a few and pack on top of them. When the packing was done, the lids were put on and the barrels were then laid on their sides, the bungs were taken out and they were filled with pickle. It took four tubs to fill a barrel, maybe

A herring gutter ties 'clooties' on her fingers. Possibly in the 1940s or 1950s.

1000 herring. It didn't take a long time to fill one, maybe an hour, depending on the size of the fish. A barrel, well packed and sealed, would keep for a year or more.

At the end of a season or sometimes half-way through, Russians used to come over to buy the herring. They tested the fish by picking one from a barrel and taking a bite out of its back. If they were happy with the taste, they bought the barrel and it was branded. The brands were put on with stencils and a black brush.

We took turn about in the crew to keep the hut clean. We had to make our own food. It was the packer's job to go up before lunchtime and put the tatties on. You had to try to fit it in with the work. We ate a lot of herring.

We wore oilskins around the tubs and had cloots on all our fingers. I bandaged all my fingers because my skin was soft. I've still got the marks of the salt – they'll never go. If your hands were sore you could go to the rest hut and get them dressed. The Church of Scotland had nurses in Lerwick for hand dressing. The curers supplied the knives. They were called futtles. Women who baited lines used the same kind of knife. The blades were kept sharp for us by the coopers as a blunt knife tore the fish. It would stay sharp for a day or two.

Mrs Smith worked in Fraserburgh, Eyemouth, Gorleston, Yarmouth and Lowestoft, joining the fisherlassies' train for the journey to England:

It set off from Aberdeen full of fisher girls and we had a merry time. I suppose it took most of a day to go down and we stopped to pick up crews at various places. A lot of Irish men and women used to come over to work with us. One year one of our gutters had to go home and an Irishman worked with us. We had digs in Yarmouth where the landladies were glad to have us outside the tourist season. The landladies were mostly nice people and I went back to the same one twice, although we usually moved around. I liked Yarmouth – we had no cleaning to do, no food to make. Lowestoft was very nice as well and maybe it was a bit more homely than Yarmouth, as quite a few Scots had gone there and stayed. We didn't bother much about social life as we had our own amusements. The shops were open late and this was great for us; we bought presents for everybody at home for Christmas, as it was well into November before we returned to the north. The first of the boats would leave about the beginning of November but the girls had to stay on to fill up the barrels and pickle the herring. There was a lot to do after the fishing was actually finished – clean up the yard, scrub the tubs, all that sort of thing we had to do.

We tended to work for the same curer each season. They came to see us before it started, just after the New Year when it was a slack time for them, and agreed terms, and they gave us arles to seal the agreement. Some gutters did go from the Moray Firth to Stornoway for the winter fishing but I didn't go. I was in Yarmouth during a strike once. We went on strike for more pay. At that time we were getting tenpence a barrel between three of us. You had a lot of herring to gut before you got that. We were paid fourpence an hour when we were doing other work. That would have been in 1936 or 1937. We were on strike for a week anyway and we won. I think our pay went up to one shilling a barrel. I would say the work was well paid. If

you'd been in a shop at that time you'd have made about five shillings a week, and we usually came home after ten weeks with over £20. That was good money compared to what a shopworker would have got. Not only that, we also got a weekly wage to buy food and pay the digs. It was seven shillings, I think, in Yarmouth. In Lerwick it was slightly less as we hadn't to pay for digs. I wouldn't have changed it for anything.

Herring girls in Shetland in the 1920s.

But 1939 brought another war to Europe and, as their fathers had done a generation before, the fishermen left their home ports to serve their country. About 10,000 fishermen from Scotland served at sea in either the Royal or Merchant navies. As in 1914, boats were commandeered: 143 steam trawlers, 294 steam drifters and 234 motor boats, according to the official figures.[34]

Coull Deas from Cellardyke fished during the War and in 1940 made his first trip from Fife to Stornoway. The boat had to put in at Fraserburgh and Wick on the way, as movement at sea was restricted to daylight. No lights could be shown at night. 'I was quite a young boy then,' said Coull,

(Above) A Scots woman gutting herring at Gorleston, Yarmouth.

(Above right) Fishermen man a three-pounder gun on board the requisitioned vessel *Girl Christian* (KY 134) in 1940. In both World Wars fishing boats were armed.

'It was an adventure. We stayed in Stornoway for sixteen weeks. I was never home in that time, the whole summer fishing.' During the War prices were controlled and herring was set at £5 per cran. When the summer herring fishing finished in 1940, Coull returned to the east coast and took part in the seine net fishing, again according to restrictions imposed by the Admiralty.

Enemy aircraft were a new threat and, between attacks from the air, from U-boats and encounters with mines, 120 fishermen lost their lives while fishing, with another fifty-four presumed to have been killed by the enemy. In all there were about 200 attacks on fishing boats and twenty-nine were sunk.[35]

In 1945, the men returned to their home ports and took up the fishing once again. The Second World War marked a break with the old patterns but this was not apparent at once.

CHAPTER SEVEN

DISTANT WATERS

Three-haak halibut

George Leiper was called up in 1940 along with the boat he skippered, the Aberdeen great liner, *General Botha*. Great lining had developed along with trawling in the 1880s and in 1930 there were about thirty steam liners operating from the port, working the Atlantic to the west and north, as far as Iceland, all the year round. When George returned to Aberdeen in 1944 he went back to the fishing, this time as skipper of the *Fort Ryan*. The number of liners had diminished at that time but, as the stocks of fish had had a rest from pursuit, there was an abundance to catch. 'In 1946–8, I made tremendous catches,' said George. 'The biggest was £5600, that was a tremendous amount of money then. In the first five years, when we came back from the War, we made a quarter of a million. We made jokes about filmstar salaries.'

There were two classes of liner in the Aberdeen fleet: the smaller one comprised vessels of 80–90 tons gross, similar in size and design to steam drifters, and the larger class, of 120–160 tons, was in turn similar to the trawlers. (Some of them did switch at the right season from the lines to catching herring or trawling.) Great lining under steam was the direct descendant of the line fishing of the cod smacks of Shetland and the linesmen of the sgoth, the sixern, the yole and the fifie, and the steam linesmen drew on the extensive knowledge of methods and grounds already current among the sailing men. At the end of the nineteenth century, the steam liners and trawlers were drawing fish from all over the North Sea and were looking northward to the grounds beyond the 100-fathom line. The liners did not bring to market the great catches of the steam trawlers but the fish they landed, often larger and not damaged by being netted, almost always attracted better prices. They specialised in prime white fish, iced and landed in first-class condition.

The liner usually had a crew of ten or eleven: two engineers, one or two firemen, a cook and six fishermen each with a one-sixth share of all the gear – lines, dahns, buoys, anchors, lights, gaffs or cleps, and grappling irons. Cellardyke men were prominent in great lining and many Aberdeen boats had hands from the Fife town among their crews.[1] The liners fished the fertile spots around Rockall, the Faroes, the Bill Bailey Bank, and the

George Leiper, aged 24, as skipper of the *General Botha* (A 194) in 1939.

Outer Bailey beyond the Faroes, and moved on to Iceland and Greenland. Only occasionally did the liners go to the east of Shetland, to patches in Sea Area Viking, and then only in the days before they were big enough to carry sufficent coal for a trip to the Faroes. 'Iceland was my happy hunting ground,' said George, 'with the occasional trip to Greenland in the summer months.' A great line comprised about half a mile of the finest Italian hemp, weighing 7 lb and having, when new, a breaking strain of over 500 lb. Tanned in cutch every three voyages, a line would be expected to last four or five years before its original thickness, about that of a man's pinkie, would thin and it would grow weak. Snoods of sisal were attached to the line every $3^1/_2$ fathoms; thinner cotton lines were then attached to the snoods and the hooks bound to the cotton with linen thread. The individual

Aberdeen liner
Mount Keen (A 411).

lines, each with 128 large hooks, were tied together to make up the full great line, several miles in length.

After about two years on the *Fort Ryan*, George Leiper became skipper of the larger, more modern *Mount Keen*. When she sailed from Aberdeen for a 28-day trip to Iceland, she carried 160 tons of coal in her bunkers, another 20 tons on deck, 30 tons of ice in the fish room, and ten cran of fresh herring to serve as bait. The destination might be the halibut grounds on the Arctic Circle to the north-west of Iceland, a voyage of 900 miles from Aberdeen, past Peterhead, through the Pentland Firth, across the open sea for the first landfall at the Vestmann Islands, along the coast to Reykjanes Point, and then across another 140 miles of open water. If the weather was good, the men would take advantage of the almost continual summer daylight to start fishing at once. Let George take up the story:

> You placed all your lines in baskets along the deck before you started
> fishing and got your bait from the fish room – herring, or maybe
> tusk, cut like fish fingers. All the gear is prepared because you haven't
> got time when you're shooting to do anything else. When you start,

you put away an anchored dahn with the line attached. Then, when
you start shooting the lines, four or five men stand round the basket,
picking the hooks in sequence out of the cork rim, baiting each one
and throwing it over the side. As each line comes to an end, the next
is attached. The ship is steaming at maybe half-speed. The line is paid
out until maybe eight or ten miles have been shot, with an anchor
and buoy marking the end.

The steady rythmn of baiting might be interrupted by a sudden tangle in
the line or by the greater danger of a hook piercing a man's hand. In the
event of the first mishap, the engine would be immediately stopped to
allow the tangle to be sorted out; another crewman stood ready to grab the
line rapidly disappearing over the side, should one of his companions be
hooked.

> We shot at depths depending on what we were after – anything from
> 60 fathoms down to 400. Halibut, or 'geni' as we called them, lay in
> deep water but cod were on shallower ground. Except on Faroe Bank
> or some of the small banks there, where you got small halibut in
> maybe 50 or 70 fathoms, we worked at over the 200 mark. It used to
> be about 140–150 but it started to become cleaned up and we went
> deeper and deeper all the time. The deepest I've gone was 420
> fathoms. It took about two hours to shoot the gear and, after
> shooting, the line was left lying, maybe three to four hours for halibut
> – for cod, maybe just a couple of hours. Then you start hauling, back
> the way you've shot. It would take a whole day to haul back – you'd
> start maybe at ten or eleven in the forenoon and work all day right up
> till midnight.

A steam-line hauler assisted the work but it was a hard job, needing a great
deal of strength from the men. They wore three-inch-wide strips of cloth
called 'dogs' on their hands to prevent the hemp cutting into the flesh and
gaffed the fish as they appeared on the surface, taking care to hook them as
close to the mouth as possible so that no wound would reduce their value.
Each fish was thoroughly washed and thrown down to the fishroom where
the mate would be in charge of sorting and stowing the catch.

> If you got a fish on every hook, you wouldn't manage. Your ship
> wouldn't carry them. If you had a heavy fishing, say of cod or ling,
> there would be a fish on every third hook. That would be doing well.
> If you had one on every second hook, you'd have to stop, you
> wouldn't have time to unhook them all. It did happen, but that was
> before the War, when we were at the cod down at Iceland in the
> autumn – I've seen me fill up and be away home after two and a half
> days' fishing. It was big cod but that's the sort of thing that happened

then. But with the usual fishing we had, I'd say if you got two or three halibut on every line you'd be doing well. They were big ones. A 20-stone halibut is six feet long and a foot thick, solid flesh and bone. The biggest halibut I caught was 23 stone – it was a nuisance, far too big, you couldn't handle it.

The hemp line had a breaking strain of maybe 500 lb. The big halibut, however, did not always put up much of a fight – when they felt the pull of the line, they just swam up – but very often a big one would be docile until it came to the surface, and then it would start threshing about, and you had to get your hook in and your clep in

An Aberdeen liner hauling among icebergs in the Arctic.

and get it aboard. A skate, now, comes up flat. I remember one time on the west coast of Iceland, we came in a lot of skate. We started hauling middle of the forenoon and were still hauling that same gear next morning in the forenoon, just with skate, great grey skate, and when they got off the hook you had to chase them all round the ship – it was a good job it was a calm day. There were lots of sharks on the west coast of Iceland. When you were hauling, the gutter couldn't throw the guts over the side, you had to put them in a special place on the deck. After a couple of days it started to get smelly and we had to steam away maybe five or six miles into deep water, away from the fishing ground to dump it. Otherwise the sharks were at it all the time and they also took your fish on the line. We had halibut coming in with a piece taken out of them – that happened quite a lot – or halibut with the mark of a shark's teeth in them.

Up round Iceland in the summer time we got a lot of fine weather but from October onwards right up till April–May, it was dirty, bad. We had problems with icing in Greenland – one year we had problems with ice in Iceland. We were over in Greenland but it was so bad with ice coming down that we came back to Iceland. It was a north-east blizzard, and that was the time two Hull trawlers

Aberdeen liner hauling halibut.

capsized.[2] We were frozen up, completely frozen, we could do nothing: there was a gale of wind and the spray as it came aboard froze immediately and, of course, the ship got heavier and heavier all the time until she was so laden she would hardly rise to the sea. We had one wheel-house window open a little bit – we could neither shut it nor open it further – and we could look out.

We just kept the wind on the port bow until we came into calmer water, and then we started chipping the ice. With a north-east wind, the west coast of Iceland was the worst of the lot. It really gets bad weather. We had the same superstructure as a trawler – the only difference was we hadn't a winch, that was all. The old-fashioned steam trawlers were no higher out of the water than we were.

When the liner skipper was satisfied with the catch, his priority was to steam back to Aberdeen as fast as possible. It was not unknown for a race to develop between skippers. Once George set sail for home at the same time as two other liners:

> I said to the chief engineer: 'We'll have to get in first.' If you're last you'd get the tail end of the buyers. As we came down the Iceland coast, we approached a great big rock, only four mile of distance between it and the land. We were coming in at an angle – too shallow an angle and we would hit this reef, too wide an angle and we would hit the land. When we were going near the coast, thick fog came down. Well I spent the whole night on the bridge, navigating that ship through that channel, just taking direction findings, soundings – we'd been back and fore there umpteen thousand times – and we got through there and away we went. Now my other two pals, they didn't do that: they stopped and when daylight came they came through, but by that time I was away ahead. That was one thing – if you wanted to be a success, you'd got to make an effort.

The line fishermen worked on a share basis. According to George Wood, whose father was a line skipper:

> In 1955, a reasonable average catch was 200 boxes of halibut, which might sell for £3000, a good shot at that time. What you had was a settling sheet – fish sales £3000 – then you started taking off for so many tons of oil, so many tons of ice and water, everything that was charged for. Say there was a ten-man crew. Then you took off the wages of the chief engineer, the second engineer, the cook, and the fireman, as he was called, although he gutted the fish – these four men got wages, guaranteed at that time £2 a day or £4 for the chief, plus maybe 7s 6d in each £100 the catch made. So the gross wages for the four went into the expenses as well. That was all totalled up, put on the settling sheet. The total might be £1200, and the £1800 left was then divided so that £900 went to the person who owned the boat, and the last £900 was divided by six to give £150 to each man on a share. Then, of course, the value of the food eaten aboard was divided, and that was taken off each man, along with income tax and National Insurance, and you were finally left with your wage. That wasn't sheer profit, because the six baskets of lines per man had to be maintained, kept up to standard so as they wouldn't break. Each man had to see that his six baskets were in good order because his companions wouldn't tolerate anything else: one bad line breaking

could lose the whole lot. A herring drifter would be the only other vessel I can think of where the fisherman is separated from all the gear. When you shoot the lines, all the fishing gear is off the ship and you're not attached to it in any way. Not like a trawler. If the weather breaks, it might be too bad to start hauling and you've really got a problem. Then, if you do lose lines, that's to be suffered by the six of them.

Great lining from Aberdeen reached its peak in the late 1940s, when over forty boats were working, and this lasted until 1960. Although the expenses of operating a liner were considerably less than for a trawler — all the gear belonged to the fishermen themselves — the advent of motor trawlers in the

The liner *Mount Keen* (A 411) departing from Torry Dock for the Icelandic grounds on 15 July 1947.

1960s resulted in the newer vessels making a bigger return for less effort. A liner might be at sea for three weeks or a month while a trawler could fill her fish room in 10–12 days. A liner might make £6000 or £8000 on a trip, but the trawlers were earning £15,000 – £20,000 every ten days. By the 1970s great lining had all but died out from Aberdeen.

Line fishing was also carried on in waters nearer home, as a seasonal break from other methods. When Tom Ralston first went to sea at the age of fifteen on his father's boat *Golden Fleece* (CN 170) out of Campbeltown in 1953, the crew worked lines. After catching herring with a ring net for bait, they shot their first line in 90-fathom water east of Carradale and hauled up a conger eel on every third hook: they ended up with two tons of conger and sold the lot in Ayr for 1s 3d a stone. Tom told me they had no line hauler aboard and the twenty baskets' worth of line, weighing five tons, was dragged up by hand, a task that left the men with their fingers locked in a gripping position. After the episode with the congers, they improved their technique and went after hake for a couple of years, shooting lines with 120 hooks in 360 fathoms. Andrew Mearns fished 30 miles out in the North Sea, where the deep holes east of Stonehaven were good for skate.

David John Mackenzie and Norrie Bremner in Wick also did turns at the great lines, when the seine net fishing was slack. Halibut frequented the east coast of Caithness in those days. The last catch of halibut Alfred Mackay recalled was nine in one morning. 'They were graded according to the number of cleps needed to heave them aboard,' he said, 'one-haak, two-haak or three-haak halibut.' In the Hebrides, Murdo Maclennan and his colleagues went to the lines instead of the winter herring, shooting off Tiumpan Head and around the Shiant Isles in the Minch for cod, ling and skate:

> We used herring and mackerel for bait but herring was better because if you were in a hurry – well, you had to be in a hurry if you were shooting the lines, as the boat was travelling. If it was a big herring you could use the tail, the middle and the head – but with mackerel the skin was a bit hard and if you weren't quick enough, you see, the hook would go into your hand instead of into the fish. We always liked herring – it was softer. Two of us baiting at the same time and the boat going, and the skipper would say, 'I'm going to turn around now, watch yourselves' – somebody was behind us with a knife in case the line caught in our hand or our trousers, and then shoot at another angle. We shot on landmarks before we got echo-sounders. Watching the tide at the same time.
>
> There were quite a few accidents with hooks. One day we were fishing for skate off Shiant – huge, some of them two hundredweight, barndoors we used to call them. This one – we were just going to put the gaffs in when it went away like that, and my brother got a few hooks in his hand. One hook went right through the palm and came out the back of his hand. We had a look. 'Are we going to try to get it out or no?' He started to get white so we decided to leave the hook in. He wasn't feeling too much pain – it was kind of numb and it was swelling. We took him to the hospital. They had an electric nipper, or something like that, and they cut the hook and pulled it out. He was patched up and we went away to sea again. He didn't get home at all. Och, he was all right. There was no poison in it. It was a brand-new hook, and seawater's clean.

10s 6d a day

Trawling was the most important source of Scotland's white fish catch before the Second World War; 85 per cent or more of the cod, ling and other white fish landed came from their efforts.[3] Aberdeen was the main trawler port in Britain, after Hull and Grimsby, and remained in this high position for many years. The fleet in the inter-War years numbered around 300, although during the lean years of the 1920s and 1930s more were lost at sea or scrapped than were built.[4] Many were commandeered for War duties in 1939 but a few carried on fishing and twenty-four of them were lost through enemy action, either attacked from the air or sunk by mines. By 1950, 193 trawlers still worked from Aberdeen and two from Peterhead,[5] nearly all steam powered; the last steam trawler, the *Avondow*, built in 1946, was scrapped in 1967. By then, however, a more modern fleet of diesel-powered boats had taken their place. The first, the *Star of Scotland*, was launched from the builder's yard in 1947.[6]

The smaller trawlers, known as 'scratchers', fished in the North Sea. They sailed on Monday morning, landed often on a Wednesday, and went to sea again to make a second landing on Saturday. Around Buchanness and Rattray was where they fished, or maybe they would make a run off to the

The crew of the *General Botha* (A 194) in 1939.

Edge, 60–70 miles east of Aberdeen, where there were good turbot and lemon sole. Most of them went to the south-east of Aberdeen, to different grounds – the Doghole, conveniently close at seven miles, or the Wee Bankie, down off the Forth.

A larger class of trawlers made ten-day trips, through the Pentland Firth to drag off Strathy Point, off the Noup in Orkney's northern waters, around Cape Wrath and off the Butt of Lewis, down off Scourie, down the Minch, and at Rona or Sulisgeir. They used to catch good small codlings off the Pentland Skerries, and fish off Copinsay, North Ronaldsay, Fair Isle, Sumburgh Head and Fitful Head, off Foula, and north to Muckle Flugga or Fetlar. The largest trawlers, some 15 per cent of the total fleet, steamed straight from Aberdeen for the Faroes, where there might be only night fishing, and, in the better seasons, for the south end of Iceland.[7] Only a very few tried the Norwegian coast and, lacking the experience of the Hull and Grimsby men they never made a success of it. George Wood told me that the Aberdeen owners had to bring up Hull men as skippers to take their trawlers to the White Sea, the Barents Sea, North Cape, Svalbard or Spitsbergen, if they wanted to fish there. Aberdeen built its reputation on being a fresh-fish port and, as the landed catches still had to travel overland to London and the Midlands, it was essential to get fish to market as soon as possible after capture. The weekly 'scratchers' did best at this, landing almost live fish of the best quality; but, even with sixteen days from Faroe, the quality was still high. George Wood:

> The trawlers worked down at Iceland from January to March and they would fill the boat in six to seven days. It was very good fishing at the south end of Iceland and the prices would drop because of the sheer quantity that came in. They would nearly all have over 1000 boxes, and

Fish being dry cured at Allen & Dey Ltd, Aberdeen.

> the bigger ones maybe 1400–1500 boxes. That was the spring fishing down at Iceland. Some of the bigger boats might go right round where the line boats were working, to the west and north-west, off Isafjord, the west cape of Iceland. Then, in April, some of them made a beeline from Aberdeen for the Bill Bailey Bank, away down south-west of Faroe. That was a place for lovely halibut, all the same size.

As the Aberdeen steam trawlers aged, they were replaced by diesel-powered vessels. The price of coal was steadily rising, but diesel fuel was still cheap and the new vessels could tow heavier gear. The trawlers differed from the line boats also in the way the men were paid. The skipper and the mate were classed as share fishermen but the crew – the 'second fisherman' (equivalent to the second mate), the six deckhands, the cook, and the chief and second engineers – were all on daily rates, although they also received what was called poundage, a percentage of the value of the catch. It was regarded as a fairly good living and, from the 1880s up until the First World War, there wasn't much to tempt young men away from the fishing. As George Wood explained:

to be making maybe 10s 6d working in a sawmill or a butcher's shop
– really no future, just steady until you retired. At the fishing,
although it was a much harder life and the hours were terrible, you
could make progress if you wanted, if you studied and knew all the
grounds. It was a challenge. There's a tremendous amount of
knowledge involved.

The second largest fleet of Scottish trawlers, numbering sixty-nine boats in
1950, worked out of Granton and Leith, and a smaller number had Dundee
as their home port, although by 1950 only seven were based in the latter
city.[8]

John Robb, born and brought up in Newhaven, used to play truant to
fish for mackerel and went to sea on a herring boat as soon as he officially
left the school. After six months he found a berth as an apprentice on the
Granton trawler *Oystermouth Castle*: 'It was 10s 6d a day, quite a good wage in
1947.' The *Oystermouth Castle* belonged to the Boyle Company, one of about a
dozen trawler companies based on Granton and Leith. 'It was all North Sea
and west coast in those days,' said John. 'North Sea in the winter and, as the
weather got better, we gradually went round to the Butt and as far as St
Kilda.' A fishing trip usually lasted twelve days but if the fishing was good
the boat might return in a shorter time, to make what was called a 'half-
landing'. Normally the crew had two days ashore between trips but it was
common to spend 320 days at sea in one year. The longest break, the closest
thing to a holiday for most fishermen, came at New Year: 'We used to get a
week. Granton and Leith ships were always at sea for Christmas but every
trawler was in for New Year. We used to sail again on 3 or 4 January.' The
crew liked to settle up on Hogmanay and have a pocketful of money to buy
their New Year's bottle and have a good time. Not every boat could land fish
on Hogmanay and to keep the catch over the holiday period the hold would
be filled with a lorryload of ice and 'dry ice'. When the market opened
again on 3 January the crew would take crowbars to break the frozen mass
under the hatches.

As an apprentice with a Board of Trade logbook to keep track of his seatime, John went on to progress up the trawlerman's career ladder. The
official working hours at sea were from 6 a.m. to 6 p.m. but this
arrangement quickly was forgotten if there was a heavy fishing and all
hands turned to to gut the catch. It was normal for the apprentice to stand
watches with the mate, steering and fishing. 'Steering was good, you would
get the whole three-hour watch to yourself,' but, as Iain Smith, another
Newhaven trawler skipper who followed the same career pattern, said,
'You'd get your backside kicked if you were a quarter point off course; the
skipper would give you a course, say running north-east by east, three-
quarters east, and he would come up and check and say "You're no on it."
The crew generally looked after the apprentices; the sense of community

that pervaded life in Newhaven and Granton carried itself to sea and, although on the trawlers for safety reasons, close relatives were not encouraged to sail with each other, the men already knew each other.

The first step up from apprentice was to become trimmer, that is having the duty of trimming the 70 or 80 tons of coal in the ship's bunkers. From that a man progressed to deckhand and then to second fisherman. At the age of nineteen and with four years' experience, John attended classes in seamanship, signals, navigation, lifeboat drill and first aid at Leith Nautical College and sat the exams for his mate's ticket. Iain had to do two years' National Service but he was posted to a trawler working as a wreck dispersal vessel and that counted towards his sea-time. To move from being a mate to being a skipper, a man had to serve one full year at sea as mate – and it

Hauling the cod end on the stern trawler *Grampian City* (A 544) at Rockall in 1988.

might take two or three years to fulfil this requirement, as a berth at that rank was not always guaranteed – and pass more exams. Then there might ensue another period of waiting, until a skipper's berth fell vacant. Iain Smith worked as mate on the *Malcolm Croan*: 'I didn't really want to go as skipper because I was doing very well as mate but I had to take the boat away, as the skipper was going to Tenerife for holidays two or three times a year – skippers were quite well off at that time. It worked out all right and eventually I took her away.' John Robb got his start as skipper in 1957, on the *Finlay Paton*, a steam trawler bought from Aberdeen where she had originally been the *Barbara Robb*, when the previous skipper fell ill and he was asked to take the ship away.

In the mid-1950s the steam trawlers in Granton were growing old and inefficient. The first diesel trawlers, vessels such as the *Gregor Paton*, the *Joe Croan* and the *Granton Falcon*, began to appear in 1955. As John Robb explained to me:

The congested quay at
Aberdeen fishmarket,
probably in the 1940s.

One diesel trawler could probably catch as much as three steam
trawlers. They were more efficient. On an old steam trawler, if the
steam went back, the boat was just bobbing up and down, but with
the diesel engine everything was steady power, faster. They used the
same nets but they were more efficient and more powerful. As the
price of fish went down and the price of coal rose, the diesels cost
less to run. The last steam trawler here was the *Fort Rannoch* in about
1957. If the steam trawler went home with 500 or 600 boxes the
diesel would be bringing in 1000. And it was cleaner, with no coal to
shovel and no ashes to haul up.

It was customary to work three-hour watches although this could extend to
three and a half hours on occasion. When steaming to the grounds, the crew
adhered to the schedule but once the fish started coming aboard it was all

hands to the gutting and sleep was snatched when the chance presented itself. The diesel trawlers normally carried a crew of twelve men whereas some of the smaller steam trawlers had only ten men on board; also fewer men, only the chief and second engineer, needed to work below tending the engine, leaving more men to handle the catch. 'Sometimes the engineers could come up to give you a hand if you were getting a lot of fish,' said Iain Smith, 'and the cook would maybe come in. You could shift a lot in a three-hour watch if the mate could keep up with the boxing – maybe sixty or eighty boxes of middle-size haddocks.' The ideal trip comprised a steady fishing, hauling forty to fifty boxes each shot, the amount that could be cleared and still leave an hour for a sleep.

> You never stopped work for sleep but after twenty-four hours most skippers would call a break, and you left the gear on the deck, got your head down for three hours and then shot again. But to land fish on fish was no good: you had to try to clear the deck between hauls. Say you had a really big haul and you had fish left when the next bag came up on the staboard side, then you would put the first lot over on the port side and leave them until you had time to gut them or, if there was no time, you might hose them through the scuppers.

After the War the fish were a good size and plentiful everywhere. Hauls of 80-100 boxes were common. The Granton trawlers would go north to the Out Skerries in the spring and then away to the east of Isle of May to the 30 or 40 fathoms of the Fisher Bank in the summer. Bad weather in winter encouraged them to move to deeper water, to the 100 fathoms of the Out Skerries, what the men called 'the edge', less boisterous than the breaking seas on shallow banks, and in a gale the ship would dodge until it grew more calm, touching her head to the sea. As John Robb explained:

John Robb in the wheelhouse of the *Grampian City* (A 544).

> Force 9 or 10 was too much for the steam trawlers, but the diesels could keep going a bit longer. Later, with the stern trawlers, it would be a hurricane before you would stop. Force 10 was pushing it, but the steam trawlers were good sea boats and tended to stay dry on the deck. The diesels, with all the weight of fuel, tended to have more washing and you had to be careful because the waves washing over could take the fish out of the pounds. In the winter we started working closer to Shetland and Orkney and I can mind sometimes on the west coast, if there was a really bad forecast, nipping into Stornoway or coming back through the Pentland Firth to save coal.

The steam trawler skipper had to keep a close eye on the coal and try to save as much as possible, but the diesel trawlers carried enough fuel for a month. Some of the Granton trawlers used to go round as far as Oban or Ayr – a voyage that took forty-eight hours, as they were too large to take the

The trawler *Arctic Hunter* (GW 9) leaving Castlebay for Rockall in 1975, with Iain Smith as skipper.

short-cut through the Caledonian Canal. Two landings might be made at Oban and then, after re-coaling – two or three wagonloads on the deck – a third landing might be swung ashore at Ayr before the homeward trip and the settling up. These longer trips lasted 28–30 days. From Granton to the 90-fathom grounds at Rockall might take fifty-six hours of normal steaming and, in good weather, the steam trawler might find herself running out of ice. Melting was particularly fast in the summer months when she cleared the Butt of Lewis and ran into the warm flow of the North Atlantic Drift. The only west coast port with ice for sale at that time was Stornoway – the development of Kinlochbervie and Lochinver came later – and it might be necessary to call in at the Hebridean port or dodge into Scrabster on the way home for a top-up. Landing at Ayr or Troon was another way of avoiding fish spoilage through lack of ice.

(Below) Crew of the trawler *Malcolm Croan* (A 444) repairing a torn net at the Faroes in 1968.

(Below left) The crew of a trawler having a meal in their cabin, probably in the late 1940s.

The Granton trawler companies paid their men in a similar way to their northern neighbours in Aberdeen, with daily rates for all the crew and a scale of bonuses according to the value of the fish landed. The deckhand would gain an extra penny for each pound the ship earned, the second fisherman would get 2d, and the apprentice would go home with a handsome farthing on top of his daily 10s 6d. Another scale of bonuses came into operation if the catch topped a certain level. In the late 1940s and early 1950s a trawler might average between £800 and £1300 per trip. The skipper and the mate were paid according to a percentage of this figure, 5 per cent for the skipper and a little less for the mate. In Aberdeen the skipper could earn an extra bonus for saving gear but this did not operate in Granton. The engineers and the cook were on fixed wages. In the early days the ship's food bill, which, with a careful cook laying in the stores, might run up to £5, was taken off the men's income but, after disputes with the owners, the food came to be provided at the company's expense. The men had to supply their own clothing and boots and, if they had none, the owners might provide the first outfit and deduct the cost from the first few months' wages.

Migratory, nomadic fishermen

In the late 1940s and early 1950s the seine net emerged as the predominant inshore method for catching white fish on the east coast, with one or two boats operating from many harbours and larger fleets from Eyemouth, Port Seton, Newhaven, the East Neuk towns, Arbroath, Montrose and the Moray Firth ports. White fish landings also increased in Campbeltown. Many of the fishermen on the seiners lived in the chain of villages around the coast but kept their boats in the larger harbours and travelled back and fore to the quayside. The east coast seiners also began to fish more on the west, making use of the Caledonian Canal or taking the longer northabout route through the Pentland Firth. Seine net landings in 1948 totalled almost 900,000 hundredweight, worth over £2 million; 54 per cent of this came ashore in Peterhead, Fraserburgh, Wick, Lossiemouth and Mallaig.

The Inshore Fishing Industry Act of 1945 and the White Fish and Herring Industry Act in 1948 brought in schemes to provide fishermen with grants and loans to refurbish the fleet and, by the end of 1948, 134 new motor boats had been built and about another 350 adapted or reconditioned.[9] The size of the seine netters began to increase so that they could fish further offshore and carry bigger catches. The new vessels were over 60 ft with a cruiser stern and a full-bodied beaminess that gave them a handsome, almost plump appearance with a gentle upsweep towards the vertical bow. The Lossiemouth fishermen, in particular, proved to be enterprising in exploring new grounds for the seine net, as William Stewart recorded, no doubt with some pride:

Lossie, Hopeman, Burghead and Nairn fishermen maintained a superiority in numbers working on the Oban, Mallaig and Clyde grounds, and for a while in the Lochinver area. For many years upwards of thirty Lossie seiners worked Stormy Bank, Sulisgeir, Noup Deeps and Hoy grounds, and landed their catches back home in Lossie. Foula grounds were also worked from January to April, and East Shetland and Fair Isle as well. Summer months saw several boats working [the] Ling and Fisher Banks.[10]

William Stewart formed a partnership with three nephews and ordered a new seiner – ' an 8-cylinder, 152 hp Gardner engine, which at that time was the most powerful engine that Gardner's were producing'.[11] It was now

Aberdeen trawler *Aberdeen Progress* (A 157) outward bound.

becoming usual to install echo-sounders and other electronic instruments, all of which served to increase the catching power and fuel the fisherman's perpetual dream of a 'big shot'.

And some big shots there were, as this item from *The Northern Scot* (22 Feb. 1947), recorded:

Six thousand boxes of cod and haddock, valued at £10,800, were landed at Lossiemouth during the first four days of this week. An all-time weekly record for the port both in weight and value of catch is expected. Approximately fifty seine boats have been fishing, the average earnings per boat being in the region of £200. Among the highest single-day catches was one of 146 boxes, worth over £250, landed by the *Ajax*, skippered by Mr George Campbell. Recent heavy south-east gales are said to have driven extra fish into the Moray Firth.

In September 1952, the *Silver Rock*, skippered by William Jappy, hauled up 10 tons of fish in her seine but could take only 3 tons aboard; she sailed in to her home port of Helmsdale, towing the other 7 tons astern, and beached the net.[12]

Sandy Miller and Bill Murray joined boats from their home village of Hopeman when they left the school. At that time, most of the fishing by the twenty or so Hopeman boats was on the west coast with the ring net in the winter and the seine or trawl at other times. In February and March they would go down to Ayr to seine for cod. Oban was often their base later in the year, from where they would travel home every third weekend in a chartered bus; to reduce the six hours needed for the road journey, they sometimes left the boats in Fort William. It took a week to alter the deck layout of their dual-purpose boats to make the switch from ring net fishing to seine net fishing.

John Thomson was to become one of the prominent Lossiemouth skippers but in the early 1950s he was also newly out of school and enjoying the adventure of the sea as a young deckhand:

The boats from Lossiemouth went as a fleet and the more progressive reached all around Scotland and to Ireland. When we went to the Clyde and Ireland we went mainly through the Caledonian Canal. When we got bigger boats it was always by the Pentland Firth. Five hours it took from Lossie to Inverness and you had to have a good tide. You needed a flat tide to get into the lock at Muirtown. It was very rare to do the Canal in a day – usually it was a day and a bit. At first it was physical labour, with the crews pushing the poles to open the locks, but later the gates were electrically operated. Of course the boats were always racing. Loch Ness is over 20 miles long but we had a pretty fast boat, the *Guide On*, and it took two hours three minutes.

The main port in Northern Ireland used by our fishermen was Ardglass near Downpatrick. Everywhere the men went in the fishing usually one or two somehow took home wives and that happened in Ireland – there were three wives from Ardglass. There were Orkney wives and Whitehaven wives in Lossie as well. Later, in Ireland, we went down to Killybegs, and we fished further south, often weekending in Dublin and using the harbours of Howth or Dun Laoghaire. In the Irish Sea we had whiting in the winter. They were prolific. We worked a pattern of three weeks away and would come home on the train for a weekend. But we used to catch whiting and gut to all hours of the morning in some Irish harbour, and the next night run across the Irish Sea to Stranraer, or Portpatrick if the weather was suitable – it was a tricky harbour to enter, a tremendous rise and fall. The whiting were all dispatched to the Glasgow market but from our point of view I'm afraid it was also a corrupt market – the prices were determined and it was sometimes a bit of a heartbreak what you'd get for all that work. If we got 30 shillings for a box, that was something – most times we got 15 shillings or even

12s 6d. Gutting whiting all night in an Irish port and then running the Irish Sea next day – very hard work for little return. But the men were home from the War, they had new boats, they were so glad to be home and making a living, and at that time, too, you know, if you did get a good week you were doing well – I suppose a good week was twice as much as wages ashore for tradesmen. But it was a struggle for a lot of people. For us, as boys, we'd have gone to sea for nothing. We got £3 when we started. Every boat had a boy as a cook. We didn't get cookery classes at the school, as our fathers had, but we had to

start cooking. Then we were deck apprentices – but it was a long time before you got a full share of earnings. You had to be proficient, you had to be gutting well, know your job, and be an able net mender and splicer – it took time to learn. But I would say that when we went to sea as boys – and we were just boys, maybe not as good as we should have been – they made men of us pretty quick. You had to pull your weight.

(Above left) The *St Kilda* (INS 47), John Thomson's boat, at sea. The *St Kilda* set a Scottish record for seine-net in January 1981 when she grossed £27,554 in one week, making five landings between 3 and 8 January of about 6000 stone of fish.

(Above right) John Thomson in the wheelhouse of the *St Kilda* (INS 47) in 1984.

The Caithness seine-net fleet was also growing at this time, with thirty-five boats over 30 ft based in Wick and seventeen in Thurso and Scrabster.[13] Norrie Bremner started in the *Laurel* in 1943, and then had a berth on the *Solace*, and later the *Spray* when she came home from War service, before going on to become one of the successful northern skippers. There is also the example of David John Mackenzie, who went to sea in 1947 on his father's boat:

Working out of Wick we went as far north as Copinsay, sometimes in Deer Sound; and our southern limit was the end of the Smith Bank opposite Helmsdale. The furthest outside we would go was about 36 miles. We would steam at 8 or 8½ knots. Generally in the late 1940s and early 1950s, the Wick boats worked about one hour's steaming south or south-east of the harbour. There was one year we hardly needed to buy coal – as our nets took up enough coal from the seabed. There was no radar or echo-sounders in the old boat. My father relied on meezes. In clear weather this was okay but in hazy weather you could easily go in the bottom – hit the seabed and stones, and damage the nets. There's much less damage to nets now, with good navigational aids. At first we worked with six coil of rope per side but the newer boats worked with ten per side (each coil is 240 yds long) – but now they work with twelve per side, that's about two miles.

During the 1950s the stocks of white fish in the Moray Firth itself declined. Golspie saw its first seiner in the early 1930s, the 30-ft *Silver Rock* with a 26-30 hp Kelvin engine, when catches of good cod could be hauled within a few miles of Dunrobin Castle on a ground called the Dottle. After the War, with the aid of the government assistance schemes, some of the fishermen invested in larger boats. Donald MacDonald's uncle acquired the *Devotion*, with a 44 hp engine thought at the time to be 'a tremendous example of progress'. Donald thinks she cost about £7000, a very considerable investment for the men. But the boats in the smaller ports around the Firth began to fail to make a living. Embo lost its little fleet, and then Inver, and then Brora. 'We could see the demise of the Dornoch Firth in the 1950s,' said Donald, 'and then it was the Moray Firth, all swept clean by the seiners. There's nothing in the Moray Firth now except a few pelagic fish. The last haddies caught by a Moray Firth seiner was about twenty-two years ago; even the small haddies are gone now, and there's only the occasional small cod.' George Wood of Macduff, however, remembers big shots of 60–70 boxes of plaice, worth £5 or £6 a box, being taken in the outer fringes of the Moray Firth in the 1960s, five or seven miles offshore.

In the summer of 1947, the crew on a small fishing boat called the *Ivy* had a go with the ripper and the seine net in the Minch close to their home at Kinlochbervie, then a small, somewhat remote village. They found good catches of white fish. The news of this rich fishing ground spread to the east coast skippers and before long boats from Buckie, Helmsdale and Banff were shooting in the Minch and using the harbour at Kinlochbervie. The village was on its way to being one of the top ports in Scotland. Just a short distance from the old wooden jetty in Loch Clash that served as Kinlochbervie's harbour was an anchorage in Loch Bervie where the boats could be safely left over a weekend while the crew went off on the long journey right across the Highlands to their homes in Moray or Banff. A single-track B-road connected the village to the outside world and in the early years it could barely cope with the increased traffic as fish lorries began regular runs through the depopulated Sutherland hills to the fishbuyers' auction. A new wooden pier was built in 1961 and new shore businesses were established to claim a share of the sea's wealth. Some distance to the south, the harbour of Lochinver also saw greater activity. Built as a herring station in the nineteenth century, Lochinver's harbour comprised little more than the Culag pier when Lossiemouth boats began landing white fish there in 1948. The facilities became totally congested when as many as sixty boats could be landing in one day.[14]

'We became migratory, nomadic fishermen – we could be in Aberdeen or Orkney or on the west coast,' said John Thomson. 'We built up the ports of Kinlochbervie and Lochinver, as we explored new grounds and new fisheries and developed new marketing. The decline in the Moray Firth was for various reasons but one was that the inner Moray Firth, through sheer high efficiency and catching power, became overfished. A nucleus of small boats manned by older men stayed here but the younger men with the better vessels foraged far afield. We went as far as St Kilda and Rockall.'

Some sma' line fishing persisted among a repertoire of techniques the fishermen could draw on, according to circumstances. In Ferryden, Andrew Mearns' father had worked the seine net:

Away back when they had to pull it by hand, before winches, they didn't have much rope – only a coil and a half or something like that – but it was a long net. They closed the net and hauled it aboard by hand. Before they got a winch, it must have been murder – I tried it, and it wasn't easy. He was born in 1901, so it was at the start – in the early 1920s, inshore, in the bays and shallow water, less than 20 fathoms. I started off with him in a boat called the *Boy Andrew* [named after myself], a few years before we changed over to the *Angus Rose* I. He got another one after that, the *Angus Rose* II, and when I got one she was the *Angus Rose* III. She was ME 19 and one inch under 50 ft long. You were allowed to fish inside the three-mile limit with a seine net, if the boat was under 50 ft. We worked the seine net but mostly it was cod nets, not the cod nets they have now for hard bottom and shot with the tide: the ones we had were on soft bottom and they were anchored across the tide with a dahn at each end, where they were left and pulled each day.

When we got *Angus Rose* II, we started trawling – light trawling for haddock and cod, and we also went prawn fishing – that was about the start of it. The cod started in October, depending on the weather. What we call thick weather was when the bottom got stirred up with a storm. When the weather cleared you wouldn't catch cod with the lines, but you could catch them with the seine net. We used to mix it a bit – we'd go seine netting if it wasn't suitable for the lines. I've seen a race of small cod – 'daggers' I used to call them, about 30 to a box, they didn't have roes and were possibly adolescent fish – in

March–April on the lines and that would be it, but you would get them with the seine net until the end of May. Then we would have to think about going off the land. The fish just disappeared. There would be no codlings caught from the end of May up to October again, but there was codlings there on the hard bottom and on the wrecks – divers have seen them – but we couldn't catch them with the lug lines. It could be the fish behaviour. During the summer we did seine netting – until we started trawling which was away about 1966.

The seine net was a hard job. It's easier now with power blocks. Trawling was easier because the gear comes right aboard. We always fished on the east coast. I went to the west coast three times but it was a disaster, I should have stayed where I was. Prawn fishing in Mallaig. We went through the Canal. It took quite a while, to get up to Inverness and back down to the latitude of Montrose again, in fact beyond that. Ardnamurchan is opposite Scurdieness. You don't get through the Canal in one day now but when I first started you could; now, once five o'clock comes, that's it.

We went east as far as 50 miles off, trawling. In a normal week we would go off at eleven o'clock on Sunday night, because the crew had maybe a bit too much to drink and if they got into bed you wouldn't get them out, and I used to sail before they got into bed. I never fished on a Sunday, my father never fished on a Sunday. I like to know when one week finishes and the next one starts, that was my main reason. I think the fishermen needed time off, the crew needed time off. Nowadays they're crazy. The older fishermen here were religiously minded. Some wouldn't sail until one minute after midnight. When I was trawling I went out at eleven on Sunday night, back in at six on Tuesday night, set sail again at eleven and came in again on Thursday or Friday morning. Worked all day Friday, sometimes all day Saturday, sorting gear. I was working a hundred hours a week.

In Newhaven, the fishermen were still concentrating on herring but, as Jim Wilson recalled, 'In the summer we could go seine netting, with a mile of rope on each side, and that was for haddies, cod, whiting, flatfish. We could go off 30 miles, off St Abb's Head.' Mixed fishing was also the rule in the south-east, in Eyemouth. Peter Burgon started his career on a seine netter called the *Golden Dawn* at the same time as the line fishing ended: 'The seine net started and the line fishing stopped. My brother, myself and another chap had a small yole and, in fact, I think we actually would be the last at the lines. We used to bait two. That would be in 1948. The majority [of fishermen] had started the seine net.' Peter Patterson also started in Eyemouth at this time on the *Milky Way*: 'We fished as far off as the Wee Bankie, 20 miles east-north-east, or as far as 50 miles due east, or 90 miles in the summer time – out on a Monday, land in the middle of the week, and out again' – and continued to use the seine net until he retired. In the late 1940s, Peter Patterson's father had said to him, 'What are you going to do with a new boat? The fishing's finished!', but he stuck to his ambition, suppressed any fears that he might not be able to pay back his costs, and bought a twelve-year-old seiner from Banff in 1956, the *Maureen*, for £2800 and sailed her for the next twenty-seven years.

It was hard work at the sea but the fishermen were prepared to do it. In Macduff, William West told me how he began his fishing career:

> The boat was finished about two or three months before I was demobbed in 1958. I came home from the RAF on the Friday and on the Monday morning I was 75 miles south-east of Aberdeen, and to say I was sick would be an understatement. On my first day, I left home at seven on Sunday evening on a local bus, away to Aberdeen and out to sea. We used to come in on a Wednesday and land so much fish, and away out and come in on Saturday again. So I used to get home to the house here about three o'clock on a Saturday afternoon and just die – into bed – and I slept on the bus from Aberdeen and got the conductress to give me a shake when we reached Macduff – and away again at seven on Sunday evening. We did that for the first two or three years. It was just a wee boatie, only 53 ft, but we were still 75–100 miles south-east of Aberdeen. That size of boat wasn't fit really for the job but a 75-ft boat was a huge boat in those days. To start with, I was the only Macduff man in the crew – the rest of them were from Portknockie and the skipper was from Cullen. She was called the *Ocean Crest*. I was on her for eleven, nearly twelve, years. When my first partner reached the age of sixty-four, he stopped; and I took over as skipper myself, about nine years after we started. In the summer time we could knock in eleven hauls per day – that was hard going, but if it was daylight you were at it. From when you left Macduff for Aberdeen, you worked all the time. The only time you got a rest was if the fishing petered out a bit and you had to shift the ground – for a couple of hours. You just collapsed where you were, oilskins and everything on. If you found a soft net to lie on, you were fine – but you died as soon as you closed your eyes.
>
> It was hard work and we were making good wages, although we were knocking in long hours. When I left the RAF I was making about £2.50 a week. After my first trip to Aberdeen I came home on Saturday and put £9 in my wife's hand. It looked like £1000. 'What'll I do with it?' she asked. An awful lot of boats did a lot better than we did at that time. We averaged about £30 a week. Good money. On the work side of it you were tired, aye moaning and groaning, but I don't know any men on it at that time who, looking back, didn't have great times.

A fixed way of life

Herring fishing was much reduced during the War but in 1946 the old seasonal pattern started up again, with 203 steam drifters and fifty-seven motor drifters steaming south from the Scottish ports to join the fleets in East Anglia. The fishermen were less prepared than they had been during the War years to put up with restrictions and there were several strikes as they campaigned for full seamen's food rations and better deals from the buyers. The gutting crews also went on strike for higher wages. The Herring Industry Board was now the government body with responsibility for the industry.

Herring landings in Scotland in 1948 added up to 2,913,000 cwt, barely more than the total in 1938; almost half of this catch was taken by steam drifters, and amazingly enough there were still some sailing drifters at work – they caught a total of 700 cwt. By contrast, 660,000 cwt were caught by the ringnetters, most of this in the Clyde area and the west coast, with only a small amount (7000 cwt) being taken in the Firth of Forth. The industry still provided employment to almost 4800 gutters and packers, and 376 coopers.[15] A fleet of eighty-eight drifters was based in Peterhead, the largest single fleet, but Fraserburgh saw the busiest season, with over 200 boats landing each day at the height of the fishing. The steam-drifter fleet dwindled quickly in the early 1950s – Buckie's fleet fell from twenty-two in 1951 to none two years later, Peterhead's from twenty-nine in 1953 to one in 1955.[16]

In the south-west the ringnetters began to look more and more beyond the boundaries of the Firth of Clyde. They were as nomadic as their brethren in other parts of the country. The *Integrity* built in Girvan in 1948 belonged to Tom Shields's father and uncle. As he told me:

> I would say there were about thirty boats working out of Girvan in the late 1940s, each with six or seven men. They all worked as pairs more or less but sometimes when away from home, for example in the north, the shortest steam was to Mallaig, six hours each way, or Oban, nine hours each way, and it was customary for the boats to make up a foursome, so that two could go to market and not be back until the next night, while the other two could fish on. You very often got them passing each other going in different directions across the Minch. The *Integrity* neighboured the *Avail* all the year round but when we went north in the winter we very often mated up with the *Incentive* and the *Arctic Moon*, two other Girvan boats, and we worked together. It was a way to maximise the fishing effort. If left on occasion on your own and there was another boat – she could well be from Campbeltown, Dunure or Maidens – you would go alongside and say let's mate up until the neighbours come back.

We often landed in Stornoway and we used to fish Broad Bay and Harris Sound. The most herring I ever saw in my life was at Isle Martin in Loch Broom. There was no herring processing in Girvan. The catch was landed here only if the Ballantrae Banks fishing was on and buyers collected here sometimes. The buyers usually came to the designated landing ports. The catch was discharged into lorries and taken away. My father fished the Solway for herring, very difficult because of the tides.

There was a season in the Clyde, but we went all over the country. In the month of May, when the boats were finished their cleaning, depending on how things were, they would try having a look around Arran here but coming up to June they fished the west side of the Isle of Man, off Port Erin, down off the Chickens. That could last right to September and they used to land at Portpatrick or go across to Kilkeel, occasionally to Portavogie in County Down and sometimes Whitehaven. We have actually landed in four countries in the one week – Holyhead, Whitehaven, Kilkeel – we landed in southern Ireland as well – and Portpatrick on the way home. It depended on how quickly you got your herring: if you got them early, you could make longer passages and try to be back for the next night. If you got smaller amounts you would try to go not so far. After the Isle of Man, we would fish sometimes for a week or two in the Clyde and then we went to the Outer Hebrides. Sometimes we went to the east coast of England, down at Whitby. We used the Forth & Clyde Canal but after that was closed at the start of 1963 we went up the Caledonian Canal. The last time we were through we stopped at Seahouses and fished off the Farnes, and then went further south and fished off Whitby. One season we fished almost exclusively out of Scarborough. When you came home from that, at the end of October or thereabouts, the winter fishing was starting in the Hebrides and we went up there. We tried to get home for Christmas. In those days we came home with the boat, a twenty-four-hour steam each way, but latterly you could leave the boat at the north end of the Crinan Canal, in the basin or the canal itself, and get a bus home. We used to do this at the end of a fishing but latterly we came home every second weekend.

The Hebridean fishing would go on until the beginning of February and then we came back into the Clyde for spawning herring. There were two main spawning areas: the Ballantrae Banks, and the Brown Head at the south-west corner of Arran. We could use ring nets in both places, although the Ballantrae Banks are shallow with a rough, pebbly bottom, and we used to change to shallower nets for working there. Some boats used trammel nets – like an anchored drift of shallow nets, 70 mesh deep, upright in the water but of no great depth: as the herring poked their heads in, they brought the nets down.

That was the standard pattern for Girvan, Maidens and Dunure boats especially. Some of the boats from Campbeltown, Tarbert and Carradale did not go to the Isle of Man as much as we did. Some went north but the Argyll boats did not go regularly to the east coast of England.

The ring net men and the drifter men were still sometimes at loggerheads in the Firth of Forth. For example, if two drifters were lying at the end of their casts of net, a ringnetter could shoot and circle a shoal of herring in the quarter-mile gap between the drift nets, an action that understandably roused the ire of the drifter men who would shout, swear and blow their whistles.[17] But some close relationships were also formed between the west- and east-coasters, as Alex Watson recalled for me in Cellardyke: 'I've seen my mother having half a dozen of the Campbeltown men up to the house on a Sunday night for their tea. My father and another boat from here worked a foursome with two boats from Girvan, when they were fishing quite a distance up the top of Loch Fyne.'

Angus McCrindle ordered a new boat in 1951 from Noble of Girvan. She was the *Saffron* (BA 182), 58 ft long with a canoe stern and one of the first ringers to have a 8L3 152 hp Gardner diesel installed:

The length to that time had been a maximum of 56 ft but with the extra two cylinders in the engine we thought it best to add the two feet in length. Noble had built two ringers before, the *Integrity* and the *Elizabeth Campbell* – but they had cruiser sterns and were flatter, with less sheer. My brother Willie drew in the stern post we wanted and it shows just how desperate Noble was for an order that he allowed us to do this. The end result was the proof, a lovely-looking boat. Mr Noble said we wanted a gondola with a lot of sheer. The cost was £7100 and half was paid on deposit in cash. I would say this was one of the most successful designs, equal to those from the Weatherhead yard in the early years and the proof in the following years was that Noble never looked back and turned out a huge number of this model up to the demise of ringnetting in the 1970s. He built another boat for us in 1962 for £17,500 – the 59-ft *Sapphire* (BA 174).

At the end of the reign of the ringnetters, the *Saffron* and *Sapphire* were the only pair of ringers to prosecute the Isle of Man fishery. The Isle of Man Fishery Board sent their representative to Prestwick to meet us and offer us a subsidy to fish the Isle of Man to supply their kipper market. We declined, saying that if they informed us of drifters landing, we would come down but we did not want to tie ourselves to landing all our catches on the island. Four or five times that season we split our catches between Portpatrick and Douglas and gained considerably on our gross earnings. But give honour where it is due, the kipperers treated us very well. In one of the last years of the Isle of Man fishery we landed 180 crans in Portpatrick from the Douglas

Bank and on that passage we passed two drifters shot north-west of Peel. We were late getting back and decided to try where the drifters were working, and we finished up with 250 cran of mixed herring for our night's work. That year we followed those herring across the Irish Sea to off Carlingford Loch in a month of big fishing. When the herring got to the Irish coast they went deeper and we had to adopt a semi-sunk method, giving the buoys 10-fathom straps to get down to them. This method was also used one year for spawning herring on the Coll Bank in the Hebrides.

The Clyde fishermen used the slack time of the year between the winter herring fishing finishing on the Ballantrae Banks at the end of March and the start of the summer fishing to refit their boats. It was usual to take all the boats ashore, 'put them on their legs,' in Angus McCrindle's words, that is, propped up, and scrape and revarnish them. This operation took about six weeks to complete and was almost a universal custom in the area up until the late 1950s. As Alex Watson explained:

The *Cosmea* (KY 21), later renamed the *Coriedalis*, in Anstruther. She was the last steam drifter from Scotland to fish at Great Yarmouth, in 1956.

> In the Firth of Forth the boats were all varnished then, because there was a slack period in the spring when the boats could be overhauled. It was only after the start of the seine net and the daily grind of five or six days a week that they didn't have time for that and started to paint them instead. Going back before that, the boats were tarred. Of course at that time every place had its small gasworks and they had no difficulty in getting tar. The Fisherrow boats were varnished as well. The boats were like yachts, they really were at the start of the summer fishing, with garnishing in white and the metalwork all silverised.

Down below even the wood panelling of the cabin was varnished. All
the boards separating the pens in the hold were taken on the pier,
washed, scrubbed and all painted over. It was a more leisurely way of
life. The men did the work themselves and the only expense was the
materials. The seine net boats used to be painted twice a year – early
on, at the end of May, and again in September. The crews used to do it
until they thought that they shouldn't be painting the owners' boats
without pay. They were painted on the beach, listed to one side and
then to the other, in the harbour at Anstruther. Below the waterline
was usually red lead, and then they became more technical with
plastic paint that was more difficult to put on but lasted longer.

Ring nets and drift nets had to be prepared as well, as Murdo Maclennan
described:

The season [in the Minch] started on the nearest Monday to 10 May. We
had to prepare the boats, beach them down here and paint them. There
was very little overhauling of engines then but we did a little – take off
the cylinder head and grind the valves, and things like that. We had nets
and buoys to prepare. We had to paint the buoys then, they were made of
canvas and had tar inside. Every man had his own share of nets and his
own share of buoys. Each man had his own colour for buoys. Mine were
blue and white. Some had grey, some red, everybody had a different
colour. On the nets too, we had a different colour, on what we called the
picket, where we tied the nets together, with a spot of white paint, or
blue, or whatever colour. We used to buy nets from the east coast and
they were painted. The nearest cork to the picket had an R or a W or a J or
whatever for the fellow the nets belonged to. I had a spot of white paint
on the first cork – that's how we used to do it – my brother had a D, and
the other fellow had an orange cork on. Och, when you got used to the
nets you could recognise them, hauling at night in the darkness, by
feeling them, like anybody handling a tweed or a sheep. Some of the nets
were rougher than others, depending on the factories they came from.
     New cotton nets, when I started first, cost about £2 10s. They
came from Lowestoft, I think; we took them in bulk. Sometimes we
had what we called the 'slinks', just the net itself. They weren't rigged
at all, we couldn't afford to buy a rigged net, so we got the slink
much cheaper, about £2, and we got ropes and corks ourselves and
rigged up the nets. There was a lot of work attached to it, so finally
we just bought the nets ready for sea.
     The nets were fixed together in order. We used what we called
ossils to tie the corks to the net and to the cork rope. The corks were
spaced by the width of your hand with the thumb outstretched, about
6 in. apart. The net was rigged so that the meshes would hang properly
in the water, in a diamond shape. You had to have a good eye for it.

When the net was hanging outside on posts, you'd notice straight away that something was wrong, if one part was tighter than another or if something had slipped, and you'd start measuring again. Since I was very young I got the feel of it and I could rig a net just as good as anybody in the area. I was really interested in it. My father and my uncle showed me and I was better than my brothers at rigging a net. It was about 55 yds long and six and a half fathoms deep.

Then we had to prepare stoppers and buoy ropes to tie the tops together. A stopper tied two nets and, when we were shooting, somebody was with the stopper waiting for the end of the net, and two half hitches went on the stopper and the rope was running all the time. The man had to put on the half-hitches pretty quick but not too tight, you see, because if they were too tight and not even, the net would be squint. The two half-hitches would slide on the rope a wee bit and the net would be even. When the tide started the knot would come into its proper place. When we started hauling the nets, the half-hitches tightened up with the weight.

[When hauling the drift net took place] one man stood at the cork rope and one at the foot rope, with another fellow standing at the winch, opening the stoppers as they were coming in. Three men were in the hold shaking the net. We did that every night. Somebody was down below coiling that heavy leader rope, 3 in. in circumference, in a dark hole full of tar. We used to tar the rope before we started the fishing — say, in April, and leave it for a couple of weeks down at the shore under cover, but if there was any sun you took off the covers and the tar would seep into the rope. What a mess the first few nights. If there was a fresh wind and a bit of motion, the tar was squeezing out of the rope. The winch was full of tar, the deck was full of tar, and anybody going near the rope — and the poor man in the coiling box down below, he was just black.

We barked the nets with cutch before the fishing started. Throughout the fishing there was a hulk in Stornoway and we used to go there every second or third Saturday to bark the nets again. It cured the nets and kept them softish. At the start of the fishing it was smaller meshed nets we used. Coming into July and August we had to change our gear and use wider nets because we fished at the Shiant Isles and the herring there were bigger. We got new nets or used last year's nets — they were still soft — and wide and that was for the bigger herring. We used to work the South Bank off Harris, and that was wider nets as well. If we started in May, we used to pack up then at the end of September. There was a theory that the herring was getting kind of thin and the buyers were not too keen. It was coming near spawning time. Most of the fishers had crofts and they wanted to gather the harvest in the months of September and October, and some of the fishermen here, after the harvest, went to the East Anglian fishing. I went to Yarmouth —

October and part of November – it was really a good fishing. We crossed by the ferry and travelled down by train from Peterhead. The first time I went, there were thirty Lewismen there and thirty women at the gutting. It was in 1956. When we came back in November, with our own boats we started on the winter fishing. There was a rush from Yarmouth, as a lot of boats wanted to get home early to get to the west coast fishing. The fishing went on to the end of January or February.

The herring fishermen from Avoch worked the drift net on the west coast in summer when Lewis Patience at the age of fourteen joined his father and grandfather on their boat in 1946:

Shetland herring fishermen haul a drift net on board the *Research* in the 1950s. On this occasion there was so much herring that the nets went to the bottom with the weight of the fish, and 12 nets were lost.

We went through the Caledonian Canal to Stornoway. It was a big push across the Minch in a north-west gale and it took fourteen hours to reach Stornoway from Kyle. I lay across dry nets on top of the hold, sick most of the time. There weren't many comforts in a 30-ft boat with five men and a small forecastle with bunks. We stayed away for long periods – five weeks before a weekend home, we came across on the ferry. The catches were smaller than they are now – we were content to work for six weeks for £100 per man, that was a good fishing then.

The Avoch fishing was based on Kessock herring. The season was September to April. I fished for them in the last weeks of September myself, up in the Beauly Firth. They came that early but sometimes not until January or February – a late fishing – some of the heaviest fishings of the lot have been late fishings, a big lump of herring coming up into the Firth when the real bad weather sets in in the Moray Firth out there. I remember 1966 being the last big year of Kessock herring. Boats came from Peterhead and other ports in the

Moray Firth and some days the ferry from North Kessock to Inverness had trouble crossing among them. From 1949 through the 1950s Avoch got new boats through grant and loan schemes. These were classed as ring net boats and Avoch produced some of the best ring net fishermen that went to Isle of Man, Seahouses and Whitby.

The Kessock herring had always been thought of as a distinct, small species of herring but it was discovered that they were, in fact, immature herring. A ban was placed on fishing for them in 1968.

During the first few seasons after 1945, the herring fishery in Shetland prospered. The number of boats rose from fifty-three in 1946 to 120 in

Whalsay fishing boat
Serene (LK 63).

1948 and the catch more than doubled over the same period, from 22,000 to 48,000 cwt.[17] The Herring Industry Board built a quick-freezing plant and cold store in Lerwick, and experimented with kippering; and, most importantly, offered to buy all the herring at a fixed price, sending any surplus to a fish-meal factory on Bressay. The Board's schemes, however, began to fall apart after 1948 when the herring became scarce. There were several years of fluctuating catches and the unpredictability of the shoals exacerbated the decline of the fishery.

William Anderson of Whalsay, after being demobbed in the spring of 1946, rejoined the crew to rig out the *Research* again for fishing:

> My father had a share in her. I was in the *Research* every summer from 1946 until 1968, the last year I was at the herring. I stayed on with the old crews. Some of the older men were retiring and new men were coming in but the nucleus of the crew were the original owners. In 1955, two young lads on the *Research* decided they would like a boat of their own, and applied for a loan and grant from the Herring

Industry Board. Because they were young and inexperienced I took a one-third share in the ownership of the new boat, although I stayed on the *Research*. The new boat was the *Serene*, the first of the *Serenes* — there's one today. She was wooden, 70 ft long, and built by Summers in Fraserburgh.

The driftnetting was a fixed way of life at that time. We started to rig out the boats at the end of April or the beginning of May. Some years there were German boats, klondikers, who came across and took herring from us early before they were of a quality to cure, and that would make the fishing start two or three weeks earlier than usual. It didn't always happen but in the pre-War years they nearly always came across. They put the herring in boxes with ice and salt, loaded up in possibly two days and sailed back home to sell them fresh.

In the rigging out we tarred the bush rope and painted the buoys, and got the ropes and nets all prepared. The boat was painted. We started fishing in the middle of May and usually fished for about fourteen weeks, although it varied a bit from year to year. At about the end of August a lot of small herring came in — we called them spent herring — and the quality dropped just like that, from a full herring to a spent herring overnight. The weather controlled it — if you got a jumbly breezy night you'd get more spents than if you had a spell of fine weather. Then they stayed full a bit longer. By and large, at the end of August there were quite a lot of spents here and that marked more or less the end of the driftnetting.

The end coincided in September with the harvest. A lot of the men had crofts. The women had done the summer work and had possibly been at the gutting. When it came to September the hay was being cut and the peats brought home — that sort of thing — and the sheep were dipped. Then in November we started rigging out the haddock lines.

The summer herring boats were big — about 70 ft long — and we put them to anchor in safe places for the winter. The anchorages were throughout Shetland. We always went to Burravoe, Yell, and anchored there for the winter, but some went to Vidland, some to Catfirth, some to drydock in Lerwick if there was major work to be done. We didn't keep any here on Whalsay because there's no safe anchorage. In the winter we mended the herring nets. The drifters carried 70–75 nets each and there were possibly seven net owners in a boat. Everyone had ten nets. For that ten-net share, they would use about twenty-five nets during the summer, because the older nets went on early when the herring were smaller and, as the herring filled, they would put on the better nets and at the end of the season you always tried to cure some new nets. To keep your fleet right. It kept moving — putting on at this end and taking off at that end. As you barked the nets year after year, they got harder and they shrank in the hot cutch.

There were always 25–30 nets to mend in the winter, and that went on at the same time as the line fishing.

The herring fishermen kept a wary eye on the curers who bought their fish and who might, at any opportunity, try to bid down the price they offered. When a boat came in, it was normal for a man to go to the curers with a sample of herring, a small amount of carefully chosen fish in a basket, and a price based on the quality of the sample would be agreed for the whole catch. The curers stuck to an old belief that 'If there was a scale or two off the herring it couldn't cure' to knock the price down, but when the purse seiners started there were no scales at all left on the herring and the curers had to admit that loss of scales preventing curing was an old wives' tale. As William Anderson explained:

The curers were up to all the tricks to pay a reduced price. They would buy a shot of herring and take them to the station and if they found one or two with the heads off then that was broken herring and they couldn't cure them and they'd say, 'We paid for good herring. We saw your sample.' If there wasn't a broken herring in the sample and there was one in the shot they'd say we can't take this, it's below the quality of the sample. They would break the boat. For example they would say we can't give you 30 shillings per cran, we'll give you 25 shillings for them. We had the alternative: take the 25 shillings or go back to the market and try to resell the fish, but then it would be the end of the day and everybody had got what they wanted, and there was a chance you wouldn't be able to sell them at all. The curers had you over a barrel in lots of ways. Oh yes, they would break the boats.'

There was an arbiter whom you could call on to negotiate, who would say whether or not the curer's complaint was justified and who could ask him to take another sample. There was a lot of that went on. Contracting to a curer beforehand was a system before that, when the older smaller boats were at it, in what they called the early and the late fishing. The early fishing was to the north of Shetland on the west side and the boat would be contracted to a curer to land a certain amount of herring at a settled price, irrespective of the market.

We landed mostly in Lerwick. We went there for the sale but you could take them back to Whalsay. There were curing stations here. It didn't always work that way. There were curing stations in the early years in Collafirth and at Cullivoe. If you had, say, five or ten cran you could go in and land there. With any sizeable shot you usually went to Lerwick. In the early years, before the War and possibly immediately after it, the catch was mainly cured. There were a few kippers and fresh herring. But after that they started running herring south in carriers – just a chartered fishing boat – that way they got a better price. The carrier was filled and got away as fast as possible, so the buyers were prepared to pay a bit more to get the herring. If you had, say, 40–50 cran you'd go to Lerwick and hope to sell them as boxed herring. The *Research* wasn't really rigged out for boxing but some of the more modern boats had more space below the nets and they could work at boxing.

Uncertainty marked the herring fishing throughout the 1950s but the situation began to pick up as the decade ended. The December fishing in 1960 in the Minch was good, with each pair of ringnetters hauling in about 100 crans a day. Gairloch, Oban and Mallaig were finding it difficult to cope with the catches, and Tarbert and Greenock also saw good landings.[18] On one occasion a dozen ringnetters landed more herring at Oban than were caught by fifty-seven drifters at Ullapool. The number of drifters fell, as smaller ones converted to seine netting. Boats from the east coast and from England began not to go north to Shetland for the summer fishing, with the result that the home Shetland boats, by then about twenty in number, enjoyed some recovery in fortune. But the future of the drift net was to prove to be a short one.

CHAPTER EIGHT

CHANGES AT SEA

A total adventure

In 1947, Frank Bruce went to sea on the *Ocean Ranger*, a steam drifter out of Fraserburgh: 'All my antecedents, all my father's folk, were fishermen – out of Fraserburgh, but they came from St Combs. I didn't go to sea with any relatives, so I didn't have support of that kind. It was a bit harder, I think, as you didn't get any advice.' Being brought up in a fishing community, of course, prepared boys for the life and the moment of joining a crew stood as a rite of passage to manhood. John Thomson of Lossiemouth cherishes his heritage: 'Since ever I kent o' being, I wanted to go to the sea. Every forebear ever known to the family, everyone, was a fisherman. My father was one of eight sons, all fishermen. I went to sea with my mother's brothers, the Campbells, on the *Guide On* in 1950 when I left the school. The post-War building boom had just happened. She was 63 ft long. We fished the Moray Firth, the Clyde and the Irish Sea, and Orkney in summer – so, we got around.' To reach the west coast, the Moray Firth boats passed through the Caledonian Canal. 'That was a marvellous trip for young lads. For us, leaving the school post-War, it was a total adventure.'

Skipper John Buchan on the Aberdeen steam trawler *Yorick* (A 247) in about 1960.

George Wood in Aberdeen spoke for many fishermen when he told me: 'I've got the sea in my blood.' Growing up in Torry, he and his pals spent all their time at the harbour:

> During the summer holidays I just about lived down there, all we did was fishing and going over the trawlers, all that area the oil industry has taken over now. At that time it was all steam and sometimes on a Friday night when the school was finished we would jump on a trawler going down to Granton for cheap coal. All the old guys, retired men, would get that job – when the trawler landed fish on a Friday night, a scratch crew would take over and we would get a trip down to Granton on Friday night and back maybe on Saturday night or Sunday, with the boat filled up with coal, ready for Monday. We used to jump on as well when they were going out to adjust compasses. So we were always used to the fishing.

For some, however, the love of the sea needed more time to develop. William West of Macduff didn't like the sea, although his father and grandfather – 'as far back as you can go' – were at the fishing in Gamrie. To his father's disappointment, William said no to the sea, served his time as an electrician and did National Service in the RAF before the opportunity came again to answer the call of the fishing:

> When I came out of the RAF, there were no jobs here. There was work in Corby but my wife said that if you're going there you're going yourself. My father came up with an idea – that I should take a half-share in a new boat on the stocks in Macduff with a skipper friend of his, a man with stacks of experience. I wasn't very keen to say the least to take a half-share in a new boat but I went along with the idea. It took three or four months to get clear of the sea-sickness and nearly a year and a half to get into the work. I loved the sea after that. It was in my blood and it gets a hold of you. It's a fresh start every week and you're looking ahead. It's a challenge. As far as I'm concerned, there's nothing like seeing a big bag of fish coming up in the tow. You've seen them in your sounder, you've trawled and you've caught them. It gets the adrenalin going. There's nothing like it. I think the hunter is bred into the fisher folk.

Other men took to the sea, although there was no family link. Gordon Fraser sailed at the end of the 1960s on the trawler *Diligent* out of Buckie. 'My family had no connection with the fishing,' he told me. 'My people belong to Aberdeenshire and Caithness but it was something I always wanted to do. I was in hospital with sinus problems and missed sailing on one of the last Salvesen whaling voyages. I was always doing a bit of fishing along the shore. The Buckie men regarded me as a landlubber and called me

The crew of the *Yorick*
(A 247) hauling the trawl net.

the ploughman.' For all the ribbing, Gordon persevered and became accepted. Jimmy Gregor in Macduff also had no fishing background and had served his time as a painter and decorator before he married and joined a boat in his mid-twenties: 'I never thought about the sea before but I liked it. It gets a hold on you somehow. The first crew – a herring drifter out of Fraserburgh – were all strangers to me, although there was one Macduff man on board and it was through him I got the berth. I suppose they did look down on me as a landlubber but I wasn't long in picking things up.' David Lees, who now operates shellfishing boats out of Dunbar, started as a miner, perhaps one other type of community that resembled the fishing community in its close-knit nature and sharing of danger:

I lasted in the mines for only about a year and a half. My father had been a chief engineer on a trawler but he didn't start there – his family were miners. Where I was brought up – in Port Seton – there was a mixture of fishermen and miners. I went to the mines at Prestongrange when I left the school. I wasn't making good enough money there, I didn't like the job, I got headaches underground. I went to the trawling after that out of Granton. I was only sixteen. I was at that for about six months and then I got on to the local inshore boats, which I'd tried to do when I left the pit but they wouldn't take me because I had no experience. I came here to Dunbar when I got married, about thirty-eight years now, and I've been fishing nearly all that time.

The sea always provided a freedom denied in other walks of life. The north-east loon who shipped with his relatives on a fifie in the nineteenth century probably felt himself a cut above his contemporaries who laboured behind a shop counter or worked on the ferm touns at the beck and call of a harrying grieve from dawn to dusk. The sea could also bring great material success and there are recorded instances of fishermen earning comparatively large amounts. Some Gardenstown men were bringing in £250 a year from line fishing in the late 1700s.[1] The east coast herring boom hauled in large earnings for some, and the ringnetting of herring, as it developed in the Firth of Clyde, was also lucrative: the crew of one boat in the mid-nineteenth century earned £34 in one week at a time when the best-paid tradesmen, such as stonemasons, could expect only £1 per week.[2] 'The fishing gave you a freedom of expression as well,' thought Alex Watson in Cellardyke. 'If anything went wrong, everybody's view was taken into account. You were listened to – your suggestion might not be right but you were listened to and you felt part of the scheme of things.'

To the adventurous and ambitious, the sea promised chances of getting on. From a half-share in a line or a net, a boy could progress to a full share and, perhaps quite soon in his twenties, a share in a boat or even ownership and taking the helm as skipper. For those of a philosophical or religious turn of mind, the fishing carried with it a biblical sanction – the Apostles were fishermen – and this undoubtedly was a source of pride for many. Even when the fishing was poor, as it frequently was, the fishermen could look to the future with a certain amount of hope, for the sea was above all unpredictable.

But it needed some powers of endurance, especially at the start. Crewing on a family boat did not always carry advantages, as David John Mackenzie of Wick, who started on his father's seine-netter, *Loyalty*, recalled: 'I was a year out of the school when I went to sea. I was very sick – sick for eight weeks. I had a pair of boots and an oilskin that cost £2 each and I thought that if I didn't hang on in at it that £4 would be lost. I was okay after the first eight weeks but they [the crew] were hard on me. They had no mercy. When I was down having food everybody would be having a pipe and they would blow smoke on me.' Sandy Hepburn in Gardenstown remembers being a little sick at the beginning, maybe three or four times, before he got used to the continual heaving of the boat but even then, 'It took about ten years to get used to it on a Monday morning, if the weather was bad. I would be a wee bit squeamish, not sick, but I didn't like being thrown out of my bed. You went away whatever the weather, unless it was really bad – a Force 7 didn't bother you.' First-timers or visitors would notice the close, fuggy smell in the crew's quarters, an effluvium that claimed many a victim. 'On Mondays when we left that was the worst time of the week with the smell,' said Murdo Maclennan. 'If you had had some herring on Saturday, that left dirty water in the bilges, and the smell of that, and the smell of paraffin – anybody would be seasick. Once you got over that, and you got a cup of tea or something, you were all right.' William Mitchell remembered the forecastle on a Fraserburgh drifter in 1939: 'The atmosphere struck me just like that and I couldn't get up quick enough. It was warm, warm, down below, with the smell of cooking and the men smoking.'

The custom whereby most youngsters started their sea-going career as cook, on a half-share or even on a quarter-share for example in Campbeltown, must have been a daunting test. Apart from the obvious problems of coping with hot frying pans on a cooker that does not stay still for any length of time, there must have been some worries over what the hungry eaters would say.

On the smaller inshore boats, cooking facilities were often limited. 'Food was a dry piece,' said Donald MacDonald in Golspie. 'There was a coal stove for boiling tea; it was more like tar, with a mass of sugar in each cup.' Jim Wilson in Newhaven described the catering arrangements on the herring boats working in the Firth of Forth:

If you were away at Bo'ness or Grangemouth, you went ashore to the Co-op or the butchers, and bought something to carry you over and then you came away. It was no use coming down from Bo'ness to Newhaven and having to go away up again. That was all time and fuel. You always had tea and sugar and tinned milk aboard. That was bought once a week, on the Saturday. Otherwise, the wives bought the food, unless you were a stranger in which case you bought your own. We had a fire. It was the size of a big pressure cooker. We called it a bogey fire, solid iron, with a lid on the top that you lifted to put the coal in. There was a small chimney up through the deck. Five or six men had to fry chops or whatever in turn on the fire. That's all we had. It was red hot sometimes. For water, we had a milk churn, filled on the Saturday and that would normally do all week. We had a jamjar on a piece of string that you put into the churn and brought out the water to fill the kettle. You didn't wash. You had your wash when you got home next morning.

When we went to Anstruther in March, if my father was the cook, he went up to the butchers and he bought everything for the men. When you came in at breakfast time occasionally you got ham and eggs but otherwise you got herring. A big frying pan full of

Scottish herring fishermen having a wash 'up the burn' at Peel, Isle of Man, in about 1930. This was often the only opportunity to wash in fresh water.

herring – maybe three each, or six if you wanted. That was a good breakfast in those days. We had a good dinner – always soup, maybe boiling beef, or chops, or meat of any kind, after we'd landed the herring. At tea time you'd maybe have herring again. In the 1930s, the bigger boat had a table to sit at, in the den as it was called, in the bow of the boat. That had six bunks. You had lockers for your food and seats. All lovely wood, all pine, all clean. The fire had an oven. You could even take a steak pie for your meal. There was a tank for water and a well and sink aboard. All mod cons.

By the 1960s, the seiners and larger vessels could provide good food with little trouble. 'We had bread for the first two days and after that the cook made rolls every morning,' said Gordon Fraser about his Buckie boat. 'There

was no fridge and we kept the beef in the ice locker. We ate very well and
had fish only once a week, and all the leftovers were thrown overboard.' If
the cooking arrangements were usually adequate or better, this could not
always be said for the washing and toilet facilities, especially before the
1960s.

It was a galvanised bucket [said Angus McCrindle] with a piece of
rubber hose split and laced round the top – the honey bucket. But,
after 1947, the Simpson Lawrence toilet was fitted aboard most boats
and it had a special seacock and its own discharge pipe. You had to
remember to shut off the seacock as you couldn't rely on the non-
return valve, and to put no matches or fag ends down it. Before the
War water had to be carried in a five-gallon galvanised drum from a
tap ashore. I always remember once in Lochboisdale on a Saturday
morning when the fleet was in for the weekend and everybody was
waiting his turn at the tap. Aboard, 25- or 30-gallon tanks were filled
up and the five-gallon carrier was kept full on deck. Once the boats'
tanks were all filled, we queued at the tap to have a wash. Any port
such as Carradale or Lochranza which had a burn was popular – a bar
of soap, towel, and sometimes a clean change of underwear was
taken, and the dirty ones washed at the same time, without a blush.

After the War tanks were larger and most ports provided a hose
which was included in the price of the harbour dues. The hotels in
most ports provided a bath at a nominal fee. Up to the War it was
common to have your first wash and shave of the week after you
came home after a week's fishing. If you had been in Carradale or
Lochranza during the week you were lucky.'

In Mallaig at weekends, pubs and dances were the favourite
pastimes of the visiting fishermen and really at that time there was not
much else to do. Sundays, if the weather was good, you took a walk
along the railway line to Arisaig and on a clear day the view was
magnificent. The church was usually well attended for the evening
service. On Canna, walking was the only recreation and many a time
we circumnavigated the island, and again the view was magnificent. In
Lochboisdale the hotel was handy and on Saturday night the cry was
for more sawdust. On Sunday again the church was well attended and
a walk to the west side was a must. It was similar at Castlebay but
North Bay, Barra, had no pub and the boys had to hire a taxi to get to
Castlebay. All these places had a phone box, some a couple of miles'
walk from the pier but hail, rain or shine they were always well
attended, as mail to Mallaig was erratic, owing to bad weather, slack
fishing, sometimes ten days between landings. It was normal in the
1940s and 1950s to be three weekends away and home for the fourth,
so the wives in those days really were the mainstays of the family.

Football was always an option and five-a-side was popular – get a field somewhere, take off your jerseys for the goalposts, and the game was on. In the spring fishing in the Minch, if you were near an island where birds nested, collecting gulls' eggs was a popular pastime and often around eleven o'clock on a Saturday night omelettes were on the menu after a session at the pub. In the Isle of Man in the early days, one boat would stay in Peel for the weekend with all the single men aboard, and the other would go to Portpatrick or even Girvan for the weekend with all the married and courting fishermen. By the time you did get home it was nearly time to go away again – Sunday was

The Whalsay drifter *Swan* (LK 243) photographed after the Second World War.

really your only free day. By the 1960s, with every boat having what was called a boat car, probably a big Vauxhall or a Ford – it had to take six men, it was easier to get home. In Whitby, in the late 1940s, the only recreation was the pub, and it showed. Some of the boys just out of the services with their Post Office Service Gratuity book had it emptied in six weeks. One chap I knew had three haircuts in one day – needless to say, the barber was a female.

At sea the men worked long hours, as Jim Wilson described:

Normally we would be away out of Oban on Monday and worked until the Wednesday; then out again on the Wednesday and back in on the Friday. If the weather was good, you were working from three o'clock in the morning, daylight, till eleven o'clock at night; and if the weather stayed calm, you went away down below to your bed and left the boat. All the lights on but otherwise unattended. You set your alarm for three o'clock and got up again. Otherwise, you left a man on watch. He did three hours and then he came off, and he could get a long lie and another man took over. If it started to blow up, he didn't wake anybody, he just took the boat into shelter.

Storms were not the only form of risky weather, as George Leiper recalled his days on the great liners:

There was one time we left Aberdeen and it was thick with fog. The last we saw was the North Pier and the first thing we saw that whole

Saffron (BA 182) hauling 40 cran of herring from a midwater pair trawl in Lochboisdale in 1972.

trip was the North Pier again on the way back. We saw nothing – right through the Pentland Firth, out to Iceland, fished, came back – and it was still fog. It was in the summer time. We just used compass, direction finder (it was before Decca), depth sounder and experience. Coming from Iceland with the *Mount Keen*, if it was dirty weather, you'd say you'd run so many miles, and tell the watch 'When you reach 100 fathoms, call me.' So, whenever he reached 100 fathoms depth, maybe after coming 1000 miles from the north, you could be anywhere, so you'd need to spend a lot of time on the bridge to look for land. Nowadays you don't need to rise out of your bed, you just have to look at your dials and know exactly where you are.

The young fishermen took to their environment very well on the whole, and only a few men had to give up the sea through the inability to adjust to seasickness. There were plenty of other hazards. Apart from the obvious dangers associated with bad weather, men were injured by the heavy gear. The continual hauling on wet rope was cruel to the hands. It took Jim

Wilson two weeks every winter to toughen up his hands; he said wearing mittens at work did not help but some men used to urinate on their mittens and wear them wet while they slept as this took some of the sting out of their flesh. In the summer, swarms of jellyfish could become entangled in nets, burning the hands of the men – it was not for nothing that jellyfish were known as 'scalders' in some parts.

Hanging on his sitting-room wall in Arbroath, John Swankie has a blackly humorous verse that sums up the fisherman's lot:

> A fisherman stood at the pearly gates, his face was lined and old;
> He stood before St Peter there for admission to the fold.
> What have you done, St Peter said, to gain admission here?
> I went to the seine net, sir, for thirty or forty year.
> The pearly gates flew wide open, St Peter rang the bell.
> Come in, he said, you stupid …, you've had your share of Hell.

Fishermen had to watch their footing on deck. In his time at sea, George Wood from Macduff was knocked overboard three times: the second occasion was perhaps the closest shave:

> We had about 800 cran of sprats. I never saw nothing like it. You could have walked on them for a quarter mile. The warp snapped and got me across the chest. I somersaulted and landed 20 ft from the boat. I had to swim for it. They made four attempts to get me … my boots were full of water. The first thing a fisherman does is to clap his arms around his body to try to trap some buoyancy in the oilskins and kick his boots off, but the swell prevented me doing this. I kicked and got towards the side of the boat. They put a block around me and lifted me in with the winch.

The Jungle and the Burma Road

The fisheries charts of the waters around the British Isles name scores of fishing grounds and banks, from the Far Balta and the Halibut Bank to the north-east of Muckle Flugga, down to the Wee Bankie near the mouth of the Firth of Forth and the Berwick Bank and the Swallow Hole to the south-east. And then there are the North Hake Ground and the Brierley Ground beyond the 200m line to the north of Sula Sgeir, and the Bryony Bank and the Empress of Britain Bank far to the west, to the south of Rockall. Many of the names are simply descriptive but they all have a poetry in them and beg the question of how they came to be so called: the Mermaid Shoal to the west of the Ballantrae Banks, the Sandy Riddle in the eastern jaws of the Pentland Firth and the Dog Hole off Aberdeen.

The fishermen have many names that do not appear on the official charts. This is particularly true for the coast, where in some stretches it seemed that every rock, geo and cave had a name at one time, but areas of open water are also named. William West referred to one ground to the north-east of Scotland as the Jungle: 'I'm not really sure of the origin of the name,' he said, 'but it was aye wild weather there and it needed wild men to go there. It was always bad weather when we fished there [in January]. The water was shallow and there was a bigger kick in the sea. I've seen us leave there, steam a couple of hours and find the weather calmer. But when we would call a boat still in the Jungle, we would be told "Dinna come back".'

There can be no doubt that many names have been lost or forgotten as the fishing has moved on and the old seafarers who shot their lines or nets there have themselves passed on. Naming, though, seems to continue and the men draw on various sources in this process. The Genoa ground, off Wick, was named because the city was in the news at the time it was

Icelanders working a purse net in 1940 for herring.

identified. Another ground near Wick, found during the Second World War, was called the Burma Road; according to some, in grudging reference to the obstacles on the bottom, though some say it was named by a man when the gurnards he caught there reminded him of the Japanese. There was a place off the south end at Wick called Ma Kelly's, and Alfred Mackay told me how it and some other local grounds acquired their titles:

> A chap called Robertson was asked where he was going one day. The song 'On Mother Kelly's Doorstep' was a hit at the time and Robertson said, 'Where do you think? Mother Kelly's Doorstep', and it was called Ma Kelly's since then. Many grounds were called after landmarks – the Warth Hill and the White Hooses – but the more distant ones were too far off for landmarks to be of much use. The 55 Minutes got its name because that was the time required to steam to it.

Another Wick ground was found by accident off Sarclett Head. The *Rose in June* was shifting from South Head to the Barney, the only two places they worked at that time. The skipper told the crew to dump rubbish over the side but one of the men mistakenly threw the dahn over and by the time the error was realised the nets were half shot. Making the best of a supposed bad job, they took a turn with the seine and hauled in a good catch. Skippers had their favourite grounds and some became associated with particular boats although, once a ground was found, it became common to all.

Andrew Mearns listed some of the grounds off Montrose:

We've got the Leads at the lighthouse: the Inner Leads and the Outer Leads. Then there was the Keelie – a strange affair, it was called after a dredger that was here away back I don't know when, called the *Kyle*, and she dumped the stones about a mile outside the lighthouse, and each year the cod would come to that area, and we would get them there in the seine net. If you were there at the right time, maybe just after low water, you'd get a good lot of boxes, but only one boat could fish it, and there would be fun and games queueing up to see who would get there first, a sort of race – a friendly competition. There's a ground about six miles off called the Castle Ness. The great fishing bank was called the Shaal Watter – it's on the chart as the Scalp. There was only 17 fathoms there, whereas most of the grounds were 25. You got a lot of cod there. Mars Reef, and then again there's a Mar Bank – not the same place. An interesting one is called Turry, and it's called after the Turin Hill at Forfar. You can see Turin Hill [from the sea], a very good landmark. There's the Ettles, of course – most harbours had an Ettles – the Gourdon Ettles, and the Arbroath Ettle. [This word varies along the east coast, 'heckle' and 'hettle' being other forms.] The Coastguard asked me if I would put these names down on a chart; they're dying out of general use now but the names still carry on among the boats that are fishing. We have satellite readings but, with the names, the fishermen and the lifeboatmen know exactly where they are.

The killer method

Catches of herring fell off in the early 1960s: for example, landings at Peterhead dropped from 108,900 crans in 1952 to under 7000 in 1964[3] and the future looked bleak for the drifters. The response in the industry was to increase the catching effort, to shift from the passive technique of the drift net to more active pursuit of the fish. Ringnetting was already established on the west coast as an active method of hunting. Some European fishermen, notably the Dutch and some Scandinavians, trawled for herring and, in the late 1950s and early 1960s, the Herring Industry Board sponsored fishermen to go to see how this was done. In 1948 a Dane called Robert Larsen had invented a trawl to be named after him to catch pelagic species off the Jutland coast; it consisted of a square-meshed wingless net that could be towed between two boats, an early form of the pair trawl.[4] Two Fraserburgh skippers, George Watt and William Cowe, were among the first to try midwater trawling in home waters, in the *Flourish* and the *Argosy*. As the engines in most of the Scottish boats were too weak to pull a midwater trawl successfully, pair trawling, with the net being towed by two vessels, became the norm – as it had been with the ringnetters, only now the nets were bigger and the power greater. The *Argosy/Flourish* partnership took good hauls of herring and sprats in the North Sea in 1963–4.[5] In 1965, two Peterhead skippers, Jim Pirie and John Alec Buchan, in the *Shemara* and the *Fairweather*, used pair trawling successfully in the Minch.[6]

The *Julie Anne* (BF 250) hauling a purse seine.

Another new method – capable of netting much larger shoals of herring – made its appearance in Scottish waters in 1965. As William Anderson in Shetland recalled: 'The Norwegians came here and just devastated the place. They just appeared overnight; 1000-ton catches were usual. They would fill three or four boats.' The method was the purse net or purse seine. 'There was a fleet of purse netters and a fleet of carriers, smaller boats, that came with them.' The new gear in the hands of the Norwegian fishermen was efficient to an alarming degree – shoals of herring were located on sonars, and encircled with a large wall of net, and then, using wire ropes running through rings, the bottom of the net was drawn tight to create the 'purse', a completely enclosed pocket. The principle of the technique was not new: it had been used in several places, and interestingly there is a record of an Aberdeen man called Bruce who 'contrived' such a design in about the 1760s.[7] Some ring net fishermen had tried fitting rings to the bottom of their nets so that they could be 'pursed' to enclose a shoal but generally the depth of a ring net was not enough and the top would be pulled down, allowing the herring to escape.[8] What astonished the driftermen in the 1960s was the scale of the operation. The deployed purse net enclosed a column of sea 240 or 260 fathoms in circumference and 75 fathoms deep before it was closed. Hauling these large nets would have been impossible without another invention, the hydraulic power block, in effect a crane with a large rubber roller with a V-shaped cross-section on the end which gripped the folds of the purse net and drew it aboard.

The purse net had been developed in the sheltered fiords on the Norwegian coast for use with inshore boats but innovations allowed it to be used in open water. The early purse nets were quite small and used in a similar way to the ring net by a pair of boats. In the ring net the bag part of the net is in the middle and the net is towed from both ends whereas in the purse the bag lies towards one end and the net is pulled from the other. Gradually the Scandinavian fishermen looked further afield for fresh shoals to exploit and so made their notorious descent on the Shetland grounds. In home waters they had taken 33,000 tonnes in 1963, and 184,000 tonnes in 1964; and in 1965 it was stated in the *Fishing News* that 259 Norwegian pursers caught 615,000 tonnes off Shetland – the entire catch of the UK fleet at that time was only about 10,000 tonnes.[9] The Icelanders were also very skilled with the purse and fished herring, sprats and cod with it. It was estimated that the Norwegian and Icelandic fishermen took over 200,000 cran (about 30,000 tonnes) of herring off Shetland in one week in January 1966.[10] The annual Shetland catch at that time was about 5000 tons.[11] An average purse-net haul was 200 tons – a drifter might think itself doing well to catch 30.[12]

The Scottish fishermen saw at once that they had to 'power up' to compete with the Scandinavians. Two Peterhead skippers, Donald Anderson of the *Glenugie III* and William Buchan of the *Lunar Bow*, went to Norway in February 1966 to see the power block and the purse net in action. Converting a drifter to a purse seiner was estimated to cost about £20,000, including £10,000 for the net, £3000 for the winch and £2000 for the power block.[13] *Glenugie III* obtained her first nylon purse seine in May – 240 fathoms long and 70 fathoms deep, with a mesh of $1\frac{1}{2}$ in., and when fully rigged weighing over 5 tons.

Alex Buchan, William Buchan's son, recalled for me what happened:

In 1954 my father had built a wooden motor drifter and called her the *Lunar Bow* – she was built in Tommy Summers's yard in Fraserburgh. That was the boat in which we first went to the purse net. We only used her as what they then called a bumboat, meaning that she went alongside the *Glenugie III*, which was a much more modern boat, and helped tow her off the net, and shared the catch. In May the *Glenugie* was put across to the island of Askøy outside Bergen to get fitted with a power block and winch. I was there along with another two of the crew and Mr Anderson, while the boat was being rigged out, for about six weeks. There was another boat during that time, the *Princess Anne*, rigged out in Norway. I remember her in that year coming into Bergen harbour for some gear.

The *Princess Anne* was a Fleetwood midwater trawler, in fact the first British boat to try the purse seine, although in the early days she failed to make very large catches. The Buchans saw that the purse seine was the way the fishing was going. The drift net was rather quickly becoming obsolete, although a few hardy old-timers, such as Robert Polson of Whalsay on the zulu *Research* was still using it and landing catches of 120 cran in 1966.[14] As Alex Buchan explained to me:

The purse seine didn't develop that quick. There were a few from Gardenstown, maybe two or three boats, within the first few years, and one or two Fraserburgh and Shetland boats started. Within the first five years there were probably no more than six or eight boats fishing the purse net. It was a pretty expensive thing to get started and this made fishermen a bit wary. You had to get this hanging power block – it was just like a crane with a V-shaped hydraulic-power-driven block, and a wheel. In fact, if the net was difficult to haul a man had to go up and stand on the net and push it into the V. We had a kind of safety ring he stood inside and as the net was being hauled he walked and pushed the net. Then they got what they called a jockey wheel which was just like a rubber tyre with a hydraulic ram putting a bit of pressure on the net to make it pull. It's just the friction of the net on the rubber, you see. In poorer weather or when the net was heavy with jellies [jellyfish] and it was slipping on the block, that's when the man went up and walked on the net. Then they developed the type of power blocks we have now with three rollers, and a transport roller which was situated more or less just above the net bin.

We met snags at first. The *Glenugie III* was built as a seine net boat for white fish. It had a wooden mast forward and we had to brail the fish out of the net, from half a ton to a ton at a time. The wooden mast just wasn't strong enough to lift more. The first time we shot the net we left out a stopper ring that kept the bouyed end of the net afloat and we finished up with the buoy under the water. We couldn't pick it up, so we had to purse the net from one end instead of from two ends. The winch was big enough but we were stuck, so someone had to go down the wire and hook on the rings one at a time just under the water. The water was coming up maybe to his middle and he was standing on the rings. We eventually got the net pulled but we thought we were going to lose it.

Our first shot was in the Scalloway Deeps – I think we got 60 cran of herring – west of Shetland between Foula and the Mainland. We were surprised at the quantity – that was a good shot in those days, 60 cran in a drift net was a lot of work. We went down the east side of Shetland on the next trip and that's where we mainly fished, down off Fetlar. That was a favourite place for the purse net. I've seen us shooting twelve or fourteen times and not getting anything, the fish finding their way out before we got the net pursed. So we didn't always get the fish but when we did it was always a good haul in comparison with the drift net.

It took about 10–15 minutes to shoot the net. If the fish were moving towards the spawning ground, you had to try to find out the direction they were taking and you had different methods for doing that – sometimes we threw a fishbox into the water and, if the fish moved away, watched what direction they took, and we knew that was the way they were going. We tried different things but the main idea, the best idea, was to circle the shoal – we picked this up from the Iceland and Faroese fishermen. We circled the shoal a few times and we could see their wake in the sea, especially in daylight. We shot the net up in front of them, maybe a quarter of a mile in front – the secret was to try to get the net to sink in front of the fish so that when they reached it they hadn't time to turn and come back out. If you shot too near in front they were up to the net before you got it closed and they turned and came back out. In the dark it was different – normally the fish were up, milling around, on the top of the water. At night, especially early in the summer, it was no use with the purse net because the fish were too spread. The purse net needs the fish to be a bit concentrated in shoals. Later on in the season, when the fish are near the spawning grounds they tend to shoal up all during the day, whether daylight or dark.

We shot the net in front of the shoal and then came round behind them to close the net. Within half an hour we had shot and pursed up. Once you'd pursed up the bottom of the net, there was no way the fish could get out – that was the bottom where all the purse rings were and the wire went through them – and you started pulling the net in from the last end you'd shot – and slowly made the size of the net smaller until you came to the bag end and there was really no room for the fish to swim. That was the time you either brailed them or put in the pump. Brailing took quite a long time, lifting up to one ton at a time. Because we worked as a pair – the *Glenugie III* shooting and pursing, and the *Lunar Bow* towing him off the net, we had no side thrusters then – in poorer weather it was always difficult to get some fish aboard the *Lunar Bow*. In finer weather the *Lunar Bow* came along the port side of the *Glenugie III* and they brailed out of the net on the starboard side and swung the fish across and dropped them on to the *Lunar Bow*'s deck. In those days, for human consumption, we put all the herring into boxes. During the brailing the crew were all down in the fish hold boxing and icing.

The men learned the tricks of the new technique and by July were able to land for two weeks' work over 1500 cran of herring, worth £12,000. That year, interestingly enough, the Shetland herring season was more prosperous than it had been in 1965. Bad weather kept 100 Norwegian pursers storm-bound in Lerwick for five days in August but the drifters were able to fish in the rough conditions, something that may have provided some solace to those who looked on the new method with dismay. The purse seine was, however, here to stay. In August the *Glenugie III* landed 1230 cran in Fraserburgh and Aberdeen; in October, they hauled over 1300 cran in the Minch and landed four times in Ullapool, one night netting the biggest single catch so far by a British purser: 680 cran.[15]

The number of purse seiners and drifters in the Scottish herring fleet

The *Seafarer* (SY 210) alongside the pier at Marvig, Lewis, in June 1979.

by 1969 was equal, fifteen of each; and there were forty-three midwater trawlers and fifty-three ringnetters.[16] John Alec Buchan had a new wooden vessel built in 1967, especially designed for purse seining: the *Vigilant*, 82 ft long, with a 410 hp Caterpillar engine and winches powered by a 85 hp hydraulic pump.

> She was built here in Irvin's in Peterhead [said Alex Buchan], more on the same lines as a white-fish boat, but beamier and bigger. She was called the *Vigilant*, because our grandfather had a boat called the *Vigilant*, that's what we did in those days, the names ran in families. The only difference from the *Lunar Bow/Glenugie* III partnership was that we used the *Vigilant* as a single boat with a small towing boat, a dory with a 60 hp engine – that was enough to tow the boat off the gear, although we were restricted a bit as to when we were able to work it. We built our first steel boat in 1970, as a replacement for the *Lunar Bow* – we sold the wooden *Lunar Bow* and built the steel *Lunar Bow* in

Norway. She was equipped with bow and stern thrusters and had a triplex power block – she was built more or less solely for purse seine. Then we were less restricted as regards the weather we could work in – we didn't have to launch a boat every time we shot the net.

But we were still rigged for boxing the fish. The next development was the equipping of boats with fish pumps. Instead of brailing the fish aboard, the pump went into the bag and pumped the fish aboard. Instead of boxing the fish we started putting them into chilled seawater – just a solution of seawater and ice – the fish were dead but they were kept in a fresher condition. The seawater and ice wasn't really a great success. The temperature of the water in the summertime, especially round about here, was such that you needed huge quantities of ice. If you didn't break up the ice into a slushy texture, the lumps damaged the fish if there was any movement in the tank. We had some bad experiences with circulating the water and big lumps of ice crushing the fish. The fish hold was divided: to start with, we had three tanks in the fish room, and then it became six – two centre tanks and four side tanks – and now the bigger boats have nine: three in the centre and three at each side. In those days the tanks would take 30–40 ton; now tanks hold 150 ton.

Murdo Maclennan, who owned the *Seafarer*, the last herring drifter to work out of Stornoway, saw at first hand what the purse net could do and did not like it:

It was too stormy for us to go out, so the skipper said come out for a night and see how it works. Oh, what a carry-on! The small herring and the big ones were all in a pond there. None was getting out. That was the killer, it's the killer method of fishing, the purse seine. It took everything. A pump going into the middle of the net and sucking it all up. What a mess! Money-making while it lasted, but they were cutting their own throats at the same time. I remember that night going out to sea. The skipper said, 'We're going to fish off Priest Island, off Ullapool there, off the Stoer.' I said: 'If you're going straight across there, you go to bed, I'll take the boat across.' I knew the area well. 'Well,' he said, 'stop her about seven miles off. Give me a shout. The cook'll be up then anyway.' I said, 'That's all right, I'll take the boat across, I'll not look at any of your gadgets or anything, I'll just follow the course.' But I was watching the echo-sounder, and there were good marks on the way across – I took a note of them on a bit of paper. When I showed them to the skipper, he said, 'Oh that's only about 200 cran, that's nothing.' 'That would do a week for us,' I said. 'Oh,' he said, 'we want to get a proper one and just get away with it.' Well, that was about four or five o'clock in the afternoon, in the wintertime – it was dark anyway – but it was four o'clock in the morning before he found a proper mark that was worthwhile that he could get 600–700 cran out of. He started shooting the net but something went wrong with one of the shackles and he had to stop and before they got that sorted out and completed the circle the herring had gone down. He only got 200 cran out of it. It was daylight then, and he was very disappointed. 'Well,' I said, 'you've got to put me back to Stornoway. I don't want to land in Ullapool.' He landed in Stornoway and he gave me £60 for the night. 'Oh,' I said, 'I don't want anything. What about your own boys?' He said, 'Och, they get £600 or £700 every week anyway.' He just put his hand in his pocket and gave me £60. For doing nothing. They were making a fortune then but now there's nothing left for them.

The stern of the *Astral* (INS 116) at Oban in 1988, showing the power block, nets and the heavy steel trawl door hanging on the quarter.

The Scottish pursers went after only herring in the early years, fishing in Shetland in summer and in the Minches during the winter, but in the early 1970s they began to hunt for mackerel. At the beginning the pursers had switched to the seine net outside the herring season, from January to May, but then they found it better to pair trawl for herring in the winter months in the sea lochs. Smaller purse nets, about 40 fathoms deep and 180 fathoms long, were designed for shallow water and the east-coast men used this size when they began to visit the English Channel to catch mackerel. A purse net generally fished to about half its depth – a net 75 fathoms deep would fish to about 30 fathoms maximum – as allowance had to be made for the net coming in at the bottom to close the 'purse'. In shallow water, the pair trawl was more versatile.

Purse seining and pair trawling on the west coast brought a boom time to the ports there. Mallaig rapidly became the premier herring port in Europe. In 1969, 168,622 cran were landed there; and in 1970 over 196,700 cran. A one-day record was set on 1 December 1970 when forty-three boats landed 7000 cran. The congestion in the small harbour under the Morar braes became acute, with ringers, trawlers and pursers queueing to unload their catches. Only eleven could berth at one time, and sales went on from six in the morning until eight at night to cope with the flow of herring, with lorries shunting and jostling. A new pier and fish market were built in 1972 and the old quays extended.[17] Scottish herring landings in 1970 at Oban and Mallaig topped the million-cran mark, and Stornoway and Ullapool between them saw another 800,000 cran ashore.[18]

More power

The purse seine and the pair trawl signified the introduction of new methods of fishing but along with them in the 1960s and 1970s came changes in many aspects of the fishermen's lives. The boats themselves began to alter. The shape of the seine netter – vertical bow, cruiser stern, housing aft, and a long graceful sweep of open deck – began to give way to chunkier, beamier lines. More powerful engines began to be fitted – 300 hp and more became common. Nets grew larger and natural fibres became almost entirely a thing of the past to be replaced by synthetics coloured orange or grey or black. Hydraulic winches and power blocks were installed, one of the first winches being tested on the Buckie seiner *Opportune II* in 1966. The hydraulic winch allowed variable control of the speed of towing, independent of the speed of the boat's engine. The seiners *Argonaut II* of Anstruther and *Ocean Gain* of Peterhead were fitted with power blocks in 1968[17] – the hauling of the seine net was made much easier and safer – and adoption of the new device spread quickly from boat to boat. By the end of 1969, over forty boats had them.[18]

Transom sterns made their appearance in the 1950s but it took a little time for the new design to become widely accepted amongst Scottish boats, perhaps because skippers felt reluctant to abandon the existing seaworthy hull shape that descended from the sailing fifie and ringnetter. The transom stern, however, provided more working space aft and more storage room below decks. The *Constellation* was launched in 1964 from the Forbes yard as the first seiner trawler with a transom stern and in the following few years this hull shape became as common as the older cruiser-sterned hulls. New designs began to appear as well among the small inshore boats. Whereas in the 1950s many of these had been small fifies or yoles, now transom sterns, clear working spaces aft of forward wheelhouses and new building materials became common. Gordon Easingwood told me that his father, Robert, in Dunbar had the first GRP (glass-reinforced plastic) hull in Scotland in 1968. Ferro-cement hulls were manufactured in Scrabster and elsewhere.

Some other more subtle changes were taking place: the modern boats began to be decorated in a more varied manner than their predecessors. In the 1950s most of the inshore boats I can recall were black with red lead below the waterline and a long white flash at the level where the bow cut through the water. Decks were often red but a little bit of artistry could be seen in the typography of the name or in the scumbling of the wheelhouse varnish. Seine-netters came in a larger range of colours but these do not match the palette now in use. In Lerwick harbour in 1996 I made notes on the colour schemes of the larger boats. That day I saw the *Julie Anne* of Gardenstown again with her pale emerald hull with a white stripe; the *Renown* from the Out Skerries, bright blue; the *Arcturus*, dark blue; the *Ariane*, dark red with a yellow stripe; the *Medalia* with her orange hull and cream upperworks, a style now being imitated, I was told; the blue and white *Sunbeam*. Some boats have figureheads: the *Arcturus* has a map of Shetland in a roundel containing five sets of initials, presumably those of her share owners. Bows are commonly highlighted with 'speed wings'; and many

The seiner *Harvest Hope* (PD 148) at sea in heavy weather, in about 1982.

boats display their names in heraldic banners on the wheelhouse front. The *Julie Anne* has initials in a shield on the bow. The saltire is a common motif on Scottish vessels. The *Alison Kay* sports a black cat with green eyes on the side of her wheelhouse.

Apart from the large trawlers, steam drifters and liners, almost all the Scottish boats were built of wood until the late 1960s but, as the hulls grew larger to handle the new purse nets and pair trawls, and the crews began to fish farther offshore and spend longer periods at sea, steel began to be favoured. A well-made wooden hull could have a long life — around the coast there were scores of yoles, fifies and seiners that were happily afloat and seaworthy after sixty years or more of use — but the strains and stresses of the new fishing methods, for example when partner boats came together to handle a full purse net and hulls might be thrown against each other, convinced many fishermen that steel had to be the material of choice. Modern building methods, involving prefrabrication and welding, and the rising cost of good timber also encouraged the shift. John Alec Buchan's new vessel, the *Fairweather IV*, built in 1969 in the Fairmile yard in Berwick, was steel; and the new Campbeltown Shipyard built in 1970 the steel stern trawler *Crimson Arrow* for James MacDonald. The Campbeltown yard was to become a prolific builder of steel vessels and many other yards around the coast and abroad were to turn out steel fishing boats during the 1970s.[18]

New designs of deepwater trawler made their appearance. A new class of small trawler began to be built in 1959 which were only half the size of the older trawlers and very economical to run. The prototype was the French-designed *Coral Isle* but they were turned out by the Fairmile yard for Granton, Aberdeen and English owners in some numbers. With a crew of eight working on a share basis, the Fair Isle boats as they were called – they were dubbed 'sputniks' by the Aberdeen fishmarket workers – were capable of fishing in Faroese waters in winter.[19] Aberdeen also received a new design

The seiner *Aspire* (LK 239) at sea in 1982.

of stern trawler in 1959, the *Universal Star*, again designed to continue to work in heavy seas.[20] So-called 'pocket' trawlers were built in the 1970s for fishing off the west coast.[21] There was a speedy scrapping of steam trawlers – the number in Aberdeen dropped from 152 in 1956 to only nine by 1964 – and a replacing of them with new diesel-powered boats; by 1967 the port had 114 motor trawlers.[22]

A successful boat, in terms of earnings from fishing, could have a considerable influence on the design of new vessels. This happened in the case of the *Argonaut III*, a wooden seine netter built in Buckie in 1969 for David Smith of Anstruther, an enterprising skipper who had been the first to use a power block to haul his seine net on his earlier boat, the *Argonaut II*. In 1970 the *Argonaut III* was dragging enough white fish out of the North Sea to push her into becoming the first Scottish seine net vessel to earn over £100,000 in one year; by 1974, benefitting from the boom in fish prices at the time, she was earning over £200,000.[23] Skipper Smith installed a gutting shelter on the foredeck of the *Argonaut III* in 1970, a curving white whaleback roof at first made from glass-reinforced plastic but later rebuilt in aluminium, and also put in large reels for storage of the seine net warps. The coils of rope, laid along either side of the deck, had been until then a characteristic feature of the appearance of the seiner. The shelter deck and the reels made the handling of the nets much easier and safer for the crew. Much deck work became automated, with the winch and reels hauling the net warps and coiling them, and these operations being controlled from under the shelter-deck or the wheel-house. Storage bins below deck for the coils of rope were introduced in the early 1970s. Additional shelter decks were added to some boats so that they were provided with cover over the foredeck and the midships area. Over the following fifteen years complete weathertight shelter decking was to become the norm on larger fishing boats.

During this time there was a great deal of experimentation by skippers. William West described some innovations of his own:

In 1972–3 I had a new boat built down here in Macduff. She was a small trawler, the *Atlas*. My brother was trawling before that on the new *Seagull* and, by that time, my father had retired. My brother advised me to put in more power as he had seen that more power equalled more fish. He had 240 hp and he advised me to go for 320 hp, and that was unheard of at the time. I went to the builders. No way, they said, a 320 hp engine in that size of boat would just shake her apart. They wouldn't hear of it and suggested 260 hp. I told them that any damage would be on my own head and they agreed to start. Of course a 320 hp engine burns a lot more fuel than the 240 hp and once, when I came home and went down to see how things were coming along, I saw two oil tanks lying beside the hull. I was told they were my tanks: 'I need double that size,' I said. The tanks were made to hold 700–800 gallons of diesel; now, if I went to the ground we called the Jungle, ten hours' steaming north-east of Macduff, and fished from Monday to Thursday I would need a tow back in – I needed at least 1400-gallon tanks. At that time tanks were square in shape and that left a big gap beside the curve of the hull. My brother and I designed a tank that would fit the curve and go right down into the bilges and, although it was the same size to look at, the greater volume gave us 1300 gallons. They were harder to make, of course, but all tanks are built that way now.

When we started trawling we went off east from Rattray Head. There was plenty of fish at that time but it was a very tidal place, like the Pentland Firth. Boats with small engines could tow but they couldn't fish and we had a great advantage down there with 320 hp. If a fellow was getting ten boxes with the small engines, I could get three times that just with the extra power and bigger doors on the trawl. It was great to start with. When I started the trawl, our net would have stood about 3 $^{1}/_{2}$ ft high. If there was anything 6 ft off the bottom we would miss it. Now the nets are 28 ft high. The width has increased, too, from 40–50 ft to 250–300 ft. You can't compare them. The power block made the difference, in allowing the hauling of a big net. When we first started we had no power block but we had a winch to heave in the wires. To start with, one man could handle the haul but as the winch went to high speed two men went forrad to it. We pulled the bag aboard by hand and if you did that eleven times a day you felt your hands were down past your ankles.

The thing that has given modern boats the edge is the computerised winch. It heaves in and lets out as the boat rises and falls, so that the mouth of the net is wide open all the time. Back in 1970, if we hit a lump of sea while we were towing, the boat staggered back a bit, the towing wires went slack and the doors flopped to the bottom. We had no more power to give and it took 15–20 minutes to get back into a fishing mode. You could feel it in the wires as they struggled to get the doors up and the net open again. And then you'd hit another lump and that was you back to square one. If it was Force 6 that was us about finished – you could shoot and you could tow but you didn't catch anything – now they're fishing up to Force 11; maybe they don't get as much as at Force 2 or 3 but they still fish.

In the old days, if we got, say a 50-box haul, and the deck was full of fish, we had to start shovelling them up with scoops, clean them ourselves, fill the boxes, stack them, tie them down. Fifty boxes meant three, maybe four, lifts of the cod end. Now a 50-box haul is two lifts. The fish go into hoppers – big steel bins. They come up on conveyor belt and when they are gutted the guts go into a channel and are washed right over the side again. True enough, there is bad weather to contend with but the work isn't in it anymore. The young fellows don't think that, mind; if I tell my son, he just laughs.

Gordon Fraser went to sea on the *Diligent* out of Buckie, one of the first boats in the 60-ft class to switch from seine to trawl in 1969. They had to steam six to eight hours to reach their fishing ground off the northern coast and to the west of Orkney. Under Fishery Board regulations, the Moray Firth was off-limits to British trawlers and the men could not understand why French and Spanish boats were allowed to fish there (foreigners were not subject to national by-law at the time). On one trip they saw an oil rig in the Firth lit up like a Christmas tree, a sign of things to come in the North Sea. Gordon found the work all new to him but he developed an interest in the technical aspects of the gear and, once he grew familiar with it, 'got on fine'. He eventually found himself in charge of the shooting of the gear and deck machinery. The trawl was shot quite fast with the towing cables through the pair of gallows; after the doors were let go, one of the crew had to run aft with a steel hook with the cable from the forrad gallows and pass it to the man on the aft gallows who placed it into a snatch block so that the two cables ran out together. As this was done, Gordon kept a careful eye on the winch to keep the wire cables at the proper tension to hold the doors in position but still allow the slack required to shift them. He also counted the spliced-in rope markers at regular intervals along the cables to know the length paid out – one mark at 25 fathoms, two at 50, three at 75, four at 100, and one again at 125, and so on – and at the sight of the mark for the last 25 fathoms, he would shout to the skipper to ease off the engine.

In the Noup ground, off the west coast of Orkney, they would catch skate and hake in 100 fathoms. At the Noup, they could haul 300 fathoms of wire, empty the cod end, set the net again and shoot it all in about 20 minutes of fast, skilful work. The tows lasted for about four hours there but generally they were shorter, maybe one and a half to two hours. The direction of towing was decided according to the run of the tide and might involve 60-degree turns. This judgement, taking into account the currents and the Noup ground as laid out on the chart, fascinated Gordon. It was the custom after the net was shot for the men to sleep, leaving only one man on watch, and during his trick at the wheel Gordon had the satisfaction of knowing that all they caught had really been caught by himself.

The developments in hull design brought greater comfort to the men working aboard but then a series of tragic accidents occurred. Some boats disappeared in bad weather, going down with all hands and leaving no witnesses to testify what might have gone wrong. In October 1974, the Peterhead steel trawler *Trident*, 85 ft long, sank off Caithness, nine miles to the south-east of Duncansby Head, while homeward bound from the herring fishing at the Isle of Man. Her crew of seven were all lost.[24] The official verdict of the Court of Inquiry was that she had foundered after taking on board a heavy sea or series of seas and that instability inherent in her design might have contributed to the disaster. The stability of fishing boats was subjected to thorough investigation, test and discussion. Stability criteria were established by the Inter-governmental Maritime Consultative Organisation; in 1975 the Department of Trade ruled that all fishing vessels over 12m had to abide by these. A few Scottish boats were found not to match up and steps had to be taken to make them more stable.

The burning

O f all the innovations that increased the catching power of fishing boats so dramatically during the middle of the twentieth century, the introduction of electronic instruments must be a contender for the most important. In the old days fishermen relied on their own experience, luck and signs. The luck was in the nature of things ungovernable and unaccountable, but the experience could be extensive and detailed, including knowledge of tides, currents, weather, landmarks, seamanship and fish behaviour. It was learned during long, wet, cold hours on tossing decks or passed on from generation to generation in pierhead yarns. The older men were repositories of this wisdom; youngsters sought it eagerly, listened and watched.

The pursuit of herring shoals was attended by careful observations of a whole gamut of signs: gannets diving, thin oily smears on the surface, herring 'playing'. The presence of whales or a basking shark, also known as the sailfish or 'mulldonn', were also good signs, although it might be necessary later to pour small quantities of diesel into the sea to discourage the shark from hanging around and damaging the ring net.[25] Tom Ralston records that a heavy shoal of herring in a sea-loch might be detected by the 'raw smell' of them.[26] 'Up in the lochs in the Hebrides in winter the water was brackish,' said Angus McCrindle in Girvan, 'and you could see where the herring were from the bubbles they put up from their swim bladders. That was a sure sign, the surface of the water covered with millions of bubbles as if the sea was a glass of champagne. That sign was used in Ayr Bay in the 1920s.' Another way was for the boat to lie still while a man in the bows would listen for the fish. Some men looked for herring in what they called the 'burning', the glow of phosphorescence on the water, in the period from June to September when the plankton was on the surface. The interpretation of the burning was a task for the specialist. On a very dark night you could see the sea light up for half a mile around, especially with spots of mackerel. The clang of the steel shod on the heel of a leather boot against the deck could reverberate down through the water and scare a spot of herring, making them move and reveal themselves in a dim flash, or a man might strike the anchor or the gunwale with a marlin spike. Part of Lord Leverhulme's plan was to use aircraft to spot the shoals and this actually happened in July 1938 when a plane, piloted by Sam Reid of Orkney, successfully guided drifters off Shetland towards the herring.[27] The feeling wire was introduced in about 1928 or 1929 in the Firth of Clyde; its use spread to the east coast and replaced the older, though similar, technique of feeling for the fish with an oar.

The first electronic apparatus to appear in fishing boats was, of course, radio. First fitted to the Hull trawler *Othello* in 1913, it was many years before it became a standard piece of gear.[28] Various experiments with direction-finding equipment, incorporating radio signals with compass bearings, were made in the 1920s and 1930s but in general these machines were fitted only in the larger trawlers. In 1933, Ronnie Balls of Yarmouth fitted an echometer in his drifter *Violet and Rose* and tried to use it to find herring shoals, with some success. Around 400 sets were installed in trawlers and liners at that time.[29] An echo-sounder had, in fact, been tried in a Campbeltown boat, the *Nobles*, in 1932 but had been discarded in 1934. Again, however, it was not until after the Second World War that the apparatus became more common.

The fishermen had to learn how to interpret the marks the device registered on the paper trace. 'The problem was when they saw the herring on the sounder they didn't know what was what,' explained Tom Shields, 'and very often they got a lot of torn nets, as they were not able to distinguish between shoals of herring and peaks of ground. If they'd known how to work the sounder properly they should have made a lot of money because you could steam and look for herring at the same time.'

Angus McCrindle said that it was in 1948–9 that echometers were introduced to the Clyde ringnetters:

> Kelvin Hughes was the favourite, with Marconi second. Thereafter foreign firms began to be active, like Simrad and Atlas. The first sonar, a Kelvin Hughes, was fitted to *Sapphire* (BA 174) before launching in

The Arbroath seiner *Morning Star* (AH 84), skippered by Jim Swankie.

> 1962. The first large independent *fischlupe* [the German term means 'fish lens' and it marked an innovation in displaying the readings on a screen instead of printing marks on paper] was also Kelvin Hughes and fitted aboard the boat in 1963. Nowadays you have the option on the fishfinder to blow up any part of the display and an option as to what scale you wish to use, as from 1, 5 or 10 fathoms. This facility was especially useful on Ballantrae Banks where the herring were spawning, hard on the bottom, and gave the death knell to the feeling wire, and speeded up detection methods.

Murdo Maclennan had his first echo-sounder in the *Seafarer* in 1963:

> We took a while to believe it, to make out what it meant. If you saw a stroke this way and a stroke that way, you had to study what it was. If you could see a lot of fish, it could be sile [small fish], it could be whitebait, it could be white fish or mackerel. It took about a year to get used to it, but when it proved to us it was right we kept the

marks on the paper and compared them to other signs we saw. But when there's herring around, you'll easily know – the birds, they're the best sign. They won't be sitting there for nothing at all. They always felt the oil coming up from the herring or the mackerel and they were feeding on that.

The development of electronic fish-finding gear became more and more crucial to the success of fishermen. When Norrie Bremner in Wick and William West in Macduff were building new boats, they both wanted what they called 'something on the electronic side better than anybody else'.

Alex Mackenzie (left) and Alastair MacPherson aboard the *Betty* with prawn boxes at Badachro in 1968.

I spoke to Norrie on the phone a few times [said William West], and we were in touch with this German firm, Atlas Electronics, a common firm now but at that time they weren't, and we found only one problem – the stuff was excellent, the fishfinders and sounders, expensive but good – and that problem was service. There were no engineers or depots nearer than Glasgow (a one-man operation) but Norrie and I installed it in Aberdeen. The firm put in writing that they would be in Kinlochbervie if I needed them there as soon as I got in from the sea. We never regretted putting in this gear. We could pick up fish when other boats were sailing over the top of them. The Atlas stuff paid for itself in no time at all.

It was very new in the early 1970s. We took a big chance with it, both of us. Norrie was the first in the north and I was the first in the east to put it in. After that, about 15–20 boats built down here had the stuff. The Atlas gear is still dearer than other makes but it's really good. Repairs next to nil – it ticks awa'. I can't mind the cost. I think we spent about £14,000. It would cost £200,000–£300,000 now.

With the fishfinder I couldn't tell at first what species it was. The old sounders would show fish if they were tight in the school as a wee hump on the bottom, with a different shade. The new sounders have different colours. The denser the reading the redder the trace. From the density and experience you can guess what fish it is. Sand-eels give a fluffy hazy trace – haddock or cod appear as a solid lump. You can see what depth they are.

Direction finding before the Second World War relied on the radio signals emitted from five stations around the coast – at Isle of May, Kinnaird Head, North Ronaldsay, Sulisgeir and the Butt of Lewis – but on the

A prawn trawler hauling her gear.

outbreak of hostilities in 1939 this system was closed down. After the War, Decca navigation systems became standard equipment in the fishing fleet, but Decca now seems likely to be phased out in favour of satellite navigation.[30]

New fishing boats have their electronics installed on building. The wheel-house of a large trawler now resembles the flight deck of an aircraft with its array of screens, switches and meters. Some vessels have several computers to monitor sensors on the nets far below in the water and to regulate towing and hauling. The wheel-house has become a bridge with weather instruments, a digital compass, rudder controls, fish-finding sonars, radar, trackplotters, winch controls, engine controls, side-thruster controls, radiotelephone, television, position plotters, satellite navigation systems and steering gear. Current indicators show the speed and direction of the tide at selected depths and there are systems to indicate the nature of the seabed in great detail. A joystick, not much larger than a match, may have replaced the traditional steering wheel; and charts can be consulted on CD. In the North Atlantic Fisheries College in Scalloway, a mock bridge allows student skippers to practise in simulation.

At the prawns

Up until about 1950, the Scottish fishing industry could be divided fairly neatly into a limited number of categories: an inshore fishing for crabs and lobsters, seine-netting for white fish on grounds close to home, drift netting and ring netting for herring, and trawling and great lining for white fish on more distant grounds. The last forty years, however, have been marked by increasing diversification as more species have become prey of the hunter and new fishing methods have appeared to catch them.

The catching of prawns is now a major item in the statistics and the mainstay of several local fleets. The prawn (*Nephrops norvegicus*) is very common in British waters, large communities of them occupying muddy bottoms where they can burrow out of sight. Line fishermen used to haul them up on their hooks, curse them for a nuisance and knock them off. Only a few people seemed to appreciate that they were good eating and in general there was no market for them before the consumption of scampi became fashionable. Before 1950 they were not counted separately in the fishery statistics but lumped under 'Miscellaneous shellfish' with other less desirable species; in that year, however, the total catch was described for the first time in its own right: 2994 cwt that sold for an average price of 37 shillings each. The catching of prawns took off after that. Stornoway, Lossiemouth and the East Lothian ports saw big landings in the 1950s, and by 1959 the annual catch had reached around 40,000 cwt, now selling for £6 or £7 each.[31]

Jimmy Gregor started going to the prawns when he got his own boat, the *Silver Cloud*, in Macduff in the early 1970s:

> We fished on the west coast and on the east, down south as far as Pittenweem and Northumberland – Shields and Blyth – in the winter between September and January. We went up the Firth of Forth just about as far as the bridges, where somebody lost gear once to a destroyer probably heading for Rosyth.
>
> The prawn trawl has smaller mesh, as small as 70mm at the start but it went up later, and rubbers on the footrope to dig into the bottom and make the prawns rise up. There are a lot of good grounds. You need a muddy bottom. There are lots of bits and pieces in the Moray Firth. It was a fairly new fishery at the time. When I started at the sea [only a decade earlier in the early 1960s], prawns, like monkfish, were thrown overboard. The towing time was usually about four hours. You shot away out before daylight. The crew of four or five took quite a while to tail all the catch. You could be there all day. If you were working locally you could be in every night but usually we were at sea for two days. Now the prawns are landed whole but we had to tail ours. At Pittenweem and Eyemouth they never tailed the prawns. They said it was bad for the grounds but it's not really because prawns are cannibals. You never pick up heads in the trawl

because the prawns take them down their holes. The only time you get prawn heads on the ground is if the fishery is failing, if the prawns have gone. If you get heads or tails you know it's time to shift the ground. But the Fife men didn't agree with dumping heads.

We usually towed along the sides of a square, according to the Decca lanes, keeping within the area you know to be soft bottom. There was a spot on the west coast I knew where I used to go round two and a half times – it was a small spot nobody else was interested in but I remembered it from my seine-net days as a place where we used to haul up a lot of prawns. The tow took three hours at a speed of about four knots. Twenty boxes a haul would give a good-enough living but there were lots of times we didn't get that. We fished the

Prawn trawlers in Pittenweem, March 1998.

whole year round. Usually the prawns are in deeper water during the day – 60–100 fathoms in the Minch – but sometimes we'd get them in shallower water, 40 or 50 fathoms. We used to fish on the west of the Stanton Banks, a good steam of 10–11 hours from Mallaig, but we didn't go to the west side of the Long Island.

Tom Shields fished for prawns out of Girvan:

There was no season, it was all the year round. Certain conditions were better for them – dull overcast weather in summer, not bright sunshine – and I didn't always fish conventional grounds. I looked for quality rather than quantity and worked around wrecks and on rocky bottoms – if you get in amongst rocks you can get much larger prawns in the muddy gutters between the outcrops. I would spend half my time trawling on the bad ground, the reefs, over there at Brodick. I remember getting prawns there – quite a few boxes – and we measured them, as long as 13 inches.

Others, including Hector Macleod in Kyle of Lochalsh, turned to catching prawns in creels. These were similar in design to the creels for lobsters but were clad in a net of smaller mesh made from finer twine.

> The first boat I can remember that started on the prawns like that was in 1952, a boat from Kyleakin called the *Sweet Home* [said Hector]. But there was a boat in Stornoway after the War, and one fellow – he was a Mackay, he had the *Girl Norma* – he did a great fishing with her, down at Barra for the prawns. That was virgin ground then – some of them were like small lobsters in size – beautiful king prawns, I don't see any of that size nowadays.
>
> Working out of Kyle here, I used to go up Raasay way, then back

The Silver Lining (CN 175) in 1983 at the scallops to the south-west of Mull. Two units of the dredge hang on the side, filled with the catch, and the crew are working on one on the deck.

> down to Loch Hourn and Loch Nevis and round the south end of Skye. Just for prawns. My son and myself were at them. In the winter it was very difficult because a lot of the trawlers used to come in, especially the east coasters, and I lost three fleets in one night – 150 creels. It was about £5 a creel then. There's a lot of that kind of thing. These creels nowadays are about £20 each. If you lose a fleet of that it fair knocks you back. For bait, it was salt herring but I always found that spent herring was better, stiffer. I used mackerel sometimes but I don't know what – the lobster would go for the mackerel before the herring, maybe there was more oil coming off the mackerel bait. There was a character here at one time and he says, for the prawns, he put bits of cup and saucer in and the prawns were going for it. That was only a joke. I went further south than Loch Hourn, to Morar, south of Mallaig, and then across to the Point of Sleat – we got very good prawns there – and up Loch Nevis – a very, very good fishing. I would do the trip to Loch Nevis in an hour. Ullapool would take about six hours, with the 72 hp Perkins I had in her. She was pretty fast. You see, if you don't

respect the sea, the sea won't respect you. You can't rush a boat through and expect to divide the sea. We would go up there on a Monday and fish until Friday, and come home for the weekend.

Landings of prawns in Scotland now run at around 40,000 tonnes per year.[32]

Queer fish

Dredging for clams has also grown into an important fishery in recent years. The word 'clam' is used as a blanket term for several species of bivalve but the most important are the scallop (*Pecten maximus*) and the

Cockenzie and Port Seton Fishermen's Society with their banner, taken probably before the First World War. Fishermen often formed societies to protect their own interests.

smaller queenie (*Chlamys opercularis*). A fishery for the latter started in Scapa Flow in 1968 after a market for queenies opened up in the United States; and from Orkney the fishery spread to fruitful grounds in the Firth of Clyde.[33] In about 1960, Jackie Johnston started to dredge for scallops in the Firth of Clyde out of Girvan. The Girvan boats had traditionally gone to the scallops, especially the old ringnetters in the off-season, not fit to run across the Minch in the winter: they would tow 4-, 5- or 6-ft dredges, depending on the horsepower, on single ropes in the Firth of Clyde, Isle of Man and on the Irish coast but never working deeper than 10 fathoms. Dredging is now on a much larger scale, as Jackie explained:

We had four dredges. The longest had 65 fathoms of warp on it, and the next one had 60 fathoms, the next 55, the next 50, so that the four of them were coming along a wee piece in front of and to the side of the next one. The longest one was on the starboard side, towing from the middle of the boat; the next two were from the ends of the beam, with a wee bit of overlap; and the fourth was from the middle of the boat on the port side. Nearly always you found that the long dredge fished the best, unless you were in very shallow water. It had better contact with the ground. They used to think that you couldn't catch scallops any deeper than ten fathoms. When I bought the *Velena*, we put a trawl winch on the boat and I had the first scalloper in Scotland working a bar and two dredges on each side. We started with two 5-ft dredges and towed them from the stern, one a little shorter than the other. When you're coming round you could foul them so you always turn next the longer wire, to starboard if that was its position. Nowadays they work with beams and they can keep the dredges well apart.

The tow bar was very efficient because it ensured the gear stayed on the bottom in bad weather when the boat rose and fell. Light tubes were used at first but when one was bent Jackie had it replaced with an old car shaft with four lugs welded on it.

> It was the best thing I ever had [said Jackie]. It held the bottom terribly well. That was the start of the scalloping in multiples. A lot of boats were built at that time and fitted out with the same rig – two others in Girvan, and one in Portpatrick. In the early days we never dreamed of going deeper than 15 or 20 fathoms but last winter my son was working in 90 fathoms on the north side of Rathlin Island there, between Rathlin and Islay where nobody had ever worked. You can get scallops at any depth provided the nature of the bottom is suitable. Not every boat can work in deep water – strong tide, the length of warp, the winch – it needs a big boat, and the boat he has is 90 ft with 750 hp. In quiet weather the warp can be as little as twice the depth. In motion or strong tides you need to give more wire. I've seen it up to three times the depth. Towing speed now is greater.
>
> When you haul the bag you can have two ton of stones, more than the weight of clams. You don't want too much weed. It blocks the dredges. Nowadays there are very sophisticated echo sounders and sonars, showing the nature of the bottom in different colours and you know which colour or which shade gives scallops. On the old black-and-white sets, you got a shading or a double-echo or whatever. I'm convinced to this day, although we didn't know it at the time, that on the old sounder we were actually seeing scallops at one bit – there was the seabed there and in below the seabed you were getting heavy shading – the scallops were so thick, and we worked there for ten days, getting seven bags in a short distance. We cleaned it up. I'm convinced there were that many scallops there they were showing like stones to begin with. If I hadn't tried it there I would have said this is too stony.
>
> The ideal bottom is gravel or gritty 'coral'. Clean sand is no use.

You tow back and fore in an area about the size of a football pitch.
The scallops shift about – they feed in from areas at the side that you can't get to, the really rugged bottom. When we first went to Jura and Tobermory the scallops were poor, real rubbish, and they've greatly improved because the young ones are not getting deprived of feeding or a spot to settle. Having said they fill in from the sides [of the towed areas], there are places – not so much for scallops I don't think – there are a few places where they've been hammered and cleaned out and there's never been any left, but I think those were places where a precarious few were hanging on.

Queenies are a different thing – they fly about like flocks of starlings. In the summertime they can be hard to catch with dredges and you can catch them better with the net. I don't know if they can hear the dredge coming or sense it but the net is a much better thing, more stealth in effect. In one spot the catch is predominantly one [species] but you do get other things with them. There are not many queenies on the west of Scotland – a few, for example in the Sound of Gigha and other places – but nothing compared to the east side of the Irish Sea and the south side of the Isle of Man. I've seen us going out for twelve hours and getting 200 bags, when we started the queenies.

My son works twelve dredges on each side. There's one boat working eighteen on each side. She has a 40-ft towbar weighing two ton and behind that three smaller bars with three sets of six – on each side. These boats have been fitted up for exploiting scallops in deep water. They go away 100 miles south of the Irish coast, 100 miles again west of Newlyn, down towards Ushant.

There are markets now for other kinds of sea life that were formerly ignored. These include the velvet crab (*Portunus* spp), the buckie (*Buccinum undatum*) and the spoot or razor shell (*Ensis ensis*), the last once being a resort of crofters in times of famine. The velvet crab market opened up in the early 1980s – over one-third of the Scottish catch was taken in the Western Isles (386 tonnes in 1988) and it is all exported to Spain.[34] The buckie is taken in baited traps which can be seen at many small harbours around the coast, made from old plastic buckets with holes drilled in the sides and cement in the bottom as a sinker. Most of these catches are sold and freighted by road to markets on the Continent.

As stocks of fish on the Continental Shelf have become depleted, some boats have begun to plunder the species to be found on the Slope, where the shallow water of the Shelf suddenly deepens and plunges from 200m to 2000m, to the floor of the Atlantic Ocean proper. The edge of the Shelf runs to the west of Britain, between Shetland and the Faroes, and the Hebrides and Rockall. The Wyville-Thompson Ridge rises to cut the deep areas and forms a link between the Shelf and the shallow waters around Iceland. On the Slope the deep sea is dark and inhabited by fish adapted to the Stygian conditions, fish with strange shapes and strange names – rabbit fish, grenadiers, scabbard fish, orange roughy, cardinal – with large eyes and often elongated bodies. George Leiper remembered hauling up some of these unusual specimens in the late 1950s on the great lines: 'We followed this ridge right out 100 miles west of Rockall, depth, I'd say, between 200 and 250 fathoms – nearly 300 fathoms – and then we got up some queer fish – ratfish, grenadiers – of course, we didn't keep them, there was no market at that time, we just threw them back.'

French and Spanish trawlers make the most effort to catch these deepwater fish, dragging their trawls at depths of 400m. The conservative British market prefers more familiar species, but landings of these unusual creatures are made regularly at the larger ports in the north-west. The Scottish Association for Marine Science published a guide to these species in 1996 in the hope that domestic fishermen might be encouraged to go after them.[35]

There has been a revival of great lining, now more commonly termed long lining, in recent years but on a much larger scale than in the past. Automated baiting machines have taken the drudgery out of the work and some boats shoot up to 40,000 hooks, although many work in shallower waters with 2000 hooks.[36] Spanish and Norwegian fishermen use this method for dogfish, hake, cod and ling. Some Faroese operate automated jigger lines, an industrialised development of the old ripper where the metal lure flashing in the sea catches fish without the use of bait.[37]

One lucrative, relatively new fishery is for Atlanto-Scandian herring, a variety of the herring that spawns along the Norwegian coast in February–April and migrates westward to feed off the Faroes and Iceland during the summer months. Their route takes them within range of boats operating from Shetland. According to William Anderson on Whalsay:

This is a new fishery, since the War. There were always a few Scottish drifters that came for what they called the winter herring. They were caught in January and I've seen them discharging in Lerwick in a blizzard. They had some very heavy catches and, although they lost some nets through bad weather, they lost more through the weight of herring. It was usual to have one buoy floating for each [standard] net but they used double buoys and sometimes a strap around the middle of the net to stop it filling, and they still lost nets. They were big heavy fish, maybe 14 in. long, and it is a question now whether they were Atlanto-Scandian rather than North Sea herring.

This early fishery was an argument when the Atlanto-Scandian quotas were being set. This year [1996] there is no quota but an overall EU limit. Norway thinks it owns the Atlanto-Scandian herring because they spawn in Norwegian waters, and Russia has a right to them because they spend a long time in part of the Barents Sea, and Iceland thinks they have a right because they circle west to Iceland within their 200-mile limit. The EU has a concession on the herring. I would imagine that future quotas will be based on present catches, on historical performance and it's important to keep this presence. Some boats are fishing only to feed the gut factories but it will help in the future negotiations when national quotas are fixed.

It's 500 miles steaming – two days – to get north to the grounds. The newer boats are fast. One day's fishing with good catches is enough to fill the boat. Quite a few land in Denmark. There is trouble in getting rid of the herring in Scotland because there are no gut factories left – there is one in Bressay and a small one in Aberdeen but they are supposed to handle exclusively offal from fish processors.

CHAPTER NINE

COD WARS

Territorial waters

At the beginning of the 1970s, Britain ranked fifteenth in the league table of world fishing nations; in Europe, only Norway, Spain and Denmark landed bigger catches.[1] Particularly since the Second World War, the nature of fishing had changed: catching power had greatly increased, the number of boats had decreased but the sums invested in vessels and gear had grown. Disputes over access to fishing grounds became more acute. Disputes there seem always to have been but, in the past, the welfare of the resource itself, the stocks of fish, was hardly ever an issue. England formed a squadron of armed ships in 1481 to defend its East Anglia fishermen against Scottish pirates.[2] James VI resented the presence of the Dutch herring fleets in the seventeenth century; he liked the idea embodied in the Latin phrase *mare clausum*, a 'closed sea' over which he had dominion. The Dutch naturally had an opposing notion – they were on an economic roll, scooping up large catches of herring around Shetland and the Hebrides, and they wanted to go on doing this. Their offer to buy Keith Inch, the little island at Peterhead that is now part of the town, was refused but their forceful presence in Shetland pushed, it is said, Scottish fishermen to sail further north, to the Faroes, where the Danish rulers of these islands were driven in turn in 1618 to forbid the Scots to fish. The Dutch jurist, Hugo Grotius, formulated laws which remain the basis of international maritime law, in which the concept of *mare liberum*, a sea open to all, is prominent. The British government tried to negotiate with the Dutch but they naturally insisted on observing the freedom of the seas to fish where they liked. Without a great deal of success, the British tried to impose a zone of territorial waters, usually 14 miles wide or following the ancient custom of foreigners not being within sight of land.[3]

In 1883, an international convention at The Hague established the standard 3-mile limit as the extent of territorial water around the coasts of most of western Europe; Norway stuck with a 4-mile limit. However, as the catching power of fishermen has increased, many fish stocks have come under pressure and communities dependent on the sea have felt moved to take action to protect their livelihoods. This has been particularly true of Iceland which relies on the sea to an extent not found in most of her

European and American neighbours. In the 1930s the Icelandic courts were regarded as being especially severe on trawlers caught fishing within her territorial limits.[4] The first extension of territorial waters came in 1952, when the limit was set at four miles, a move that excluded foreign vessels from some 5000 square miles of sea.[5] In 1958 the limit was pushed further out – to 12 miles – and this led to the first of the Cod Wars between Britain and the small northern nation lying under the Arctic Circle. The conflict was conducted amicably at first, with British skippers avoiding areas where the Icelanders set their cod nets, but in April 1959 the gunboat *Thor* chased a Fleetwood trawler, the *Carella*, to the Faroes, and the Royal Navy thwarted attempts to board British trawlers.[6] An agreement was finally reached with the British and West German governments in which these countries recognised the 12-mile limit.

The recurrences of the Cod Wars in 1972 and 1976 saw more heated action. The extension of the Icelandic limit to 50 miles on 1 September 1972 provoked the fear that it could result in half Hull's fleet of sixty-six trawlers being laid up.[7] Three-quarters of the catch of Britain's distant-water fleet came from Icelandic waters and trawler owners wanted continued access by foreign vessels to Iceland's territorial waters on the basis of national quotas. As if to underline Iceland's arguments, the North East Atlantic Fisheries Commission and the International Council for the Exploration of the Sea published research results in midsummer 1972 indicating that the cod catch in the North Atlantic should be cut by 50 per cent and that the Newfoundland Grand Banks had been overfished since 1966. Negotiations between Britain and Iceland failed to achieve much compromise and the 50-mile limit came into force. The peace lasted for only a few years and conflict broke out again when Iceland extended her limit to 200 miles in 1975.

Iceland's frontline was her gunboats, lightly armed but equipped with clipper devices like garden shears that could cut the warps of the offending trawlers, sending catch and gear to the bottom. Three gunboats – the *Aegir*, *Thor* and *Tyr* – made attempts to break through the Royal Navy screen of frigates to reach the trawlers and were successful on fifteen occasions. On 7 January 1976 the *Thor* and HMS *Andromeda* collided, and both sides claimed that the other was responsible for the ramming. Iceland threatened to break off diplomatic relations with Britain; this caused concern in NATO circles and pressure was put on both countries to settle the dispute by talks. The Iceland prime minister flew to London, after the Royal Navy withdrew to outside the 200-mile limit, and discussions took place in a somewhat strained atmosphere: the British prime minister, Harold Wilson, asked the trawlers to stop fishing on 27 January but then told them to resume but to haul their nets if they were challenged by Iceland's coastguard. Morale was reported to be low on board the thirty-five trawlers off Iceland and there was fear for the future of the industry. The politicians failed to find an acceptable compromise over what tonnage limits could be established as the British share of Iceland's cod stocks in the first session of talks which ended on 28 January (on 26 January the *Tyr* had cut the warps of the *Boston Blenheim*), and the dangerous cat-and-mouse game in the stormy northern seas continued throughout the spring. An official from MAFF flew in a Nimrod from Kinloss in March and spoke to the beleaguered trawler fleet and their escorts, trying to reassure them that the government appreciated their difficulties and was doing everything possible to address them; the trawler skippers, tossing in 35-ft waves, were not overly impressed. This phase of the Cod War finally came to an end some two months later, on 1 June, when Britain and Iceland signed an agreement in Oslo; the terms were that twenty-four British trawlers would be allowed to fish Iceland's cod not closer than 20 miles, and in some places 30 miles, to the coast for a six-month period.

A sign that things were going against Britain's position had come on 29 January when the US Senate passed a Bill to establish a 200-mile limit in their own waters, to come into force in mid-1977. The EEC issued a policy document on 18 February with the idea of a Community-wide territorial sea out to 200 miles. The trend towards the 200-mile figure was rapidly gaining momentum: Anthony Crosland, the British Foreign Secretary, described it as 'inexorable' and said that the fishing industry would just have to face it, while the Tory Opposition muttered about betrayal. The closing of Iceland waters to the British trawler fleet had swift consequences: within a month Boston Deep Sea Fisheries, a leading trawler company, had cut its fleet from sixteen to eight trawlers, and this 50 per cent reduction in capacity was predicted for the industry generally with a total loss of about sixty boats, 1500 sea jobs and 7500 shore jobs.

In the first Cod War, in May 1959, HMS *Contest* had prevented the *Thor* from boarding the Aberdeen trawler *Avon River*[8] but generally Iceland's victory did not have a great effect in Scotland. As George Wood recalled:

> Aberdeen trawlers rarely went to Iceland. I mind my father saying he would only go to Iceland at maybe the end of January when the fishing got slack here. The water was very deep — 3 miles off and they were in to 60 fathoms — and they were fishing close like that, very heavy fishing, but once that fishing passed they were back — at Shetland, Faroe, the Edge here for turbot. The weekly Aberdeen men — the 'trippers' — fished around Shetland and down the west coast, looking for good fish. So Iceland didn't affect us, but Faroe did. That would have been after the Iceland Cod War — Faroe saw that Iceland were getting away with it so they just went out and out and out.

George Leiper explained that the line boats weren't troubled by the Icelanders:

> I remember down on the south-east side, there was what we called the low shore. It was very shallow water for a long way, and the

nearer the shore the more fish you caught. Anyway, this day I was shooting away early in the morning and I looks out the window on the bridge. That's a vessel there, no lights on. It was dark, of course. Oh, that's the gunboat – we're caught now. Ach well, we're doing it now, so we might as well carry on. So we carried on shooting the lines. The gunboat came up alongside us, just sailed along, and away he went. Now if I'd been a trawler, I'd have been nabbed. I was inside the limit. It was three mile at that time.

The Faroes declared its 200-mile limit in January 1977. As well as Aberdeen trawlers, the Granton boats fished in Faroese waters, especially once they adopted diesel in place of steam. It took forty-four hours to make the voyage from the Firth of Forth to the northern archipelago, fifty hours if the trawler steamed through the fiords between the islands to reach Mykines on the west side. 'When we first started going regularly, the limit was 6 miles,' said John Robb. 'Then it was extended to 12, and then they made it point to point.' Declaring territorial waters from point to point enclosed much larger stretches of sea than simply allowing the line to follow the coast, and the 12-mile limit in effect meant that the Granton men had to keep 30 miles out on the west side between the islands of Mykines and Suđeroy. At Christmas in 1974, a Danish gunboat fired on and chased the *Aberdeen Fisher* out of Faroese waters for fishing within the limit, in a pursuit that lasted eleven hours and half-way to Shetland.[9] 'I mind one of the last trips I made up there,' said Iain Smith. 'It was the afternoon. I think it was the *Arctic Hunter* I was in. Willie Young was mate. He says, "You better get up." I says, "What's wrong?" He says, "There's a helicopter waving at me." This was the Faroese, and the guy was going "Get out! Get out!"'

Most Scottish fishermen understood why the Icelanders and the Faroese were so passionately resolved to defend their home waters. They are less charitably disposed towards European fishermen, especially since Britain joined the European Economic Community (EEC), as it was then called, in 1972. Many had grave doubts over the consequences this would have for them and the politicians took the matter of fishing rights on board. On the same day, 3 November 1971, that the Icelanders met British officials in London to discuss the extension of their limits to 50 miles, Geoffrey Ripon, the British negotiator in Brussels, announced that the present fishery regulations of the EEC prevented the signing by Britain of the treaty of accession. The EEC wanted all member states to have the right to fish right up to the beaches of member countries but Britain insisted on a 6-mile limit. A compromise was reached quite quickly in which the EEC agreed that Britain and the other applicants for membership at the time could retain the 6-mile limit for a fixed period of perhaps two years, with the possibility of extension of the period for another eight years. They also agreed that there should be a 12-mile limit in areas where fishing was a mainstay of the local economy – these favoured areas were Orkney,

Shetland, north-east Scotland, north-east England, Devon and Cornwall.

Alick Buchanan-Smith, the Scottish Under-Secretary for Agriculture and Fisheries, confidently and optimistically commended this agreement to the fishermen. The leader of the fishing delegation, Ian Stewart, the secretary of the Clyde Fishermen's Association, was less enthusiastic but accepted that the agreement was the best that could be achieved in the circumstances.

Blockade

Throughout the history of the Scottish fisherman, he appears as an individualist and, at the same time, a member of a community with a strong egalitarian spirit. This was recognised by the Revd George Donaldson in Buckie in the 1790s who wrote:

> Here we see men judging and acting for themselves. Everyone adopts those plans which best suit his circumstances and situation in life. The fishers indeed, as individuals, are placed more on a footing of equality; and their pursuits are uniformly similar. Of course their language and transactions are the language and transactions of the community rather than of individuals. All adopt the same measures and pursue similar plans in executing them. The voice of one almost always puts all in motion; and the example of one is frequently followed by all; and yet, what is singular, no one seems to possess a character decisive enough to take the lead, and rise to superiority by the strength of genius or the arts of address.'[10]

There is a fine balance between co-operation and competition displayed through all the stories of the fishing. In John Thomson's words:

The *Wellspring* (CN 207) with cod at the Bennan cod fishery off the south end of Arran in about 1974.

> When everybody was at the fishing and there wasn't much going, it was a living, it was a way of life. The folk were poor, and everybody needed everybody else. They shared the hard times and everything. The community grieved together, they physically launched boats and hauled them together. If anybody was in distress, everybody ran. If anybody was in danger on the sea, everybody did what they could, even possibly sacrificing their own lives in the rescue.

As Frank Bruce recalled:

> There was great competition between the boats but it was muted or channelled in certain ways. It was important to get a bit more fish than the next guy. There were certain people who were a bit better off in the village – the skippers, for example. They'd have bigger houses. There were almost no cars and, as far as I can recall, in the 1930s only

one fisherman, apart from the local joiner and the coal merchant, had a car.

When the old steam drifters set out for sea through the narrow harbour entrances on the east coast, there would be a tremendous jostling for position and, at sea, there was sometimes animosity about getting the best ground, with a shouting and use of strong language.

Working at sea in small groups, the men formed close-knit teams. This spilled over to the relationships between boat crews, some of whom would contain relatives in any case, and even to the relationships between communities. Fishermen might hesitate over applying to this a high-flown term such as 'brotherhood of the sea' but something akin to it existed and, to a large degree, survives to this day.

As William West in Macduff explained:

You worked with the same men for years and years and you just got to ken each other. You were living and sleeping in a place the size of a small greenhouse and you got to ken each other's moves and ways and everything. My brother was a fisherman – my sister's husband had a boat. We all worked in conjunction with each other. About a dozen boats used to fish out of here. If fishing was scarce, everybody scattered – some away across to Wick, some away out to the Jungle, some away down south. Nowadays if you did that, the first thing you would hear would be somebody coming in with his fishroom full. But when we did it we kept in touch all the time. We knew exactly what was going on in Wick, well maybe not right away – the fellow that went across would get a couple of hauls in before he phoned anybody else, but you always let your partners in the job know. Kenneth, my brother, worked in Wick waters. He landed in Wick a lot. Rattray was my main fishing area. We kept in touch all the time. We spoke in codes: if I was speaking to my brother or he was speaking to me we didn't need to mention fish, I knew by the tone of his voice, a lilt, a bit of excitement, if he was getting fish, and he knew by the tone of my voice. I would take another haul and zoom across to Wick, if he was getting – and in the same way he would come down to us. There's still a bit of that yet but not what it was. They're still sharing if somebody's in trouble – they're always there to help – but as far as fish is concerned, catching and sharing fish with somebody else, there's so much money involved in fishing nowadays.

The individualism of each skipper at sea has often meant that solidarity among fishermen is hard to achieve but there are some striking instances in the past of a whole community acting together for a common purpose. The Society of Free Fishermen of Newhaven can be traced back to 1572 but may be much older, and it has been described as the oldest trade association in

Scotland.[11] The rules of membership changed over the centuries but generally it existed to protect the rights of the Newhaven fishermen to ply their occupation in the Firth of Forth, especially in relation to access to oyster beds, and to provide some basic welfare for the fishing families, in return for membership dues. The Society at different times fought and won legal disputes, acted as a kind of local authority and even ran a school. A Fishermen's Society was founded in Nairn in 1767. The members paid dues of 6d in May, November and February and the larger sum of 1 shilling in August, when it was reckoned the line fishing would be most remunerative.[12] The Society was essentially a welfare organisation, providing some help for widows and orphans but it grew large enough to gain some property rights – a street in the fishertoun is named Society Street.

Two boats brailing herring from a pair trawl in the Firth of Clyde.

The right to use the foreshore, for landing and hauling, was vital to the fishermen and at different times in Scotland there were disputes with landowners over access. The Scots Parliament passed in June 1705 an Act for Advancing and Establishing the Fishing Trade in and about the Kingdom and, in its preamble, it states that previous acts were either 'in dissuetude defective or do not answer the present circumstances'. The new Act authorised all 'good subjects' to take and cure herring and white fish, and to have the free use of ports, shores and forelands for the task on payment of ordinary dues.[13]

The line fishermen who worked inshore grounds in the eighteenth century took care of marketing their own catches, either taking cured fish to market or selling it fresh through the efforts of their womenfolk. Fisheries on a larger scale, however, needed levels of investment and marketing that were beyond their means. Hebridean merchants had a strong hold on line fishing in their home areas and in the 1890s it was reckoned that two-thirds of the sailing drifters in the islands were owned by landsmen, mostly Stornoway merchants and curers. The fishermen tried to break free from this system but it was not until 1915 that a local fisherman had a share in a drifter and 1919 before a drifter was fully owned by her crew.[14] Merchants and lairds in Shetland likewise had a tight hold on fishing through what was termed the 'truck' system.[15] The Victorian herring boom depended on the investment of the curers. This relationship between the producers – the fishermen – and the trade – the curing and marketing of fish – has not always been a happy one. For example, there were disputes in the 1930s over details of the curers' arrangements for buying fish and the fishermen occasionally threatened to apply the ultimate sanction: stay in port and refuse to catch anything.[16]

Large catches by the whole fleet could result in such a drop in the price buyers would offer that the fishermen preferred to dump their fish. In June 1936, for example, this happened in Lerwick: one day the price offered fell to 13 shillings per cran and 1500 cran were thrown into the sea.[17] In the Clyde area in the early 1930s, so much herring was dumped in Rothesay Bay that it stank for weeks: fishermen could not get their catches sold and some sailed up to Glasgow to give the fish away as free food for the city's poor. 'They had a benefit concert for the fishermen in Rothesay,' said Duncan McArthur, 'Harry Lauder and others came down from Glasgow for it. It was pure poverty.' Skippers sometimes had to pay buyers to take their fish. This state of affairs horrified one Dunure skipper, Sammy Gemmell of the *Storm Drift*: he noticed that his crew had earned 10 shillings each as their share for the week's work while he had had to 'bribe' the buyer by paying him £3 9 shillings to purchase the fish.[18] Gemmell discussed the problem with Ian Stewart, a Campbeltown solicitor and secretary of the Clyde Fishermen's Association, formed in 1935. They devised an arrangement whereby all the boats pooled their income for herring of comparable size and quality and shared the proceeds fairly. 'There was a big fishing in the summer of 1937 and the boats teamed up so that two or three boats would stay ashore for a week and go to sea the following week, when another three would be ashore,' said Angus McCrindle. 'The fishermen put on a quota to stabilise the landings – in all probability each member of the crew of these boats would receive about £3 or £4 per man per week at this fishing.' The Clyde Fishermen's Association was the first in Scotland to introduce its own quotas, with the total limit on the herring catch being divided according to the numbers of boats and men. All the fishermen in the Firth of Clyde, on both the Kintyre and the Ayr shores, were members. Operated by the men themselves, the quotas and rules were generally respected and seen as fair and were extended to cover the catching of white fish as well as herring. The Mallaig and North-West Fishermen's Association had a similar set of rules. The system came to an end, however, in 1970 when the right of the fishermen to set their own quotas and cause others to observe them was successfully challenged in a suit brought to court under the Restrictive Trade Practices Act.[19]

Although the fishermen were often at odds with buyers – William

Anderson's views on the Lerwick buyers have already been described, and Tom Ralston writes of their tricks in *My Captains* – they have also shown solidarity with them, making arrangements which would benefit both sides of the commercial equation. William West recalled one such operation:

> We used to share hauls a lot in Kinlochbervie, especially in the wintertime, back in the late 1960s and early 1970s, when we were seine-netting. The first dogfish put their nose round the Cape [Wrath] in the last week of November. On this occasion, the Minch filled with dogfish. Everybody at Kinlochbervie was catching dogs. So, the market could have been dodgy especially coming up to Christmas. The buyers tried to get a set market: each boat catches eighty boxes of dogs per day. They could get an outlet for this. So, maybe one fellow would go out in the morning, shoot, and haul maybe 150 boxes; he would take his eighty and somebody else would take the rest. Later on, what we did was: everybody went and shot their nets – you were sure to get the fill of it – and you took your quota out of it, dahned the net, left it on the bottom, and went back the next day to get another eighty boxes. It took you two or three hours to get the fish aboard and then we went inshore to shallow water and fished for flats, codling, whatever was there. That went on up until Christmastime – you wouldn't make a fortune but your dog was £1 per box – eighty boxes, £80 – if you got maybe 10–15 boxes of other fish, even less, you'd make up your £120–£150 for a day's work. That was a good wage in those days. The crews were delighted – they knew what their wage would be before they left port. That worked away right up till the week before Christmas and suddenly one boat decided to get a big haul – they came in with 400–500 boxes of dogs. That finished everything. I think, though, that the salesman was looking for a back door to get out. He would buy the dogs because he had given his word on it but he was finding getting rid of them a bit of a job.

In 1970, fishermen became more and more disgruntled with the way dockers worked in Aberdeen, still then the main landing port and fish market on the east coast.

> Sometimes they put down dockers double the size of your own crew, with very high charges, and mucked you around [said John Thomson]. We could only participate in landing the fish, they controlled the situation. We could have eight of a crew and they would put down sixteen men. Some of them didn't work well, and there might be a man filleting fish for himself down in the hold. You were frightened to say anything. At that time dock labour was targeting ports like Lochinver and Kinlochbervie to have flying labour

there every day. Thank goodness, that came to nothing. It was a price we weren't prepared to pay. We couldn't live with it any longer, and we boycotted Aberdeen and withdrew. I remember the night boats first went into Peterhead. They didn't know what to do, so we landed in the street. The little market was overpowered. Old men came running down: 'What's happened, men, what's happened?' We said: 'We've boycotted Aberdeen, we just can't live with the dock labour.' Most of the boats around the coast joined the boycott and went to Peterhead. A few of the Fife boats lingered in Aberdeen because it was nearer home for them, but that was the start of Peterhead's growth as a white fish port. It's the biggest port now, and Aberdeen lost.

The power of concerted action was revealed in this incident and the lesson was not lost when the fishermen faced a more widespread crisis in the mid-1970s. After several years of prosperity, the industry ran into severe economic difficulties in 1974. This resulted from a number of factors, among them the OPEC hike in oil prices in 1973 which pushed fuel bills up by as much as 300 per cent and the subsequent rise in the price of manufactured nets and gear. At the same time, the whole economy was going through a recession: fish prices fell, wages ashore increased rapidly, and imports of frozen fish from European countries where fishing received more government support than it did in Britain rose to high levels, further undercutting the domestic quayside prices. The oil industry in the North Sea gushed in Aberdeen and drew men away from the fishing boats. The cost of a new boat rose dramatically, even while she was still on the stocks, and the sale prices of secondhand boats dropped. It was reported that the crews on some fishing boats went without wages for weeks. There was also concern about the prospects for the fishermen in the new EC when boats from Europe would have greater access to British waters; many were in favour of a 50-mile exclusive zone but in general there was little faith in the British government acting so forcefully. Some fish stocks were also dropping, and a quota on North Sea herring was introduced in July 1974 by the North East Atlantic Fisheries Commission.[20]

Joint action among fishermen was not an easy thing to organise, especially as the men were rarely ashore all at the same time. When they did meet, perhaps a few at a time, in ports scattered around the coast, the talk was of impending crisis. Meetings became more frequent as 1974 drew to a close and, on 22 January 1975, a group of fishermen flew from Aberdeen to London to lobby MPs. At the same time they began to talk of taking more decisive action to draw attention to their grievances by blockading the ports. The 120 men in the delegation were listened to in Westminster but not all were reassured that anything would be done. On the flight back to Aberdeen, they resolved to give Harold Wilson's government one month to reply. In February, French fishermen, with grievances of their own, staged a sit-in in Paris and then blockaded a succession of Channel ports, starting with Boulogne and spreading quickly to Dunkirk, Calais, Dieppe, Le Tréport and Bordeaux. The French government responded within days with a package of measures to alleviate the fisherman's lot. In contrast, the British government seemed to plod: it produced some half-hearted proposals on fuel subsidies but baulked at doing anything about fishing limits – Labour's renegotiation of Britain's terms of entry to the EC deliberately excluded the Common Fisheries Policy from the agenda but did much for agriculture.

Scottish fishermen were not alone in feeling angry. Their brethren in other parts of Britain were suffering as they were and, in fact, the first blockade took place on the Humber on 18 March. Grimsby and the port of Immingham were blocked by some fifty fishing boats. Skippers from North Shields listened to what was taking place on their radios and decided they also should act; on the afternoon of the 23rd they formed a barrier across the Tyne. It takes a lot to make fishermen act in this way but now the spark had turned to a flame. Fishermen in Scotland held a series of meetings as soon as they could be organised, culminating in a major planning session at the Treetops Hotel in Aberdeen on the 27th. An Action Committee, comprising twenty-four men representing all the districts from Shetland down to the Firth of Clyde, was formed. Willie Hay, from Buckie, was unanimously elected chairman, with Jake McLean from Peterhead as vice-chairman. The Committee drew up a series of rules on how the blockade would be conducted, emphasising safety and responsibility on the part of the campaigners, and set the deadline for midnight on Sunday 30 March – it was the Easter weekend and Parliament was in recess.

Early on Monday morning, before dawn broke over the coast, the boats began to move to their appointed positions. The Whitehills boat, the *Coral Strand*, put to sea first with bagpipes playing. The Action Committee had meanwhile established their HQ in the Gloucester Hotel in Aberdeen and as the night progressed reports came in from all around the coast on how things were going. At dawn the armada of trawlers and seiners were forming lines across the harbour entrances in Aberdeen, Leith, Granton, Lerwick, the Clyde at Greenock, Stornoway, the Cromarty Firth, Wick, Buckie, Macduff, Fraserburgh, Peterhead, the naval depot in Kyle of Lochalsh, Inverness and Mallaig.

John Thomson was on the Committee:

I was in Aberdeen in the blockade. Willie Campbell took my boat and I was actually in charge of the delegates for the Moray Firth and Minch fleet. The Lossiemouth fleet blockaded Invergordon, a very difficult situation in a tidal estuary. Some of them blockaded the entrances to Lossiemouth, Buckie and Macduff. The majority of boats took part in the Blockade. There were very few dissenters. It was the first time that our men had ever mobilised themselves. The force of the power of labour was abusive at that time but it was getting results and it was obvious when we saw others exerting their power to think that we could do it as well. We had won the dock labour issue. On other matters we had been given government assurances but they didn't do anything. The case was good and the men nearly all complied. It was an absolute remnant that would not take part but I don't think they fished, they stayed in port. I would say for sure 90 per cent were active.

It was pretty difficult. Willie Ross was Secretary of State – a most unyielding man. We had political talks, we had industry talks. I'll always remember the night we went to Aberdeen. The press got whiff of our threats. We had all our plans. All the men knew what was to happen. Rumours were going around. When the fleet approached Aberdeen, the Harbour Authority challenged them. The boats came in and said they were a blockade fleet.

There were many hairy moments. A little German cargo boat threatened to break out, and I think we eventually negotiated and let him go. We let trawlers in to land but we wouldn't let them out – we didn't want to do our own men any harm. We didn't want to be too disruptive: in Orkney we allowed the ferries to take cattle but not fish. There were many things that could have frightened us off. Ships could have been lost – in that instance, would they have got insurance rights? Violence could have flared up, and, worst of all, there could have been loss of life. It is a great commendation of the men that not a life was lost and not an injury was done. That had been the biggest fear, and that nothing like it happened is a great tribute to the men themselves. Some amazing things happened in that blockade. Part of the Moray fleet was at Ardersier and Inverness. The police were on our side, they really were. Bakers were putting down bread and morning rolls to the boats. Lots of people actively supported us. Telegrams of support came from Canada and the United States – one fisherman's problem is an all-fishermen's problem.

We did not expect all that support. The men found a new sense of solidarity. We were all thrown into it, we'd never broken the law before. We didn't like what we were doing because the process of law was upon us within days with injunctions. At the meetings, to save the chairman any more anxiety, I kept a pocketful of injunctions. If these had been [followed up] afterwards, we would have found ourselves very much on the end of having to square up the people who wanted compensation. Those threats lingered with us for quite a while but we had no intention of putting on the blockade indefinitely. It was a week – we knew that before we started but nobody else knew. But the injunctions were all dropped. I think the forces of law, with public opinion, had seen a very responsible situation, and the law was not enforced because public opinion would have objected.

There is no doubt that the fishermen's action stirred the public to sympathy, as images of lines of boats strung flank to flank across the harbours – the impressive results of skilful handling – appeared in the media. On Thursday 3 April, at six o'clock in the morning, as planned, the fishing boats began to disperse and steam back to their home ports.

> It's very difficult to be sure but I think it worked [said John Thomson]. We had six points at issue. One concerned territorial limits and the encroachment of European vessels. That has proved to be one of the biggest things. Eventually, in 1977, when the 12-mile limit was moved to 200 miles, and Europe gained rights inside it through the Common Fisheries Policy, it turned out to be the biggest disaster there ever was. The blockade made a point and, despite the sell-out there has been since, it was worth standing up. We had other actions after that. Prices were so poor because of imports. The men closed Peterhead for a week, blockaded and closed their own port through dissatisfaction. There were some bitter rows among ourselves and we actually warred amongst ourselves, and some said they would never come together and do an action again. One of the last concerted actions by the fleet – and I was in charge of it – and some didn't agree with it, but we did it responsibly – we went down and escorted the *Britannia* up the Firth of Forth to Leith Docks. We had about fifty boats. It was a very responsible action. At the time the *Britannia* was entering the harbour, some hotheads among the lads suggested rushing the dock to block it and make a real scene. I wouldn't allow that; it was meant to be a responsible, respectable action to gain us some credit elsewhere for other things. That was the last action. I don't think you'll get the industry ever to stand together again. It's been torn apart by politics.

Last of the drifters

Almost all fishermen now are members of some organisation. Co-operatives and local associations have been formed in many ports, encouraged by the formation in 1973 of the Scottish Federation of Fishermen's Co-operatives and provision of government funding. The co-ops have taken on different agenda but selling chandlery, marketing fish and the making of ice or nets are typical activities. Lewis Patience retired in 1997 from being manager of the Avoch Fishermen's Co-operative.

> I would say it is a typical co-op. It was set up in 1978. We had very little assistance but we had a loan, and then a grant from the Mallaig and North West Fishermen's Association. We have a shop selling chandlery and clothes and we act as a selling agent for the fish. A lot of the co-ops actually sell the fish for the fishermen but we can do it only on a secondhand basis, as home agents for the boats. We can't

get right into the fish selling because there's no fish landed here. The fishselling companies sell the catches and they contact us, and we are the settling agents rather than the selling agents. The boats, not the men, have the shares in the Co-op. It's a different thing altogether down in, for example, Pittenweem and the Firth of Forth, where every man has a share. The United Fishselling Company in Buckie is a co-operative as well and they actually work the same as we do, except they have fishselling. The Stornoway Co-op has the same idea as we've got, it's the boats and skippers that are the members – they sell fuel, they do everything in Stornoway. A salesman in Buckie used to sell all the Kessock herring in Inverness but all the fishermen thought they could do it better for themselves – all fishermen think that anyway – and that's exactly what they did.

Fishermen are also prone to blame their colleagues using a different technique for the fall-off in the stocks relevant to themselves. The drift net men accused the ringnetters of over-exploiting the herring, and then accused the trawlers of destroying herring spawn. Line fishermen resented the threat from seine netters. The same accusations can be heard today about the newer fisheries. One fisherman told me that prawn trawling was the death of the inshore fishing as the nets hauled up immature fish which were then shovelled overboard dead; square panels introduced into the trawls to allow fish to escape were not being widely used. Others have asserted that clam dredging leaves the seabed furrowed and young fish in mince.

In June 1977, some fishermen sailed up the Thames to voice their discontent close to the House of Commons. About forty-five boats, mostly English but including the Peterhead trawler *Budding Rose*, took part[21] in what proved to be one of the more notable demonstrations in a year of protest. At the beginning of 1980 there were more reports of growing militancy among the Scottish fishermen over demands for a government fuel subsidy, imports of fish and quotas, and a threat to blockade the oil terminal at Sullom Voe was rumoured.[22] The effects of the post-War improvements in fishing techniques were beginning to be felt.

Concern had been growing by the mid-1970s over the size of herring stocks around the British coast. In December 1971, the member states of the North East Atlantic Fisheries Commission (NEAFC) had agreed to reduce the catch in 1972 by 17 per cent of the 1970 level, and to make a further reduction in 1973 by 26 per cent of the 1970 baseline. They were also of a mind to limit the white fish catches in 1972 to a level equal to the yearly average of the previous decade.[23] The NEAFC had been formed in 1959 as a successor to the International Fisheries Convention, of which Britain had been a founding member, to provide a forum for the discussion of the international conservation of fish stocks.[24] It set quotas on herring in 1974 and two years later more curbs were placed on herring fishing, this time on the weight of by-catch herring that could be landed: in the North Sea, the limit for herring by-catch was set at one-tenth by weight of sprat catches and one-twentieth of catches of other species.[25] The regulations recognised that in netting fish a boat was bound to catch more than just the target species.

At this time the full quota for herring in the area governed by the NEAFC was 85,000 tons, of which Britain's share was less than 6000 tons. This was another source of complaint: on the basis of track record (the share-out of an overall quota was based on fishing history) the Danes were awarded a much greater share of the total catch, although most of what they took was destined for fishmeal plants. In April the NEAFC agreed a total quota for 1976 of 160,000 tons of herring, with Britain's share set at 9700 tons; and a minimum size of 20 cm was placed on herring landed for human consumption. By August, however, Britain was seeking release from the agreement, as the NEAFC scheme was seen to be ineffective in controlling the fishing effort – the British boats had already exceeded their quota but foreign vessels were continuing to catch herring outside the 12-mile limit. A complete ban on herring fishing was inaugurated on the North Yorkshire coast to protect the spawning stock. To escape the herring quotas, many Scottish boats switched to pair trawling for white fish.[26]

At the beginning of 1977 came the dire news that herring landings were two-thirds down on the previous year's level. There were warnings of imminent collapse of the fishery with the loss of 10,000 jobs in Scotland. Lack of herring in the Minch encouraged purse seiners to move north to Shetland waters in search of better luck but around Christmas some were forced to let netted shoals go, as the quota for the year had been exhausted.[27] A ban on herring fishing in the North Sea was introduced at the end of February and set to run until the end of April and then May. The ban was extended to the end of June and was applied for the first time in May 1977 to the waters to the west of Scotland as well. At a meeting in May, the EC agreed to consider a long-term review of the Common Fisheries Policy but only Britain supported the idea of continuing the herring ban to the end of 1977 and declared itself ready to take unilateral action. On 30 June Britain extended the ban on herring within her 200-mile zone for a further six months. Early in the morning on the following day, barely eight hours after the British ban came into force, the Royal Navy arrested a Dutch trawler, the *Johanna*, and escorted her into Lerwick. The skipper was fined £25,000 and had his gear and catch confiscated. This fine was also inflicted on another Dutch skipper, of the *Maria*, when he was arrested 50 miles east of Aberdeen at more or less the same time. The Dutch had been busy in Scottish waters in the early 1970s: according to the Herring Industry Board, they had taken twice or almost three times their allotted quota of fish in the immediately preceding years. French trawlers blockaded Boulogne on 27 October to protest against the extension of the herring ban and early in November the EC agreed to relax the rules to allow Norman and Picardy fishermen to catch 600 tonnes in their own inshore waters until the end of 1977.

The monitoring of fish stocks in EC waters was the responsibility of the

International Council for the Exploration of the Sea (ICES). This body issued statistics in July 1977 indicating that the North Sea stock of herring had fallen in 1976 from 1.2 million tonnes to 300,000 tonnes, of which only about 50 per cent were capable of breeding. The North Sea catch had declined from almost 500,000 tonnes in 1972 to less than 170,000 tonnes in 1976. The stocks on the west of Scotland were also suffering, the British catch having declined from 120,000 tons in 1973 to 53,000 in 1976, the lowest catch in ten years and well below the British quota. The EC proposed extending the North Sea ban to last through 1978 with a possible further extension to 1979. A ban on industrial fishing and reducing the amount of herring caught as a by-catch were also put forward as urgent conservation measures.

The *Vigilant* (PD 365), a modern pelagic vessel built in Norway in 1995 for the Lunar Bow Fishing Company, Peterhead.

In mid-August a quota limit of 11,900 tonnes was set on Irish Sea herring but this was soon followed by a complete ban for seven weeks starting from October. The landings of herring in England and Wales fell to only 815 tonnes in the first half of 1977. It was revealed in December that the British herring catch in 1977 was the lowest of the century, grim news that was only partially relieved by the catch also having, at £12.5 million, the highest value of the century. The total was only 42,000 tonnes where three years before the landings from the Minch alone had been 100,000 tonnes.

The British government announced at the end of June 1978, as part of a package of conservation measures, a ban on fishing for herring in west coast waters to take effect from 6 July. West Germany, Denmark and The Netherlands grumbled. The Dutch lost access to a quota of 3000 tonnes and the Germans to 3700 tonnes. The ban may have been just in time. Stocks were sadly depleted and in September, Dr D.H. Cushing, director of the MAFF lab at Lowestoft, said that there was still no sign of a recovery in the stock.

On Lewis, Murdo Maclennan remembers this period:

We had the last herring drifter in Stornoway, the *Seafarer*. Well, when the herring ban came on, we had already turned to trawling, because there was no herring around from May to July, so we took a couple of months trawling for prawns and white fish and then, once we saw signs of herring at the end of July, the trawl nets were going ashore and the drift nets were going aboard. There was another boat up in Harris at the driftnetting – the *Scaraben*, I think – and they turned to potting, creels. We were the last boat out of Stornoway with drift nets. There was another fellow but he used to go out just occasionally – maybe in the winter he would put on 12–15 nets and go out, just for a pastime. We were the last boat with a full crew making a living out of it. It was a good living when the ban came – prices were soaring then. I don't think the ban was necessary, not for driftnetting – yes for trawling and purse seining but not for driftnetting. We picked the quality in the drift nets, not quantity – there was no rubbish at all among our fish. The wee ones were going through the net, you see. But you could never explain that to the people sitting in St Andrew's House in Edinburgh. When you said driftnetting they thought it was salmon or something like that you were talking about – they hadn't a clue, and our own MP and councillors and everybody tried to explain to them but, no, it was driftnetting that was banned. It wasn't the scarcity of herring around here at all. I mind the last winter we were out, landing one of the best landings in my life. We had eighty units – the crans had stopped then – and we grossed £3000 for the one night's fishing. Say there were four boxes to a cran at one time. Before we stopped there were six boxes to a cran. The boxes were smaller, but if you put it into baskets it was just the four baskets. A unit was one of the smaller boxes. The prices were really good then. I saw one day getting £80 for one unit. It was the scarcity that did that. The buyers were desperate to get herring.

The Minch reopened in August 1981 but in September the government placed a ban on the catching of herring in the Irish Sea as the catch limit for that season of 3400 tonnes had been almost reached. When the 1982 fishery began, at midnight on Sunday 18 July, all the fishing boats were required to have licences and it was announced that the fishery would close when a total of 16,000 tonnes had been caught.

Alex Buchan was among the east coast skippers then fishing in the area:

Most of our fishing was done on the west coast. When they closed the North Sea for herring we used to fish the west coast more or less twelve months of the year, apart from the off-seasons, which were from the end of March to the beginning of May. It was the custom to land usually on a Friday in Ullapool or Mallaig. Mallaig wasn't a good harbour to leave a boat in – it wasn't so big – so we went up to Kyle where we could leave the boat alongside, or anchor in Skye in Loch na Beiste, just across Kyleakin, in a bicht there, or Ullapool – that was a favourite place for the boats. The boats that worked from Ullapool fished quite a lot up in the Lochinver/Kinlochbervie area but we fished there when the mackerel came. That was a favourite place for mackerel – they seemed to come along the north shore round Cape Wrath and down into the Minch, on their migratory route when they went down to spawn in the springtime to the west of Ireland. The boats used to fish them in all the bays. We hired a bus to drive the whole crew home at the weekends – it took about four hours. We came home on the Friday night and went back on Monday morning. We did that nearly every week. In fact, that was more or less standard practice in those days – everybody started fishing on Monday night and stopped on Thursday night and landed on Friday. We might have been in port two, three or four times in the week, landing every day. We tried to land every day to keep the fish fresh.

Pound signs in front of their eyes

The herring was not the only species to become the subject of restrictions at this time. Quotas were imposed on, for example, haddock in the North Sea. To quell protests, the government resorted on occasion to short-term measures: in November 1976, it decided to 'borrow' from the 1977 North Sea haddock quota but a few days later reimposed the ban for the rest of the year. In July 1977, Norway halted cod fishing in its waters north of 62°N, as the quotas for EC members had already been exhausted This was another blow to the English trawler fleets and, to a lesser extent, to that of Aberdeen. At about the same time, a ban was also placed on Norway pout fishing in an area of the northern North Sea, as catching pout caused damage to immature haddock, an unavoidable by-catch. The ban extended to the end of October: Britain pushed for it to last longer but the other EC members resisted this move, forcing the British government to talk once again of unilateral measures. In September 1978, after it became clear that haddock catches in England and Wales had fallen by 25 per cent in the first part of the year, the British government acted unilaterally to restrict haddock catches and began to issue licences for the North Sea, rules which applied to UK boats only. In May 1979 the catch limits on haddock and whiting were increased in Scottish waters. MAFF scientists announced in March 1980 that several fish stocks were at risk in UK waters. The prospects for cod and haddock in the Irish Sea were poor, and fishing pressure was more than the breeding stock could bear. A stricter licensing system, whereby all vessels over 40 ft would need one to catch white fish, was introduced in April 1980, and landing fish without a licence would incur a maximum fine of £50,000 on summary conviction. Stocks of skate in the

Irish Sea, hake off Cornwall, and plaice and whiting in the North Sea were also slipping to low levels.

The other main pelagic species, the mackerel, had become the target of a major fishery, especially in the waters around Cornwall. The growth of the mackerel fishery was rapid during the 1970s. Disputes over stocks erupted as the mobility of local fleets allowed them to sail further and further from home in search of fish. Mackerel fishers in Cornwall and Devon accused Scottish boats of seriously damaging stocks in the south-west. During the mackerel season, from September to March, the south-west men fished for mackerel with lines but now, in a repeat of the impact of Norwegian boats in Shetland some ten years before, Scottish boats had steamed in with purse nets and were taking 200 tons in a single shot. The Scots were also accused of undercutting the regulation prices in the French Channel ports. Landings of mackerel in Cornwall and Devon were well down on the levels of the previous five years: the purse seiners would wipe out the stock, claimed the English fishers. The Scots answered that high mackerel landings now would set a better precedent for the anticipated quotas to be set by the EC.

In September 1976, a Soviet trawler skipper was fined for fishing within limits. Soviet and eastern European vessels were also being seen as a threat to mackerel stocks. It was estimated that their catch in British waters amounted to 600,000 tons in 1976 and the EC devised a formula whereby the allowable Soviet quota would be reduced to 15 per cent less than the average annual catch between 1965 and 1974; as it was, when the new 200-mile limit was introduced in January 1977, the Soviet quota was reduced to 50,000 tons for the first three months. During 1977 the catch of cod in England and Wales fell by one-third while the take of mackerel trebled, from 56,000 tonnes in 1976 to almost 135,000 tonnes in 1977. In September, in an attempt to answer protests from fishermen in the south-west of England that Scottish and Humberside boats were taking too many mackerel, the British government introduced fishing licences. By December 1979, the pressure on the mackerel population – over 350,000 tonnes were being taken by then – was growing to an alarming extent. The weekly quotas were cut by one-fifth at the end of the month and it was decreed that fishing for mackerel by all except the smallest boats had to cease by mid-February. In August 1980, the government became concerned about mackerel stocks in the North Sea and suspended the licences of British boats six weeks earlier than usual, although this did not have any consequence for the British fleet for whom the major fishery was off the south-west. However, the catches in the south-west were very high and scientists feared that the population might also collapse there.

A feature of the rapid growth of the mackerel fishery was the klondiker. The expression arose in the fishing communities at the time of the Yukon Gold Rush in the late 1890s, when the Klondike River was in the news, to signify a source of quick wealth. In the case of the sea, it referred to the practice of sailing to the Continent with a cargo of fresh herring at the start of the season when prices were high, something akin to the fashion for tasting the first wine of the year. The practice is an old one – the Dutch were doing it in Shetland in the seventeenth century – but in modern times its origin has been ascribed to a Lowestoft fish dealer called Benjamin Bradbeer who noticed in 1887, during a visit to Hamburg, the Germans' predilection for new, fresh herring. The klondike herring were shipped in open barrels called kits, iced and lightly salted.[28] In the 1920s, klondiking was an important feature of the winter herring fishery in the Hebrides and German trawlers ran with boxes of fish from Stornoway to Altona, over 79,000 barrels crossing the North Sea in this way in the peak year of 1927.[29]

The new breed of klondiker was somewhat different. They began to operate in November 1977 when vessels from eastern Europe, unable to fish for mackerel in the British 200-mile zone, were circumventing their exclusion by buying catches directly from British boats. The EC was quick to point out that it was subverting fishing controls in the North Sea and undermining any Soviet/EC agreements on access to stocks but this did not halt it happening. Nine klondikers, some of them over 13,000 tons, were present in Cornish waters in December 1977, and the fishing boats were selling them mackerel according to a quota system of 3.5 tons per day per crewman.[30] Two-thirds of the mackerel being caught in British waters by the end of the 1970s were being sold to klondikers waiting outside the 12-mile limit. In February 1981, concern was expressed by the Scottish Office over klondikers but later that year the foreign fleet of factory ships was in Loch Broom in large numbers. Signs began to appear in Ullapool shops to say that Russian was spoken here. The Russian, East German, Bulgarian, even Egyptian, ships – large, ungainly, streaked with rust – anchored in the loch under the green Highland braes to buy from the Scottish fishing boats and process the catch onboard. The pursers could not resist the high prices being offered by the klondikers' agents, sometimes as much as double the price they could hope to earn in quayside auction. Mooring alongside a klondiker and transferring the catch through the factory ship's powerful suction pumps took only an hour or so, compared with the several hours needed to tie up and discharge ashore. There was a risk that the fishermen were being cheated – a catch discharged ashore was weighed exactly whereas the tonnage sucked into a klondiker could only be estimated – but this did not deter many. Tom Ralston reckoned that the weights of fish transferred to klondikers could be under-estimated and the fishermen consequently underpaid by as much as 30 per cent.[31]

At this time, however, most fishermen, if asked, might have pinpointed the Common Fisheries Policy as the main problem with which they had to contend. The issues arising from Britain's joining of the European Community was a major concern of the blockaders in 1975, the first of their list of six points on which they demanded some response from the government. They wanted renegotiation of the EC policy before the Referendum on British membership. Their second point was on the related issue of how much of British territorial waters would be reserved exclusively for British fishermen.

In November 1976, the EC was still hoping that a reduced fleet of British trawlers would be able to fish in Icelandic waters, ironically at the same time as fears were being expressed over the numbers of Soviet and eastern European vessels operating in EC waters. In the Fishery Limits Bill, laid before the House of Commons in November, the British government followed the example of the Icelanders in extending British territorial limits to 200 miles. Licensing for foreign vessels was to be introduced and there was to be a general crackdown on poaching by foreign vessels, with the maximum fine for a summary conviction being set at £50,000. The new limit came into force at midnight on 1 January 1977. Icelandic vessels were now banned from British waters. The Soviets, fellow-members of the EC, and a few other nationalities, including Norwegians, Faroese, Finlanders, Portuguese, Spanish and Swedish, were to be allowed access at a reduced level for a three-month period, during which it was hoped, particularly in the case of Soviet vessels, to negotiate reciprocal agreements. The new 200-mile limit, or half the distance to a neighbouring nation where the distance between countries was less than 400 miles, increased the extent of British territorial waters from 30,000 to 270,000 square miles. Interestingly, Canada extended her limits to 200 miles at the same time. The new area of British sea was divided into four zones, to be patrolled by the Royal Navy, Nimrod aircraft and fishery protection vessels of DAFS, but there was some dispute over whether the naval vessels were up to the task, especially as the new 'Island' class of patrol vessel, described as being equivalent to an armed trawler, had no helicopters and, at 16 knots, were slower than many of the trawlers they might have to catch.

In Aberdeen the trawlers were having to compete for crews with a new industry, as George Wood relates:

> When oil came, the town and the harbour just saw pound signs in front of their eyes and, apart from one Bailie McGee, who wanted to stand up and preserve old Torry – he was just shoved into the background, there was no way in the early 1970s they were going to preserve old Torry. The piers and quays were modernised. As the oil boom was starting in the early 1970s, some of the fishermen who were getting old or fed up with the hours found the oil jobs attractive. Being away fourteen days didn't bother a fisherman – he was accustomed to hard work day and night for fourteen days anyway. They took jobs such as firewatching. A lot of fishermen went off there, not immediately but once they saw the lie of the land and saw what the oil companies were needing, they went. They often got jobs as riggers because they were good at splicing steel warps, which many people couldn't do on 3-in. steel wire on a rolling boat. They got good jobs. Maybe in a fortnight out there [on the North Sea], they were working

ten-hour shifts – even twelve hours didn't bother them – they got ten hours off, in a bed, the best of food, regular times, the best of wages – all so unusual for them. The trawlers suffered with them going, they weren't being replaced. The trawlers started going away with crews with no experience, they really weren't suitable – in the mid-1970s, the companies found it wasn't economical, if they couldn't get crews to really work the trawlers. The Aberdeen trawler fleet declined then – maybe over ten years, from the early 1970s to the early 1980s. The only way you could carry on was to get genuine fishermen, experienced, and keep away from the toerags.

Altogether the Aberdeen fleet shrank from eighty-one to fifty-six vessels[32] but new trawlers were still appearing from the yards. The stern trawler *Grampian Chieftain* was launched in January 1977. Her sister ship, the *Grampian Monarch*, had done most of her first year's fishing in Icelandic waters, one of the few Aberdeen boats there during the Cod Wars, and in 1974 had been the city's top earning trawler, grossing about £280,000.[33] The White Fish Authority issued a gloomy report in June 1977, summarising how the British fishing fleet had diminished. Although English ports were the most badly hit, since 1974 Granton had lost fouteen trawlers and had only seven left, and the port's last trawler firm finally closed its doors in October 1978.[34] The number of full-time fishermen in Britain fell by over 10 per cent in the mid-1970s and the full British trawler fleet fell from almost 500 boats in 1974, the largest fleet in Europe, to fewer than 150 in early 1980.[35]

The countries in the European Community staggered acrimoniously and slowly towards the formation of a Common Fisheries Policy during the 1970s. Britain had most of the fish stocks and most of the fishermen but vested interests in the other eight member nations fought long and hard, and with some measure of success, to keep a hold on access rights. The EC issued its fisheries policy document in February 1976 in which it put forward the idea of national coastal fishing zones up to 12 miles wide within a Community-wide territorial sea out to a 200-mile limit. Within this area quotas would be scientifically worked out and assigned to the member states on the basis of existing catches. Member states would be free to trade quotas among themselves. Britain, Ireland and Denmark already had a 12-mile limit, the other member states still having a 6-mile limit. The EC policy also stated that loss of fishermen's incomes resulting from the limit changes would be compensated for from Community funds.

There was a general feeling in the fishing communities that the British government did not care about their industry. Trawlers no longer with access to the Icelandic grounds were trying to catch fish in less distant waters but half of them were being laid up or scrapped. In an article in *The Times*, Hugh Clayton expressed the view that the government had shown itself not to be committed to supporting fishing and contrasted its stance on agriculture.[36] A hundred Scottish fishermen and supporters promised to demonstrate in

Brussels in May 1977 while the EC was debating the fisheries. Britain was seeking a 50-mile exclusive zone for her own fleet but the EC did not accept this proposal, suggesting instead that there were alternative ways to deal with the 'vital needs of local populations' dependent on fishing. No one could be exact about what these alternative ways might be and the French were still supporting the principle of free fishing for all 'right up to the beaches'. Britain relaxed the call for a 50-mile exclusive zone in June 1977 and asked instead for a zone of 'dominant preference' whereby British boats would get first crack at stocks between 12 and 50 miles offshore, with EC and non-EC vessels being allowed to fish for any surplus.

In February 1978, the EC Commissioner for Fisheries appealed to the British government not to persist in blocking the evolution of a CFP. John Silkin, Minister of Agriculture and Fisheries, who is still remembered among the fishermen as being genuinely concerned about their interests, wanted guaranteed 'dominant preference' for British vessels within a 50-mile zone and argued that the conservation measures proposed were minimal. Silkin wanted a 12-mile zone reserved exclusively to British vessels and the zone between 12 and 50 miles as a preferential zone. There was deadlock over mesh sizes. British fishermen accused their European colleagues of switching nets at sea and evading mesh-size regulations, and they wanted restrictions put on the catching for industrial purposes of species fit for human consumption. In June 1978, the EC was not too happy when Silkin announced that an increase in mesh sizes was to be imposed on all vessels fishing in UK waters.

The EC tried twice in 1978 to reach agreement on a CFP. The Community's vision of a truly common policy in which the grounds would be open equally to all members was not acceptable to the British government in whose waters most of the fish swam. The Tory Party in opposition criticised the proposed CFP: John Peyton, John Silkin's shadow minister, said, 'The total allowable catch is to be parcelled out according to criteria which – I choose my words carefully and do not wish to exaggerate – seem to us to have been rigged to suit almost every country save the United Kingdom.'[37]

In May 1979, the newly elected Tory government set out what it expected from a CFP. Peter Walker, the new Minister, had similar views to those of his predecessor, John Silkin, insisting that ' ... a revised policy must provide a comprehensive policy on conservation; an adequate zone of exclusive access; a further considerable area of preferential access; a control system which enables member states to police their own waters; and a very substantial share of the total allowable catch for the UK.'[38]

The British fishermen were consistently suspicious of the behaviour of their fellow Europeans and their fears were not dissipated by what they saw happening on the ocean. For example, in April 1978 a Belgian skipper had been fined at Dover for fishing with undersized mesh, and a few months later a Spanish skipper was fined £16,000 at Plymouth for breaking the

200-mile limit in the south-west. The Spaniards were seen as being partic-ularly likely to ignore fishery legislation. In August 1979 a Spanish trawler was chased for 350 miles down the west coast, ignoring the signals from the cruiser *Westra* when she was challenged off St Kilda and finally being intercepted by the frigate HMS *Ambuscade* and escorted into Campbeltown.

The fishermen saw that European governments were doing something to support their home fleets. The French provided fuel subsidies, the Danes and Germans helped the reduction of the fleets by supporting decommis-sioning, the Dutch subsidised modernisation, but the British government was widely seen as caring nothing for the fishermen and as making matters worse by allowing the importing of cheap fish to undercut prices in the home markets. Even Icelandic boats were selling cod in English ports at very low prices because the cold stores back home were filled to capacity. The importing of lobsters from Canada provoked fishermen in the Hebrides to sail into the rocket firing range off Benbecula and to stay there for most of the day on 2 July 1980. In February 1981 Peter Walker appealed to the fishermen to end blockades and other action protesting against the dumping of cheap foreign fish and agreed to set up a working party to investigate allegations of unfair importing. Some skippers decided to go on strike, to stay at the quayside because it wasn't worth their while to put to sea.

The future of the Scottish fishing fleet did not appear overly bright in the mid-1970s at the time of the blockade but fishermen are nothing if not resilient and the ensuing years had brought renewed hopes and growth in some aspects. The total value of port landings in Scotland fell to £59 million in 1975, from the £64 million of the previous year, but as 1976 began catches and prices both started to rise again to such effect that the value of that year's catch reached almost £86 million. In the late 1970s there was a surge in the building of new boats in the middle size range – between 30 ft and 79 ft – when about 190 were laid down.[39] Better safety rules were established and there were continual developments in design and gear. Some skippers now began to have their new boats built in European yards.

The newer vessels were built with greater beam and greater draught than their predecessors. This larger hull volume improved the living and working conditions aboard and made for good stability to counter the increasing topweight from machinery and superstructure. Care was taken to meet new regulations concerning freeboard introduced in 1981. With shelterdecks now covering three-quarters or more of the working deck space, the boats were being equipped to fish further off in deeper water for longer periods and to be able to choose between different types of gear for pelagic or demersal fish. Hatches and doors were set in the shelterdeck structure to enable gear to be shot and hauled without the crew needing to go on to the exposed deck housing. Boats were thus able to continue fishing in rougher seas. By the mid-1980s vessels were being built with complete shelterdecks.

The seiners and trawlers were now looking further and further west to find new grounds and daring the elements in their pursuit of fish. The Wick boat *Boy Andrew* (WK 171) set a new record in 1982 with a total catch of white fish for the year worth £600,000 gross. Norrie Bremner had named his new boat after his son, Andrew, who was now her skipper at the age of twenty-three. The *Boy Andrew* had been built in 1979 in Campbeltown Shipyard, an 87-ft steel vessel, capable of fishing in the stormy Atlantic to the west of the Hebrides as far as Rockall. Just before Hogmanay in 1982 the *Boy Andrew* slipped from her berth in Scrabster to make another record-breaking trip. To the west of Orkney the crew shot their nets in seas heaving under the strength of gales gusting up to Force 11. The *Boy Andrew* in many ways typified the modern Scottish fleet. The ten men in the crew were all, except one, in their twenties. They were tough, determined to work round

The *Boy Andrew* (WK 170) in Wick 1997.

the clock if necessary, to make a go of it. They had to fight to control the nets, full to bursting point, and bring them aboard. From Orkney they sailed to the Bressay bank to fish some more. On 5 January the *Boy Andrew* landed over £45,000 worth of white fish in Peterhead. Her engineer recorded the record-breaking voyage on his camcorder; copies of the video became favourite home viewing in many Caithness households.

In 1985 the Bremners had a new *Boy Andrew* (WK 170) built in Campbeltown at a reported cost of £1,200,000.[40] Her namesake and predecessor was re-christened the *Opportune*, a tribute by Norrie Bremner to a long-standing friend, the Buckie fisherman, George Murray, who always gave his boats that name. A detailed description of her machinery would be out of place here but a few facts will give an impression of the power of the fishing vessels of her time. The new *Boy Andrew* was 87 ft long and 24 ft 7 in. in beam; her main engine provided 690 hp at 425 rpm. The fuel tanks held 25,800 litres of diesel, and her fishroom had a capacity of around 200 cubic metres. Crew comfort, at least when off watch, was not neglected: each man had a bunk with a reading light and the galley had a full range of appliances.

CHAPTER TEN

SAVING
THE FISH

Total *Allowable* Catch

The present form of the Common Fisheries Policy (CFP) of the European Community came into force in January 1983 and it can be safely stated that very few fishermen have been happy with it since. 'A sense of independence has always been the hallmark of fishermen,' admits an EC publication on the CFP, acknowledging that they would like to be free to hunt where they like, before going on to argue that 'Such behaviour is no longer economically, nor legally, possible'.[1] The problems with the CFP arise from the fact that the available fish stocks are not large enough to allow free-for-all access. The number of fishermen in the member states varies enormously from country to country: Spain and Portugal have around 85,000 and 38,500 respectively, while Britain has around 24,200.[2] Belgium, Denmark, France, Germany, Ireland and The Netherlands also have significant numbers of fishermen with access to the North Sea and the North Atlantic.

The CFP actually comprises four separate but interrelated policies.[3] Two of these deal with marketing and international relations and have had little direct effect on the Scottish fleet. The third, the structural policy, has been in operation since 1970 and has been concerned with funding the restructuring of fishing fleets throughout the Community. Grants for building new boats, replacing old ones and improving shore handling facilities were made available and in the years after 1970 the size of the EC's fishing capacity grew tremendously: the total tonnage of the fleet nearly trebled between 1970 and 1993, from 794,000 to over 1,940,000 gross registered tons, the Scottish fleet benefitting along with those of her neighbours. This increase in fishing capacity has had, of course, enormous implications for what is commonly thought of, and criticised, now as the CFP – the fourth policy, that concerned with conservation.

A basic principle of the EC – that discrimination on grounds of nationality is not allowed in access to fishing grounds – has been relaxed since 1973 when Britain, Ireland and Denmark joined. Coastal waters up to a limit of 6 miles were reserved for local fishermen; this zone was extended

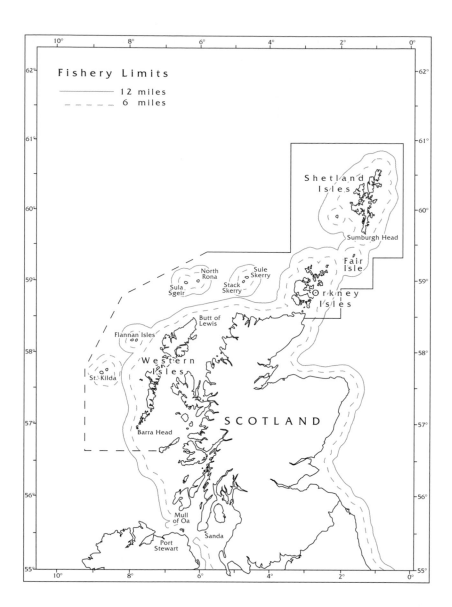

to 12 miles in 1983 to 'protect the traditional fishing rights of coastal fishermen ... [and] ensure fishing remains an essential part of the local economy'. This rule is of vital significance to much of Scotland. The 6- and 12-mile lines do not follow the coast exactly but swing out to the west of the Hebrides with further exclusive zones around St Kilda, the Flannans, Sulisgeir and other rocks. Shetland, Orkney and Fair Isle are enclosed in the so-called Shetland Box, an extensive zone around the northern islands, which some hope can be extended to the west of the Hebrides and possibly to the Moray Firth. 'It has a management system in addition to that of the UK 12-mile limit. Within the Box fishing by white fish boats over 26 metres is limited by licence. That's something we fought long and hard for in the early days of the EC and we obtained it,' explained John Goodlad of the Shetland Fishermen's Association. 'It has been of benefit to Shetland by preventing a concentration of foreign vessels in these waters. The Dutch and the Danes have no licences for the Box. When the CFP was reviewed in 1992 we put a lot of effort into protecting the Box, lobbying for months in Brussels, and the result was that the Box was retained.' On the east coast the limits follow the coast more closely but the inner part of the Moray Firth, and the Firths of Tay and Forth are counted as within the 12-mile zone. Based on their traditional fishing activities, four countries – France, Germany, Ireland and Norway – have access to parts of the zone between 6 and 12 miles. Certain areas outside the 12-mile limit are also subject to restrictions, but in essence the territorial sea of the EC is open to all vessels belonging to the EC member states.

The CFP uses the concept of quotas to share out the fish catch among the member states. This is done according to the principle of 'relative stability': the share-out is based on the track records of each country's fishing practices. Adjustments to protect the interests of regions the EC recognises as having a special dependency on fishing are made according to agreed rules, such as those of the so-called Hague Preferences. The British have historically liked to eat haddock and this is reflected in a high percentage of the North Sea haddock being recognised as Britain's share of the stock, whereas the share of the catch of saithe, less popular as food, is much lower. 'The UK always gets 78 per cent of the North Sea haddock, 58 per cent of the mackerel, and so on,' explained John Goodlad. 'We know our share but we don't know our tonnage. Shetland then gets a share of the UK quota – about 10 per cent for white fish, 25 per cent for mackerel, the high shares being an indication of the importance of Shetland in the UK context.'

The EC's own scientists and those in the International Council for the Exploration of the Sea give annual estimates of the size of the stock of the most important species of fish; these figures are used to determine the Total Allowable Catch (TAC) for each species. (The CFP, like so many of the EC's policies, is liberally endowed with technical acronyms.) The TACs are then subjected to debate and negotiation, and are shared out, usually after much wrangling and horse-trading, between the member states so that each country is awarded a share of the total, the annual quota, that the fishermen are allowed to land. About 100 species are subject to this annual share-out which is announced at the end of December. Some of the British quotas for 1998 are shown in Table 1.[4]

A quota on sand-eels was imposed for the first time in 1998; Britain's 20,000 tonnes represents about 2 per cent of the TAC of 960,000 tonnes, the bulk of which was awarded to Denmark who has, in the face of many years of controversy, caught sand-eels for industrial purposes.

The CFP tries to match fishing capacity to fish stocks in a number of ways other than fixing TACs. An important part of the structural policy has been the series of Multi Annual Guidance Programmes (MAGPs) which sets out targets for fleet sizes; under this policy, for example, fishing boats are decommissioned, an ironic admission that the enthusiasm with which fleets were encouraged to expand in the 1970s and 1980s was wrongly

TABLE 1

Sea area	Species	British quota for 1998
North Sea	herring	38,910 tonnes
	cod	58,740
	haddock	66,000
	whiting	27,415
	saithe	7790
	sand-eel	20,000
Firth of Clyde	herring	1000
West coast of Scotland	herring	46,360
	cod	5520

placed. The numbers of boats allowed to catch fish are limited by the issue of fishing licences. These were introduced for all EU vessels in January 1995. Skippers also have to keep a logbook with detailed records of the fish they catch and land. Further management of the fishing effort is achieved through such technical measures as regulations on mesh size and the construction of fishing gear.[5]

Black fish

As long as people have been catching fish there seem to have been reports of what could be termed overfishing. Examples can be found in records stretching back over the last two centuries. For instance, in 1820, it was observed of the Shetland cod smack fishery: 'the extent of the Cod Banks … has been greatly overrated and their productiveness consequently misunderstood'.[6] Lobsters seem to have become severely depleted through overfishing in the Peterhead area in the 1790s, forcing men to seek them further west.[7] At Nairn, at that time, it was recorded that 'fish of all kinds are much scarcer since 1782' and the linemen were having to go as far as the Caithness coast to catch them, forcing the price up from 3d a score twenty-five years before to 1s 6d or 2s 6d a score.[8] There are various references to white fish being scarce on the east coast, for example in St Andrews Bay in the early 1790s, but this may have been due to other factors such as shifts in the migratory routes of the fish: 'Haddock, which for some years had disappeared, have this spring been found again in considerable quantities,' wrote the minister of Cockburnspath.[9] In 1865, James Bertram found Newhaven fishermen who believed that the haddock in the Firth of Forth had been 'all eaten up'. The boats were having to go further, a night's voyage, to find them. In his time he also heard 'whispers' that the

Newfoundland cod stocks were almost exhausted. The general view persisted, however, that the sea was an inexhaustible source of food.

Although naturalists explained changes in fish stocks in terms of migratory behaviour, ideas often based more on armchair theorising than hard evidence, there were also many folk-beliefs to account for the mysterious appearance and disappearance of shoals. In St Monans the kirk bell used to be silenced during the herring season as its tolling was held to scare the fish from the bay. Gunfire was also stated to frighten shoals away from their usual haunts, and after the battle of Copenhagen herring were said to have fled the Baltic. In the Hebrides, kelp burning was blamed for driving away fish. The railways, too, were blamed for overfishing by some, as the new ease with which fish could be shifted and marketed throughout the country encouraged extra fishing effort and the landing of more perishable fish than could easily have been disposed of in the earlier days of walking and horse and cart.

There can be no doubt, however, that overfishing takes place. No population of fish, no matter how prolific or fecund they are, can withstand indefinitely the assault on their numbers from a predator equipped with modern fishing gear. The fishing effort of modern vessels can be relentless. Many have two skippers who alternate in command and duplicate crews, so that the boat is never in port for longer than necessary. William Anderson described to me how Shetland trawlers have a double crew, half working one week, half the next week. 'There are eight in the crew and four work at a time,' he said. 'The crews are too small and it's bad for conservation. Sizeable fish are being dumped because there's no crew to gut them before they're landed. In my day we thought a crew should number seven. We gutted by hand but all the boats have gutting machines now. They have better washing facilities – they gut into a trough with a continuous stream of water. A boat can land on Monday in Lerwick, takes on stores, and come on Monday afternoon by Whalsay to exchange crews for the next week.'

Fishery regulations have in the past generally been enacted more for economic than ecological benefit. They were designed to control access to fish stocks and prevent conflicts between groups of fishermen. For many years it was the general rule that trawling and seining were not allowed inside the 3-mile limit, where the creel fishermen could set their static gear without interference. Some fishermen, however, were always willing to poach, to shoot a net inside the limit.

> We used to poach in Reiss Bay [a Wick fisherman told me]. The boat was underpowered, and it was hard to compete outside. On poor days we were often in the Bay. The Baptist minister came to the house and said to my father, 'John, I believe you're doing something you shouldn't be doing. You're a member of the Baptish Church and it's illegal what you're doing.' 'Well, I must tell you this,' said my father, 'I have a wife and family, the engine is underpowered and the boat is

undersized, so when I'm unable to fish outside I fish in Reiss Bay. It doesn't say in the Bible that you aren't supposed to fish in Reiss Bay, so I'll fish there if it suits me.'

Responsibility for enforcement of fishery regulations has fallen over the years on the shoulders of various official bodies. In 1808 it was first assigned to the Commissioners of the White Herring Fishery but they soon began to share fishery protection duties with the Royal Navy. The Commissioners were reconstituted as the Fishery Board for Scotland in 1882 and given the power to create and implement by-laws for regulation of the fishing in twenty-six districts around the coast, each of which was assigned a fishery officer in overall charge. Since the late 1880s a succession

The fishery protection vessel *Suliskeir* in heavy seas off Shetland.

of fishery protection vessels have been deployed, all of which became very familiar to fishermen. The *Ulva* and the *Longa*, for example, built in 1943 and 1944, were coal burning and were known as the 'smoky joes'. There is a story that they belched such thick smoke on getting up steam that they had to use their radar to find the way out of harbour – no doubt apocryphal, although there were complaints against them for dirtying washing and curtains. These outdated boats were got rid of in the 1970s. The Department of Agriculture and Fisheries for Scotland (DAFS) took over from the Fisheries Board in 1961. At that time there were eight 'cruisers', as the protection vessels were universally known, in the Scottish fleet, assisted by minesweepers from the Royal Navy. DAFS also operated a number of fishery research vessels.[10] In 1991 the Secretary of State set up the Scottish Fisheries Protection Agency (SFPA), the body now charged with enforcing fishery regulations. The SFPA has four offshore patrol vessels, several inshore vessels and two aircraft on continual patrol on the 185,000 square miles of territorial sea, and twenty-two offices around the coast where staff monitor fish landings and ensure adherence to fishery regulations.[11]

Poaching in the old days is remembered as being a battle of wits between the fishermen and the cruisers and there are plenty of stories about these encounters that convey a certain innocence over what almost everyone would agree was law-breaking only of a technical kind. David John Mackenzie told me of one incident: 'One foggy day in Reiss Bay, we didn't know that on one end of the fog bank the cruiser was at anchor. The Noss Head lighthousemen said it was the best thing they ever saw – us fishing at one end of the bank and the cruiser at the other. Reiss Bay was a good bay – there were big hauls of haddies there. Inshore fishermen complained about their creels being destroyed but I can't recall any ever informing on the seiner skippers they knew well.' For a boat to be charged with poaching she had to be caught in the act or identified as being guilty with corroborating evidence. To avoid detection, a boat could douse all lights, even to the extent of shading the compass and using hand torches, to shoot within the limit. Attempts might be made to disguise a boat's identity, although this did not always work. Gordon Fraser told me about Aberdeen men who used a paste of flour and water to stick newspapers over the boat's name so that they could try for whiting inshore; unfortunately when they sailed into port with their catch they forgot to remove the sheets of newspaper and 'it wasn't hard to know what they'd been doing'. The fishermen, of course, kept each other informed over the radio of the positions of the cruisers. Fish carry no indication of where they were caught and once the nets were hauled and the boat was safely outside the 3-mile boundary there were no restrictions on landing.

In the old days, the fishery protection service was staffed largely by men from the fishing communities themselves. There was a common understanding, a sharing of risk – the cruiser *Freya* foundered in heavy seas off Sarclett Head, Caithness, in January 1959 and three men, including the captain, were lost.[12] Cephas Ralph, the SFPA Area Manager for the north of Scotland, is from a fishing family in Lossiemouth. He went to sea with his father on the *Fame* (INS 56) from the age of about eight every summer and Easter holiday, working mainly in the Clyde and from Kinlochbervie and Lochinver, seine netting and later trawling, before going to university to study electronics and then deciding to go back to sea. In 1981 he applied to be a fishery officer and served for a number of years in Peterhead, Oban and Shetland, with promotions through the grades until he reached his present post.

The CFP TAC system sets an upper limit on the amount of fish any vessel can land. It is, however, not at all easy to stay within the TAC limits at sea. When a skipper hauls a trawl net, he has only a vague idea of what is in the bag. If he has already reached his quota on, say, cod, what is he to do with the cod he has just caught? The law forbids them to be landed in port. The choice is starkly clear – throw them back, although they are already dead, or try to land them anyway as 'black fish'.

Dramatic reports of black fish landings have appeared from time to time in the press.[13] The image they present is of a fishing boat slipping in the dark into a small harbour, of a lorry reversing without lights on to a quay, of men in quiet haste winching box after box of illegal fish ashore, all ending with a few quiet words and a silent departure into the night. Through its very nature, it is impossible to be certain of the extent of black fishing. The illegal landings appear in no logbook. The buyers need fish to keep their processing plants working to capacity and it is tempting to buy black fish at a lower price. Fishery officers check landings but their movements are observed and word passed on when the coast is clear. It has been estimated that as much as a quarter of the fish landed is illegal but this is almost certainly an exaggeration. 'There are possibly black fish landings here [in Shetland] but it's on a small scale,' said William Anderson. 'Possibly saithe. This was considered a useless fish before – nobody here took it – but the Europeans take it, and the local boats are allowed something like 15 per cent as a by-catch. Apart from that there's very little black fish.'

The older fishermen were a very moral group of men and for many of them the dilemma presented by the CFP was too much. They had the choice of discarding extra fish or landing it; the former seemed a terrible waste, an unacceptable act in return for the sea's bounty and the labour and skill they expended in reaping it, and the latter turned them into criminals. In 1990 the editor of the *Fishing News*, Tim Oliver, quoted the words of a Scots skipper: 'It's impossible for a skipper with a boat over 80 ft to stay viable now without breaking at least one of the three main rules: misreporting, using a smaller mesh or making illegal landings. Impossible on the quotas we have now.'[14] The only way out for some was to give up the sea altogether.

Sandy Hepburn works now as a janitor but twenty-five years before I spoke to him he had passed his skipper's exams.

> I enjoyed the fishing until the last few years when quotas came in and it got political, and to make an honest living was just about impossible [he said]. Between that, and no home life. When I went to sea, everybody came home for the weekend – big catch or small catch – but the weekend fishing came in more and more and nowadays the trips are ten days at a time. The boats come in, four lads jump ashore, four lads jump on – like another half-crew – and the boat turns around and goes away to sea. There are two skippers, working twenty days on and ten days off. I gave it up altogether. Well, I was a bit sorry but I was fed up with it. A lot of lads have given it up and gone offshore on the oil rigs and there's a lot of fishermen on the stand-by boats –they are a month on and a month off but they know what they're doing. At the fishing, planning anything was very difficult, even for a Saturday. There was a lot of pressure on the men in the last few years – if you've a new boat, there's a lot of pressure.
>
> The boats can't live on quotas – everybody knows that. They are

trying to get round them and the authorities are turning a blind eye. At the herring you had to put in the amount you estimated you had aboard – you were really only allowed 20 per cent out. Then you had to make an entry of the exact amount that was landed. Two different entries for every landing. That was every day. The white fish log book was filled up once a week. It was handed in to the Fishery Office at the port you were working from. But the fishery officers came down and dipped your tanks to see what you had aboard. I got on very well with the officers – they knew what the fishermen were up against and lots of times they took a lenient view, provided you didn't just go overboard.

Alex Buchan in Peterhead said that many of the younger men saw the CFP regulations as a game and had no moral problems in finding a way around them. Other fishermen have struggled on but have found the stress too much. Faced with complying with CFP regulations and still earning enough to pay the men and repay the loans taken out to cover the costs of a new boat, several young skippers have had to seek medical help. As William West, who retired from the sea some years ago, explained:

> There's terrific strain and stress with these new rules. All this they're up against now. Some of the rules are sensible but the most of them are made up by men who don't know what they're speaking about. A 78-ft fishing boat cost £1.2 million in the early 1990s – the loans came from banks and other sources but it's all got to be paid back. The government is willing to help with the interest. Young men, all in their thirties, are attending hospital because they are cracking up under the strain. To go out into the North Sea there, to get a living out of the sea, is bad enough in itself. There's enough to contend with. It's hard enough finding fish but the hardest bit is the thought of coming back in and landing. You're coming with so much fish above your quota. The fishery officer will be there. Some fellows it doesn't appear to affect too badly and some fellows wouldn't be affected whatever happened, but most men I know are really finding it hard. They're struggling.

For all the grumbles, the SFPA statistics make it clear that the majority of fishermen still adhere to conservation laws. Only a small percentage of the almost 3000 boardings at sea and the many hours of inspection in ports by the SFPA result in the detection of infringements and prosecution in the courts. There is now, however, an increased antagonism between the fishery officers and fishermen. 'That wasn't there when I started,' said Cephas Ralph, 'but on a one-to-one basis our officers still get on well with fishermen. The potential exists for things to go badly wrong in specific instances but in general there is a good working relationship day to day. But we can't not do what we have to do.'

The fishermen also find themselves at odds with the scientific community from time to time in debates over the true size of fish stocks. Assessing fish populations is extremely difficult and establishing what percentage of a population can be removed and still leave a viable breeding nucleus is a very inexact business, particularly as human predation – fishing – is only one of a range of factors affecting the fish. It is not surprising that scientists tend to err on the side of caution but fishermen find this very frustrating. They know the importance of sustaining fish stocks but, at the same time, the evidence of their own eyes seems to contradict the scientists' conclusions.

According to Dr Nick Lake of Highland Council Development Department:

Fisheries research is under-funded and therefore the information

Various inshore boats in Wick in 1997.

available to Brussels is incomplete or not available at all. Much more basic research needs to be done on stocks. Fishermen on a day-to-day basis know what's out there. They know if there's a lot of cod but no haddock, or a lot of plaice but no megrim. The present system does not allow them to report these variations because the quotas are fixed. If quotas are fixed too low, they are being prevented from catching a lot of one species, for example they could be catching tons of cod but they have to discard it all or land black fish. The fish are already dead, so it makes no sense from a conservation point of view. We need a system whereby fishermen can feed catch information to scientists to be taken into account in stock assessment.

At present, boats over 12m keep a logbook and report all their landings. For boats under 10m, reporting is done on a voluntary basis in some areas but not at all in others. This is a huge problem. Also there is no requirement to report discards. It would be a good idea to do this but the system does not encourage fishermen to report faithfully. If he's catching a lot that has to be discarded, could he be accused of fishing for the wrong species? Although discarding works very well in single-species fisheries, most fisheries, especially for white fish, are mixed. The pelagic fishery for herring is very species specific: the big pursers can catch nothing other than herring or mackerel although problems can arise over the presence of juvenile herring or juveniles of other industrial species, but you can take juvenile herring as a by-catch in fishing for sand-eels. Reporting discards is important but it has to be done in a legal framework that does not penalise the fisherman. At the moment scientists estimate what they think may have been discarded – it's a broad-brush approach and takes no account of variation in discarding from week to week or even from day to day.

Many of the problems associated with over-fishing arise from marketing.

> The industry is market-led [said Dr Lake]. It doesn't matter if cod are scarce this week – if the market wants cod, you've got to find cod, and if you don't find it it will be imported into the UK. The market is dominant. Perhaps it hasn't been given enough credence in the industry. In the past catches were sold on the quayside on a take-it or leave-it basis. But now the consumer is king. Unless you supply what the consumer wants, there's no point in catching it. No supermarket chain is prepared to have one of its ready-made dishes go off the shelves on a weekly basis. The public has to be educated to accept variety of species. A key Scottish market is Spain where people eat a much wider variety of species.

The old-fashioned fishmonger was better placed to respond to changes in fish catches and the fishwife with her creel was more responsible in the ecological sense than the present fish-processing industry. The fishfinger was invented to overcome the British household's dislike of the unfamiliar. The *Fairtry* was launched in 1953 from John Lewis's yard in Aberdeen as the world's first stern-trawling factory ship but the frozen cod she brought back from the Grand Banks was difficult to sell as the freezing process turned the fish flesh a discouraging brown colour. The colour disappeared on cooking, hence the brainwave of turning frozen fish into fishfingers to make them acceptable to the public.[15]

Fishermen are discouraged from responding to natural changes in fish stocks by the existing CFP rules on track records.

> The system is flawed in that, if a quota exists for a species and you don't catch it, you lose your track record [said Dr Lake]. Track records are done on a three-year basis. If you lose your track record, you can't have it restored. Fishermen may be forced to hunt haddock, when

they know they're not there, to maintain their track record. This also leads to false declaration of landings – they are marked up to maintain track records or transferred to other species, for example landing 20 ton of cod but calling it 20 ton of whiting. Track record procedure is an EU ruling but the UK government has its own management of track records. It is difficult to see how to allocate quotas without track records. The quota system is very flawed, right from stock assessment to allocation between vessels. Fishermen are constantly criticised for fishing stocks under pressure but the system dictates that if they don't do that they will lose out. What can the man do? He has to play the game if he is to pay for his boat, his mortgage, and so on, but the game at the moment criminalises most fishermen. He has to break the law to survive. The crazy thing is that in 1996 there was a huge

The *William Henry II* (DH 5) of Dartmouth, Devon, and the *Vandal* (LK 337) from Shetland tied up at Ullapool, April 1998.

population of saithe in the North Sea but the UK had no quota for saithe. Boats were catching tons of saithe but having to dump them because they had no quota to land. Because they had no quota they could not build up a track record.

In Shetland, John Goodlad gave me his view on another aspect of conservation that has appeared in recent years:

The agendas of both the fishing industry and the environmental movement are identical – we both want a healthy marine ecosystem – but relations have got off to a bad start because some environmental organisations are often more interested in their own media profile and the soundbite than in science. One of the challenges over the next ten years is to build up a good working relationship with the responsible parts of the environmental movement. A good example: the sand-eel fishery in Shetland was very controversial in the early

1980s. But it has been reopened in the last few years on a tightly controlled basis, limited by quota to 3000 tonnes, limited to boats less than 20 m, and limited by season – and this has been done through co-operation between the Shetland fishermen and Scottish Natural Heritage. It has created a small sustainable fishery.

There are no fishermen in London

The older fishermen who have witnessed the changes in recent years speak with nostalgia about the old days.

Back in the 1970s it was commonplace to see from fifteen to thirty boats landing at Macduff here and the market full from end to end [said William West], but the better prices elsewhere led to landing in other ports. I would say the Macduff fleet is as big now as it was twenty years ago but it is like a garage here now – boats come in, get jobs done, if it's bad weather – a lot of them still come here at weekends but they land at Fraserburgh and Peterhead. The majority fish on the west coast. Scrabster is popular now. I was at sea for twenty-two years. I loved every year of it but now that love for the sea is kind of gone: if you ask one of the young men now, it's just a job – 'I want to make as much as I can but I've my time on and my time off.' We didn't take time off – we enjoyed the job.

Andrew Mearns was the last full-time fisherman in Ferryden. 'It's dying out in other places as well,' he said. 'There's a lot of one-man bands and I'm dead against it – folk going to the sea by themselves for clam fishing. It's very dangerous. There are very few boats out of Gourdon and small places north. I think there's one full-time man out of Johnshaven. In many places the pleasure craft have been taking precedence over the fishermen.'

The fear that today's fishermen, with high-tech gear chasing big money in the short-term, are cutting their own throats is widespread among the older generation. At the same time, there is an equally widespread opinion that the present system of TACs or quotas of the CFP is wrong-headed and damaging to the fishermen's interests. John Thomson spoke for many when he told me:

I would say now that if we had fears of what Europe was going to do to the fishing, they've been realised tenfold. Fish and fishing are the very essence of our being. We know that if we destroy stocks there will be no future. We've learned some very hard lessons in the last generation. Some fathers won't allow their sons to go through this. My two sons had a vessel and sold her – to me, that my sons are no longer fishermen strikes like a dagger to the heart. I hope they go back to the sea. Every forebear I know was a fisherman; it might end with my sons. It's very hard to accept. The old fishing communities were wonderful places. Hard work, and there was tragedy, but there were rewards and happy times in the community. A way of life is dying now. It will be retained but for how long I don't know in the main centres. We realise there's a European Union and we'll be a part of that, we're all for a single market because that's business, but we say the CFP has killed the UK fishing industry to a great extent.

In his book on the CFP, the late Mike Holden summarised it as having four major defects: it was not conceived as a coherent whole and it suffers from an internal contradiction between the structural and conservation policies, it has no specific objectives, it has been based on biological rather than economic considerations, and it is compromised through the decision-making process in the EU.[16]

All or some of these defects may be addressed when the CFP falls due for reform in the year 2002. A number of proposals have been put forward on how this might be done. Among these has been the idea of Individual Transferable Quotas (ITQs), whereby the right to fish for a particular species might be conferred on individuals as their property which they could then buy and sell. It is unlikely to be adopted by the EU on any scale, as experience with it in The Netherlands, where it has been applied to plaice and sole fisheries, has revealed that regulation has been very difficult. Strict enforcement would require designated ports and times of landing, and it would be impossible for a young man to make a start in the fishing without first buying, probably at great cost, the right to a particular stock.

Designated ports are being mooted also as an answer to the problem of black fish. It is likely that from July 1998 all fishing boats over 20m will have to land in Britain at one of a list of thirty-one designated ports;[17] for Scotland, there will be nineteen designated ports - the major ones listed in Table 2 – but not including, for example, Wick itself, Stromness, Arbroath, Macduff or any of the other smaller ports. Landing at a non-designated harbour will be allowed but prior notification of this intention must be made to the authorities. Designation will not apply to boats under 10m, at least in the first instance, but there is worry that it will be eventually extended to them. The application of these rules may spell doom for most of the smaller fishing harbours.

There is another fear: that, in 2002, the existing exclusive zones around the Scottish coast will be abolished and that a boat from any EU country will be able to fish anywhere, 'right up to the shore' in the phrase that chills the heart of the present fisherman. There is deep distrust of the extent to which skippers from other countries will respect local traditions. The fishermen also distrust the politicians. Although many Members of Parliament have fishermen in their constituencies, almost nowhere are they dependent on fishermen's votes. A few politicians in the past have been

SAVING THE FISH **225**

respected for their support of the fishing: in the 1930s, Robert, later Lord, Boothby, when he was MP for East Aberdeenshire, often spoke up on behalf of the fishermen, and in more recent times John Silkin MP and Alick Buchanan-Smith MP have been highly regarded. It was pointed out to me that, unlike Norway, Britain has no fisheries policy and support for British fishing interests in Europe has often been a matter of short-term expediency. The contrast with the level of support exerted on behalf of the farming sector has not escaped the fishermen's notice. In 1991, although the EC was offering large grants towards the cost, the Tory government refused to introduce a decommissioning scheme to reduce the size of the British fleet because it was not 'a sensible use of taxpayers' money'.[18] As John Thomson wryly observed to me, 'There are no fishermen in London.'

The issue of quota-hopping or flags of convenience has been of grave concern in recent years, especially since Spain and Portugal joined the EC in 1986. The Spanish fishing fleet is the largest in Europe, with about 85,000 fishermen, and the industry is of great importance in their national economy. Unfortunately the Continental Shelf is narrow in Spanish waters and their local fish stocks are mainly pelagic species such as sardines and tuna. Spanish and Portuguese boats have always been prominent in the Grand Banks cod fishery. Quota-hopping came about through British fishermen selling their fishing licences to agents acting on behalf of Spanish vessels.

> You might say British fishermen shouldn't sell their licences and track records [said John Thomson], but, if you've been fishing all your life, your assets are below your feet, you're not making it, you've got to get out and you're looking for a price, you don't ask the buyer the colour of his money. The bidders are agents – you don't know who's buying. Spain and The Netherlands have bought 20 per cent of the British quota from ourselves. The government can't eradicate quota hoppers. It'll grow, it's the system. We can't blame the Spaniards and the Dutch for buying the licences – it's the law that allows them. There is no instance of a British fisherman buying a Spanish licence. It's all one way. We've got the resource. In Spain they eat five times the amount of fish we do. We admire them as fishermen, we don't quarrel with them as fishermen, we have a quarrel with the politics of what's allowed.

Dr Nick Lake said that, if the British government had listened to their fishermen in the early days when licensing came in, it would have accepted that licences should not be transferable, have zero value and should revert to the government when expired. 'The government rejected these proposals because they were too complicated to manage,' said Dr Lake. 'We now have the situation where licences can be four to five times the value of the vessel, and this has led to quota hopping. It desperately needs to be resolved. We've shot ourselves in the foot. If it takes five years to resolve the quota-hopping issue, we have a real problem that faces no other country.'

Fishermen generally accept that fishing capacity has to be regulated to match the capacity of the fish stocks to support a sustained yield. How this might be done is the subject of fierce debate but in the last few years a vague consensus has been emerging in favour of a 'days-at-sea' scheme. The principle is that boats restrict their fishing and remain tied up for stipulated periods of time. In February 1991, a days-at-sea regime was made law by the EC for Fisheries Zones IV (the North Sea) and VII (the South-West Approaches and the English Channel), requiring boats over 10 m to remain in port for eight consecutive days each month. The restriction applied only to some boats, those that had caught over 100 tonnes of cod and haddock in the eighteen-month period between January 1989 and June 1990.[19] The

The *Clarnes* (INS 108) and the *Maranatha III* (UL 77) at Lochinver, April 1998.

scheme was shortlived and highly unpopular. Its application to part of the fleet was seen as unfair and the compulsory tie-up period resulted in some fishermen being forced to go to sea in times of bad weather to earn their living. After a year the rules were changed to allow a more flexible tie-up regime.[20] Compulsory tie-up was not renewed by the EU in 1993 because the Sea Fish (Conservation) Bill, passed in Westminster in 1992, allowed the British government to limit days at sea for all vessels in British waters and removed the need for legislation at the European level.

A flexible days-at-sea scheme whereby the fishermen could choose their own days to fish or stay at the quayside has some attraction. It would, say some of the older fishermen, merely regularise what used to happen anyway when bad weather and being in port every weekend punctuated the fishing routine.

Up to now Shetland has resisted days at sea [said John Goodlad]. I think days at sea, with the same number of days for each boat, would introduce economic inefficiencies, as new boats have to be worked as hard as possible. Any future days-at-sea scheme could take the form of a year's tally per boat. I think there must be some control of fishing effort. Once upon a time, in the days of sail and muscle, effort was limited. The technology now is awesome and there is no doubt that limits have to be set on fleet size. If we get the balance right.

Another idea to limit the assault on fish stocks is the setting up of 'no-take' areas. This has been done in New Zealand but there are doubts over whether it would be politically feasible in the EU. 'If North Sea areas are to be closed, they must be nursery areas,' argued John Goodlad. 'There is nothing worse than throwing back half the catch because it's under size. Mesh size regulations are not always effective, and even if the fish escape they probably die from stress.'

Within Scotland, the Scottish Fishermen's Federation (SFF), established in 1973 and having as members the main regional associations in the country, is the main body for representing the views of the industry to government. A few years ago, a smaller group, the Fishermen's Association Ltd (FAL), broke away from it to campaign for British withdrawal from the CFP. The SFF adheres to a policy of reforming the CFP from within. Apart from these there are a number of smaller, local groups which act to provide a common forum for debate and to present a united voice over fishery issues.

> These voluntary associations have tried to argue the case for management measures for their own areas [said Dr Lake], but they have no power. They negotiate with the Scottish Office to try to get things done but it's very slow and, to a large extent, ineffective. Highland Council has helped these associations in the Highlands and Islands to pull together and this has resulted in the formation of the West of 4 Fisheries Management Group. The name derives from the 4°W line of longitude, the boundary between Fisheries Zones IVA and VIA. The West of 4 Group is consulted by the Scottish Office over the implementation of fishery regulations.

Highland Council has a fisheries policy in recognition of the fact that fishing and fish farming account for 19 per cent of the region's exports, and that fishermen, albeit in many cases part-time, are a vital component of the small communities in the Highlands and Islands. Other local authorities in Scotland also have policies and schemes to support fishing. Fife and Angus Councils recognise the importance of the sea in their own economies, with over 400 men employed directly in fishing.[21] In the north-east the local authorities and industrial representatives have produced the Grampian Fisheries Strategy to deal with the impact of the CFP and the resulting socio-economic changes in that area.[22] Fish landings in Aberdeenshire and Moray make up about 40 per cent of Scottish landings by weight, and in some towns, such as Peterhead and Fraserburgh, the fishing is a major employer.

There were over 4000 fishermen in the region in 1993, almost half the total in Scotland. For example, 45 per cent of Fraserburgh's workforce and around 60 per cent of Gardenstown's is dependent on the sea.

Local or regional management of fisheries is a possible way forward through the thickets of the CFP and it would be worth exploring how management systems could evolve upwards from the fisherman level.

> Yes, I think their ideas would work [agreed Dr Lake]. Most fishermen, on whatever scale, have made a large investment in gear, vessel, etc. They want to catch fish in a sustainable manner, they want a stable management regime, with increased policing of management measures, but the measures must be appropriate to the stocks. Local fisheries management needs to be backed up with policing from a strong central agency.
>
> Europe is setting fleet sizes under the Multi Annual Guidance Programmes. The biggest fleet sector in Britain is the inshore boats under 10m. If this sector is targeted for cuts, it will have a large impact in the Highlands, in the small communities. But, on what ground is it being done? At the moment they are fishing quite happily. Knee-jerk management — we need to cut fleets, therefore we'll decommission a lot of boats — is not right. The under-10-m sector is large because the decommissioning schemes that have been brought in have not been structured properly. They have been more suitable for medium-sized vessels. As a result people have been decommissioning 12-m boats, buying licences for smaller boats and putting more pressure on inshore stocks. This does nothing for the midwater stocks as the bigger boats are working further out. The decommissioning programme has basically screwed up but it has an enormous local-level impact.

Under more localised management, for example, for North Sea stocks, the adjacent nations would be directly concerned. At the moment, when decisions are taken in Brussels, all the member states are involved but it is difficult to explain to fishermen why Luxembourg should be voting on North Sea management. Perhaps the time has come to consider an even more radical approach: to ditch the old concept of Grotius, of *mare liberum*, and consider fish stocks in the open sea as the resource of the adjacent countries rather than everybody's.

Salt in the blood

In the last two years, gathering material for this book, I visited many harbours around the coast. In some I found thriving fisheries, the problems deriving from overfishing and the CFP notwithstanding, but in others – once vibrant communities drawing a living from the sea – there was hardly a trace of a way of life now gone, except in the local heritage centre. Fishing settlements have dwindled and disappeared in the past, long before the CFP became an issue: take, for example, the old village of Ortie on Sanday, abandoned at the end of the nineteenth century, or the settlement called Usan, a small handful of miles south of Montrose. Peter Anson described it as being the home of five fishermen with five sailboats in 1930; in 1870 there had been twelve boats and thirty-nine men, presumably all fishing with lines. I found a quiet inlet between low, dark rocks with a curve of shingle and sand, and on the brae above a row of six or seven derelict cottages, roofless, with the walls slowly falling in around the empty window and door spaces. There is still a salmon fishing station here and a few creels being worked, but the old fishing community is long gone, presumably flitted to Ferryden or some other larger port. Likewise, on Lewis, one evening I watched a translucent green sea break in a clean line on the pale, empty gold of Garry beach, where once the sgoth fishermen of North Tolsta raced in with their catches.

It takes a long time usually for a fishing place to die completely. There was not much to see at Ballantrae, the little haven a doglegged pier on the Ayrshire shore with the lump of Ailsa Craig and the more distant mass of Arran lying offshore, to indicate that it was the resort of herring fishermen in the past to the extent that its port letters BA became the registration for all the vessels on this stretch of coast, but there were a few small boats and some creels. A small flock of boats – *Myra G.*, *Our Amy*, *Shangri-La*, *Valerie* – graced the harbour of Port William on the east side of Luce Bay, and the accumulation of tubs and barrels, adapted for catching buckies, on the quay showed there was still life in the place. To the south of Aberdeen, Cove was home to a few creelboats and salmon nets hung in dark curtains from poles, drying in the chilly east wind. The tide was out at Gourdon, leaving the *Emma Kathleen* and the *Sharona*, and several smaller boats, aground on the mud. There is no fishing from Crovie now and only a few inshore creel boats and pleasure craft rocked in the haven at Gardenstown. The fishing tradition continues, however, and several enterprising families still pursue the calling of their forebears from larger ports.

Some once prominent fishing harbours are now more or less completely given over to pleasure craft and filled with the sleek, expensive hulls of yachts, with cute, witty names – *Eauvation*, *Knot Sure* – that you would be unlikely to have a fisherman use. Nairn had about 400 fishermen and 105 boats in the mid-1800s[23] and in 1930 there were still twenty-four steam drifters and fifteen motor boats, manned by some 260 men. They have all gone. Lossiemouth likewise has become a marina. John Thomson has seen the decline of the fishing: 'It's a very sad thing – when you see a harbour that was such a force die and go derelict, it's very sad.'

There are still many harbours with busy fishing fleets, perhaps reduced in numbers from their heyday but comprising modern craft bringing home rich hauls of fish. In the south-east, Eyemouth has seventy-eight vessels nominally based there, a market and a boatyard. The basin of the harbour is a long, thin shape where the river Eye has cut a steep-sided valley down to the sea. When I visited it, there were fishing boats in from England as well as Scotland, the *Golden Promise*, newly built, was being fitted out for her owner in Oban, and work was progressing on the construction of a new deepwater berth and improvements to the harbour entrance. Fishing contributes 60 per cent to the local economy and the port ranks as the leading east coast market south of Aberdeen. In his 'tour' along the east coast in 1930, Peter Anson considered Ross and Burnmouth as the first fishing villages to the north of the English border; Burnmouth still has a harbour with a number of creel boats.[24] Dunbar cherishes its heritage as one

The Guernsey crabber *Our Hazel* (GU 171) unloading her catch into a refrigerated truck bound for Spain, at Ullapool, April 1998.

of the oldest ports in the country and is home to a working fleet of about a dozen prawn trawlers and almost as many two-man crab boats. In the East Neuk of Fife, Pittenweem has the central market. The harbour is busy, seeing a stream of boats from all along the east coast come in from the North Sea grounds. Freezer lorries shunt around on the quays. St Monans and Elie are home mainly to pleasure craft now but Anstruther has working boats and farthest to the east the little curve of harbour at Crail has a shellfish fleet. Arbroath harbour is still busy and Aberdeen has a fleet, although it is much reduced from the heyday of the trawlers and liners. Peterhead and Fraserburgh, or the Broch as it is generally known amongst the fishermen, are the largest ports in the north-east. Both are home to fleets of large modern vessels: 107 of over 10m registered in the former and 150 in the latter in July 1996.[25] Along the Moray Firth, Buckie and Macduff harbours are still busy.

Wick has a working fleet but the main change in Caithness recently has been the rapid development of Scrabster as a fish-landing port. The value of

Peter Anson's drawing of Burnmouth, the most southerly fishing community on the east coast of Scotland.

catches passing through Scrabster has risen from just under £3 million in 1985 to over £25 million in 1995,[26] and the Harbour Trust has extensive plans to develop the facilities for marketing and processing. The large new mart complies with EU standards. One morning when I was there, the fishing boats in the harbour were representative of the activity. Tied up were the Peterhead-registered *Morning Dawn*, her old name and home port of *Cornelia*, Texel, still distinguishable under her new livery; the *Alison Kay* from Lerwick; the *Bounty* registered in Grimsby; the *Atlas* from Macduff; and the Faroese *Polarstjørnan* from Klakksvik. The *Seagull* of Banff was oiling and taking on food supplies, while some of her crew in baseball caps and yellow oilskin breeks were laying out and checking chains and ropes along the quay. That morning, 2300 boxes of white fish had passed through the mart, most of it into large refrigerated lorries for transport south. Like Kinlochbervie, Lochinver and other large ports, Scrabster sees many boats come and go but there is also a resident fleet of small boats fishing for crabs.

Scrabster has benefited from geography, being well sited to service boats fishing off the west coast. This is also true of west coast ports such as Kinlochbervie, Lochinver, Gairloch, Ullapool, and Kyle. Lochinver is a favourite landing port among the French and Spanish boats. There are several fishing harbours on Skye, Portree being the largest, and Oban and Mallaig are important in the south-west Highlands, the latter having the largest locally based fleet in Highland Region.[27] In Kintyre, fleets operate from Tarbert, Campbeltown and other smaller ports and, across the Firth of Clyde, the Ayrshire fleet is still a sizeable entity, with a new market at Troon.

The fishing continues to develop. A notable innovation has been the adoption of the twin-rig trawl for white fish. Twin-rigging, whereby two trawl nets are towed side by side on three warps, first evolved in prawn fishing[28] as a technique more efficient than the single trawl; like the seine

Women wearing the costumes of the fishing community in the Fisherrow Walk, an annual celebration revived in the late 1960s.

net, it is of Danish origin and the *Annandale*, in the Western Isles, was experimenting with it in 1985.[29] Many of the new fishing boats being built for Moray Firth skippers are designed for twin-rigging. In shellfishing, the adoption of the parlour creel, with an extra chamber to accommodate more crabs and lobsters, and the vivier tank to keep the catch alive in pumped seawater, has increased efficiency.

The landings of all species of fish in Scotland by British vessels with fishery districts ranked in order of the catch value in 1995 are shown in Table 2. The figures for each fishery district are totals for all the ports within it.[30] The precise order of ranking in the table varies of course from year to year but it does give a general picture of the Scottish fishing industry at the present time. It is also important to bear in mind that the port giving its name to the fishery district is not necessarily the largest within that district; Wick's high position is due to the recent growth in importance of Scrabster, Pittenweem is the centre for all the East Neuk, as is Ayr for the fishing communities based in Girvan, Dunure, Maidens and all the ports in the south-west.

TABLE 2

	1991		1995	
	Weight (tonnes)	Value (£'000)	Weight (tonnes)	Value (£'000)
Peterhead	119,256	81,130	112,376	73,272
Fraserburgh	25,051	20,697	38,227	31,410
Shetland	104,824	22,710	107,192	25,738
Wick	9443	11,830	23,315	25,643
Aberdeen	32,996	26,427	27,943	24,093
Mallaig	9792	14,005	19,952	17,382
Stornoway	5984	9569	8986	14,925
Kinlochbervie	10,483	11,944	13,705	13,627
Ullapool	62,089	9818	53,469	10,599
Lochinver	6133	8211	7576	9364
Ayr	17,022	12,558	6765	8190
Campbeltown	5478	7887	5240	8134
Eyemouth	5385	7603	5450	6693
Oban	4685	7391	5048	6556
Orkney	1086	1942	3905	5368
Buckie	2658	3601	3762	5033
Pittenweem	2346	3178	3077	3789
Lossiemouth	4091	2001	3113	2134
Arbroath	1457	1,969	1331	1845
Macduff	2152	2316	1607	1472

The total number of fishing boats in Scotland officially numbered 2792 in 1995, of which 1583 were inshore craft less than 10 m in length. The number of fishermen totalled 8395, of whom 6889 were 'regularly employed', 1423 were 'partially employed', and eighty-three were classed as 'crofters'. The Scottish Office carefully warns that these figures are based on estimates.

Looking at methods of fishing, the largest number of boats are working with creels (1571), prawn trawl (316) and demersal single trawl (287). In 1995, there were ninety seine netters, 104 clam dredgers, ninety-five using the demersal pair trawl and, interestingly enough, eighty-four boats still using great and small lines. Placing Scotland within a UK-wide context reveals that most of the country's fish, some 80 per cent of it, is landed north of the Border – the figures in Table 3 are for 1994 and are taken from the Annual Report of the Sea Fish Industry Authority.[31]

In the Highlands and Islands, fishing is of vital importance, far beyond what statistics on numbers of fishermen and boats indicate. The small communities scattered around the west coast sea-lochs may only boast a handful of fishing vessels but where the population is low and geography

TABLE 3

	Weight (tonnes)			Value (£'000)		
	Demersal	Pelagic	Shellfish	Demersal	Pelagic	Shellfish
England & Wales	75,201	34,188	45,172 (approx.)	107,342	5142	36,728 (approx.)
Northern Ireland	9667	4096	6901	8400	429	8936
Scotland	189,387	224,190	45,303	175,949	28,106	75,271
Total	274,255	262,474	97,376	291,691	33,677	120,935

limits economic opportunities every job counts. In Shetland, one could argue that the sea has always been of greater economic importance than the land.

John Goodlad, the Secretary of the Shetland Fishermen's Association, has been intimately involved with the development of the fishing resources in the northern archipelago for some years.

Fishing is very very important to Shetland, notwithstanding the oil industry development, and in the last 10–15 years the reliance on fishing has probably increased. If you take fishing, fish processing and fish farming together, the number of people employed either directly or indirectly accounts for 23 per cent of the islands' workforce. If you exclude oil, fish and fish products account for 85 per cent of Shetland's exports. Fishing dominates the economy.

We are fortunate in having a fairly modern fleet, probably one of the most modern in Europe. One aspect of the Shetland fishing industry, pretty much absent from the rest of Europe, is the share-holding structure. In mainland Scotland one might tend to think that boats are share-owned but generally it is the case there that the skipper, the mate and maybe the fish salesman have shares and employ the rest of the crew. So, although the employees are on a share system, they get only a proportion of the catch and the owning of the ship is actually in the hands of the skipper and the mate. In Shetland this is not the case – the old system where virtually the entire crew have shares still exists. This is best illustrated by some of the new pelagic boats being built in Norway at a cost of £6 million or £8 million. These are owned by 'companies' but the shareholders in the companies are the seven, eight or nine men of the crew aboard. It's almost like the last bastion of Marxism, although the fishermen would be horrified at that description, but it is a unique system where most of the men

Watching a rough sea
from the deck of the
Argonaut (KY 157).

employed on the boat have an absolutely equal share.

There are two advantages: when times are hard, the men with the
shares stick with the boat but, more importantly, when times are good
the benefits are spread widely throughout the community. If you go to
Peterhead you'll find that the fishermen have all got good houses but
the skippers have really palatial mansions. In Shetland you'll find that
everybody has a fairly decent house. From the cultural point of view
this is very important, and a great strength to the industry.

The system is not under threat. It has survived and has come
right up with the most modern technology. The *Altaire* was ready to go
to the Atlanto-Scandian fishing in the far north but delayed sailing for
one week to let the crew get their peats cut. Someone said that if they
had gone to sea the profit from the one trip would have kept

Northmavine [their home district] in paraffin for twenty years, but the traditional values held firm. This incident proves that if the fishing should fail there is a resilience in the community, an appreciation that life is more than balance sheets.

We have a modern fleet of nine pelagic boats, six of them rebuilt in the last three years for a total investment of £60 million, an enormous sum for a small community; 40–50 trawlers ranging from 40-ft wooden boats to standard 70–90-ft trawlers – three new ones are being built just now [1996], one a large stern trawler being built in Spain for a partnership (150 ft, costing £4.5 million); and 50-60 shellfish boats with two-to-three-man crews. The total Shetland catch

The *Falcon* (BCK 222) heading in to her homeport of Buckie, April 1998.

is 15,000 tonnes herring, 26,000 tonnes Atlanto-Scandian herring, 35,000–40,000 tonnes of mackerel, 20,000 tonnes of white fish, and 1500 tonnes of shellfish – as well as a few bits and pieces, such as sand-eels, making a total of approximately 100,000 tonnes. Most of the white fish is landed in Shetland but most of the pelagic catch is landed in continental ports, depending on prices. The fleet can go with speed and safety to where the best price is.

From his home in Whalsay, William Anderson keeps up his close interest in the fishing, noting the changes and the continuing of traditional ways:

The year's cycle of crofting and fishing is entirely changed now. I would say that Whalsay depends more on the sea now than it did in the past. The new harbour at Symbister was built in the late 1960s, and two breakwaters have been added since to give extra shelter. There's a big building programme of pelagic boats going on. Two boats – the *Serene* and the *Charisma* – are being replaced. Four boats are being sold – the *Research* and the *Azalea* will be replaced by one big trawler, and the *Zephyr* and the *Antares* are to be replaced by two new boats. Then there's the *Fiskebas*, exclusively a purser, and the *Adenia*. That's seven in the pelagic fleet. Then, of trawlers, there's another seven (72–80 ft) – one does a little seining, although that's a thing of the past – and umpteen smaller boats at the lobsters, scallops, queens, buckies and so on. Whalsay is one of the main fishing areas in Shetland now, if not in the whole north, especially for pelagic fishing. There is a massive investment of £40 million in the five new boats.

I think the Whalsay fleet is okay for the future. In the past the rewards were very small, but what would come in was more or less the money you had for extras. Home expenses were small because you lived off the croft. Haddock lines would give a few fish and we could always go off and get some peltags. It was a spartan existence but it was good healthy plain food. Women knitted a lot at that time, even when they went to the hill for a kishie of peats they would be knitting as they went. That was bringing in cash and really the income from the fishing was extra, a bit of handy money. That's all changed. There's very little knitting now and nobody walks anywhere.

The oil did not affect the fishing, not very much in Whalsay. Very few men broke off from the fishing to go to work in the oil industry. No boats were sold. Though the oil was a great boon to Shetland in the sense that it brought in money, it didn't bring any more contentment. A lot of the social life has gone now.

Shetland's neighbouring archipelago to the south – Orkney – has a small but active fishing fleet. It is a cliché to sum up the difference between the two island groups with 'The Orcadian is a farmer with a boat, the Shetlander is a fisherman with a plough' but there is a great deal of geographical truth in it. In the old days, the Orcadians made full use of the inshore resources on their doorstep and the herring fishing for a time did bring some prosperity to Stronsay, Stromness and a few other places but, when Captain Robert ('Robbie') Sutherland returned to Stromness as a teacher of navigation in 1967, there were only two Westray boats catching white fish and a number of crab and lobster boats operating.

I started a school to encourage people to take confidence in themselves [he explained]. Our green fields denied us the wisdom to see that a rich harvest was being taken away to the north-east and Aberdeen right from our shores. They cleaned all the beautiful areas we had of lovely fish. The Rackwick fishermen used to catch fine cod long ago. There's nothing there now. We had no means of satisfying the seatime regulations of the Board of Trade. Seatime only counted if it was put in on vessels that were fully decked and spent nights at sea. I pointed out to the Board that the local men were pretty competent with small boats, and the outcome was that six years' experience on small boats could qualify a man for a special certificate to take vessels up to 50 ft and be skipper of a fishing boat. Alfie Sinclair, owner of a seine netter, was one of the few who had experience – he had worked in Scrabster on the *Primula* with Angie Mackintosh – and he later got the *Evelyn*. We needed boats of a size to allow the training of skippers to get full-time skipper's tickets. David Reid of the *Bountiful* was able to provide seatime. Secondhand boats from Buckie were the forerunner of the present fleet – purpose-built boats of 90–100 ft.

Captain Sutherland is proud of the way the fleet has developed in the last couple of decades; it comprised 211 registered boats, most of them catching shellfish, in 1995.[32] From his house hard by the sea in Stromness, he can watch some of the boats now making a living from the fishing, boats like the *Aalskere* that trawls for white fish as far as Rockall, on ten-day trips, landing anywhere, depending on the market. The inshore boats are also doing well at crabs and buckies; the shellfishing is good and there is no overfishing yet. Westray has become a centre of the fishing in Orkney: distant from Kirkwall, its isolation had made the people part-time fishermen and crofters. People were moving from the smaller islands to Kirkwall but some of the Westray men wanted to stay on their island. The sea gave them a potential and a freedom, and they produced their own processing plant mainly from capital raised on the island.

Angus Sinclair, who lives in Stromness, is the owner of the *Orcades Viking III*, the only freezer-trawler in Scotland. His father and grandfather were fishermen. His father fished out of Scrabster in the late 1940s and 1950s on the *Primula*. There was no seine netting in Orkney before that time. His grandfather worked a yole out of Stromness with lines for halibut, which could be caught close at hand. Halibut were so abundant that they could be used as leens, or runners under the keel, for hauling the boat when they could not be sold. Angus had a purser in 1980 for one year and then, in 1981, acquired another, the purser *Orcades Viking* I (K 616). Seining from Stromness they worked around the coast, off as far as two hours' steaming west in deep water. They were usually back in most nights. The boat in 1985 proved to be too small. 'We didn't have experience of the purse seine at this time and used the seine net,' said Angus. 'We had a man come with us for a while to show us the use of the purse. The *Orcades Viking II* was 190 ft – we pursed for half of the season and trawled for the other half, further offshore by this time, as far as the Minch. We always landed in Ullapool to sell to the klondikers. The *Orcades Viking III* came about because I thought it would be good to get a freezer-trawler that could stay at sea until she was full.'

The *Orcades Viking III*, built in Denmark at a cost of £9 million,[33] is almost 2500 tons, 240 ft long and with a main engine generating 2500 hp. The crew numbers thirty, mostly from Stromness, but the engineer is Faroese. The usual trip lasts 12 days, with two weeks as a maximum. 'Landing depends on price,' said Angus. 'For example, we landed in Holland a good

Landing fish at Aberdeen.

bit at one time, because that was where the freezer market was. This year [1996] we're landing in Faroe. We've landed in Germany. Marketing the fish is as much part of the operation as catching them. The freezer needs 60–70 tons a day to keep solvent. The target catch is 150 tons.'

The *Orcades Viking* III goes to the edge of the Continental Shelf to fish at up to 500 fathoms. To reach that depth they shoot approximately 1500 fathoms of warp, nearly a mile of gear hanging off the stern. A midwater trawl costs around £100,000: 'It can't be insured but we don't often lose one – and we have three sets of gear aboard. Towing need not take long, the bag can fill quickly and "eggs", the sensors on the bag that detect it filling and alert the bridge, can go off quickly. The crew comprises one deck squad and two factory shifts who work six hours on, six hours off, to process the catch.' It takes the *Orcades Viking* III twelve days to catch 1000 tons – with two trips completed in a good month.

Stornoway is the main centre of the fishing in the Western Isles. The harbour, on the north side of the estuary of the Bayhead river is next to the extensive, tree-planted grounds of Lews Castle which gives the port a benign aspect more redolent of southern waters than the reality of the wind-blasted North Atlantic. It is a busy port, with boats coming and going, nets being mended along the quay, forklifts puttering back and fore and gulls calling above the raucous splutter of generators and diesel engines. There were 393 registered fishing boats in the Western Isles in 1994, and at that time 695 fishermen, including 111 part-timers and twenty-five crofters.[34] Fishing is spread throughout the Hebrides: most boats land at Stornoway or Ardveenish in Barra but there are still many working from smaller havens and anchorages. Most of the fleet fish for shellfish, using creels, but the larger trawlers catch prawns in the Minches and two large Barra boats concentrate on pelagic species – herring and mackerel – away from their native islands. Through poor local market conditions in the past, the Hebridean fleet did not put a great effort into catching white fish and, in the allocation of pressure stock licences following the introduction of the Common Fisheries Policy in 1983, most of the smaller boats were not awarded any. Most of the white fish taken in Hebridean waters is by east coast or foreign boats. The high price of licences makes expansion into catching white fish difficult if not impossible now, and this is seen as a major obstacle in the way of developing the fishing in the area.

Fishing was said to be in crisis in the 1930s. At that time Peter Anson wrote a pamphlet with the title *The Scottish Fisheries: Are They Doomed?* which attracted a great deal of attention and ended: 'We need a new fervour of spirit – a new slogan "Back to the Sea" – a cry that shall stir the deserted fishing villages and impoverished towns from Wick to Wigtown, from Unst to Eyemouth, where at present a national tragedy is being enacted before our very eyes. For as Sir Walter Scott reminded us: "It's nae fish ye're buying. It's men's lives."'[35]

The fishing survived then, and it can survive the Common Fisheries Policy if appropriate and timely reforms are introduced. The number of fishermen, and the consequent numbers in dependent occupations, have risen and fallen over the years. In my father's day, there were eight full-time crab boats working from Keiss harbour, employing around twenty men. When Murdo Maclennan left school in the 1930s to join a drifter crew, almost all his neighbours went to sea, up to fifty men leaving on eight boats on a Monday morning. A fisheries policy that could go some way towards restoring such a situation would be worth having.

I began the journey described in this book in Fraserburgh. Nearly two years later, I was standing on the quay at Carloway on the west coast of Lewis on a wet April afternoon. The pier nestles in a hook of the land, sheltered from the west wind that comes, as a man said to me, 'straight from America'. Croft houses looked down from the braes. Two boats were tied up – half the number of registered boats which call Carloway home – and creels were stacked in a rampart on the quay. Not far away was Dun Carloway and the stone circle of Callanish. The people have been drawing a living from the sea here for thousands of years. The salt in the blood has been passed down through the generations. It is up to us to ensure it does not cease now.

NOTES ON SOURCES

ABBREVIATIONS

Ann Rep	Annual Report
DAFS	Department of Agriculture and Fisheries for Scotland
FBS	Fishery Board for Scotland
FN	*Fishing News*
NSA	*New Statistical Account of Scotland*
MGC	Macfarlane, *Geographical Collections*
OSA	Sinclair, 1791–9, *The Statistical Account of Scotland*
SO	Scottish Office

1 THE OLD COMMUNITIES

1   NSA, Gamrie.
2   Bertram, 1865.
3   Wilson, undated.
4   OSA, Lochcarron.
5   OSA, Applecross.
6   OSA, St Cyrus (Ecclesgreig).
7   NSA, Boyndie.
8   OSA, Rathven.
9   Waterman, undated.
10   Wilson, undated.
11   Anson, 1930.
12   Newhaven Heritage Museum.
13   Wilson, undated.
14   FN, 4 Jan. 1990.
15   Newhaven Heritage Museum.
16   Black, 1946.
17   Anson, 1930.
18   Sutherland, undated.
19   Inverness Public Library.
20   Information from Donald MacDonald.
21   NSA, Cullen.
22   MGC, vol. 1.
23   OSA, Rathven.
24   Ibid.
25   OSA, Avoch.
26   OSA, Gamrie.
27   OSA, Lonmay.
28   OSA, Ely.
29   OSA, Kilfinichen and Kilviceuen.
30   Information from John Thomson.
31   Information from Andrew Mearns.
32   Martin, 1981; and information from Tom Ralston.
33   OSA, Benholme.
34   OSA, Nairn.
35   OSA, Whitekirk and Tyninghame.
36   OSA, Inverbervie.
37   OSA, Gourdon.
38   McKean, 1987.
39   Signal Tower Museum, Arbroath.
40   Thompson, 1983.
41   OSA, Inveresk.
42   Signal Tower Museum, Arbroath.
43   *The Scotsman*, 18 April 1989.
44   Anson, 1969.
45   Martin, 1695.
46   Fenton, 1978.
47   Waterman, undated.
48   Martin, 1981.
49   Anson, 1950.
50   Sutherland, 1985; Slater, 1997.
51   *The Scotsman*, 11 May 1998. A statue to Willie 'Kingfisher' Spears has recently been unveiled in Eyemouth.
52   FN, 29 Oct 1938.
53   Information from George Wood, Macduff.
54   Dorian, 1985.

2 SAIL AND STORM

1   Johnstone, 1980.
2   Smith, 1984.
3   Halcrow, 1950.
4   OSA, Unst.
5   See, e.g., Halcrow, 1950; Goodlad, 1971; Sandison, 1981.
6   Macdonald, 1984.
7   Ibid.
8   Miller, 1994.
9   Calder, 1887.
10   Washington, 1848.
11   Anson, 1930.
12   Nairn Fishertown Museum.
13   Anson, 1950.
14   Ibid.
15   Scottish Fisheries Museum.
16   McKee, 1983.
17   Anson, 1950.
18   Martin, 1981.
19   Slater, 1997.
20   Dorian, 1985.
21   Bunyan, 1991.
22   Gifford, 1988.
23   MGC, Vol. 3.
24   McNeill & MacQueen, 1996.
25   Gifford, 1989.

26 NSA, Inveraray.
27 Gifford, 1990.
28 MGC, vol. III.
29 Goodlad, 1971.
30 Anson, 1930.
31 In Halcrow, 1950.
32 Stewart, 1993.
33 *Berwickshire News*, 18 Oct. 1881.
34 FN, 22 Oct. 1991; and *Press and Journal*, 2 July 1997.

3 LINES AND HOOKS

1 Ritchie, 1981; Armit, 1996; Pollard & Morrison, 1996.
2 OSA, Tongue.
3 DAFS Report, 1967.
4 MGC, vol. II.
5 MGC, vol. III.
6 *Ibid.*
7 OSA, Nesting.
8 OSA, Barra; OSA, Craignish.
9 Barrow, G.W.S. (ed), *The Acts of Malcolm IV*, Edinburgh, 1960.
10 Barrow, G.W.S. (ed), *The Acts of William I*, Edinburgh, 1960.
11 Anson, 1930.
12 Gibson, 1984.
13 Anson, 1930.
14 Hume Brown, 1893.
15 *Ibid.*
16 MGC, vol. III.
17 *Ibid.*
18 Information from Andrew Williamson.
19 MGC, vol. I.
20 *Ibid.*
21 *Ibid.*
22 OSA, Rathven.
23 Johnson, *A Journey to the Western Islands of Scotland in 1773.*
24 Barrett, 1997.
25 OSA, Slains.
26 OSA, Gamrie.
27 OSA, Peterhead.
28 OSA, Barvas; Lochs; Uig; Stornoway.
29 OSA, South Uist.
30 OSA, Barray.
31 OSA, Tiree.
32 OSA, Killarow and Kilmeny.
33 OSA, Gigha and Cara.
34 OSA, Kilbride.
35 Edmonston, 1820.
36 Information from Andrew Williamson.
37 Edmonston, 1820.
38 Information from Andrew Williamson.
39 OSA, Nigg.
40 OSA, Rathven.
41 OSA, Drainie.
42 OSA, Tarbat.
43 NSA, Fordyce.
44 NSA, Rathven.
45 NSA, Cullen.
46 NSA, Boyndie.
47 Information from Gordon Linklater, Kirkwall.
48 Bertram, 1865.
49 Dorian, 1985.
50 Stewart, 1993.

4 SILVER DARLINGS

1 Blaxter & Hunter, 1982.
2 Dunlop, 1978.
3 Fraser, 1818.
4 Halcrow, 1950.
5 MGC, vol. III.
6 Fraser, 1818.
7 Smith, 1984.
8 Rodger, 1997.
9 Anson, 1930.
10 Grant, 1930 – quoted in Dunlop, 1978.
11 Day, 1918 – quoted in Dunlop, 1978.
12 Elder, 1912.
13 Halcrow, 1950.
14 OSA, Fraserburgh.
15 MGC, vol. II.
16 MGC, vol. I.
17 MGC, vol. III.
18 Anson, 1930.
19 MGC, vol. III.
20 *Ibid.*
21 Fraser, 1818.
22 OSA, Kilfinan.
23 OSA, Inveraray.
24 OSA, Lochgoilhead and Kilmorich.
25 OSA, Campbeltown.
26 OSA, Queensferry.
27 OSA, Dalgety.
28 OSA, Queensferry.
29 OSA, Kirkbean.
30 OSA, Kilfinichen and Kilviceuen.
31 Martin, 1695.
32 OSA, Kingarth.
33 OSA, Rothesay.
34 OSA, Kilbride.
35 OSA, Glenelg.
36 OSA, Kintail; Lochalsh.
37 OSA, Stornoway.
38 OSA, Uig.
39 OSA, Culross.
40 OSA, Avoch.
41 OSA, Cromarty.
42 Dunlop, 1978.
43 Gairloch Heritage Museum.
44 Buckland, 1878.
45 Scottish Fisheries Museum.
46 NSA, Banff.
47 Anson, 1950.
48 NSA, Wick.
49 NSA, Dornoch.
50 NSA, Edderachillis.
51 NSA, Tongue.
52 NSA, Edderachillis.
53 Sutherland, undated.
54 Stromness Museum, 1976.
55 Fenton, 1978.
56 Gibson, 1984.
57 NSA, Farr; Durness; Tongue.
58 NSA, Helmsdale.
59 NSA, Rathven; Gamrie; Cullen.
60 Washington, 1848.
61 Butcher, 1987.
62 *Ibid.*
63 Anderson, 1785.
64 Martin, 1981.
65 Ralston, 1995.
66 *Ibid.*
67 Smith, 1985.

68 Newhaven Heritage Museum.
69 Gray, 1978.
70 Waterman, undated.
71 Buckland, 1878.

5 FROM SAIL TO ENGINE

1 Lossiemouth Fisheries Museum.
2 Smith, 1985.
3 Buckland, 1878.
4 Sutherland, 1985.
5 Tanner, 1996.
6 Sutherland, 1985.
7 Scottish Fisheries Museum.
8 Sutherland, 1985.
9 Anson, 1950.
10 Waterman, undated.
11 Sutherland, 1985.
12 Scottish Fisheries Museum.
13 FN, 1 Feb. 1927.
14 Wilson, 1968.
15 *Scottish Highlander*, 1 Feb 1894.
16 *Scottish Highlander*, 15 March 1894.
17 *Scottish Highlander*, 5 July 1894.
18 FN, 1 Jan. 1927.
19 Sutherland, 1985.
20 Anson, 1930.
21 Tanner, 1996.
22 Stewart, undated.
23 Stewart, 1986.
24 Scottish Fisheries Museum.
25 Sutherland, 1985.
26 FN, 1 Jan. 1927.
27 Wilson, 1995.
28 FN, 1 Jan. 1927.
29 FBS Ann Rep 1939.
30 DAFS Ann Rep 1967.
31 Scottish Fisheries Museum.
32 Sutherland, 1985.
33 Wilson, 1995.
34 Martin, 1981.
35 Scottish Fisheries Museum.
36 Anson, 1930.
37 Wilson, 1995.
38 FN, 1 Jan. 1927.
39 OSA, Nigg.
40 Baldwin, 1982.
41 Bertram, 1865.
42 OSA, Peterhead.
43 OSA, Cockburnspath.
44 Fenton, 1978.
45 NSA, Durness.
46 Information from Jim Wilson.
47 McGowran, 1985.
48 OSA, Prestonpans.
49 OSA, Petty.
50 OSA, Tranent.
51 OSA, St Andrews.
52 SO, 1995.

6 BETWEEN THE WARS

1 Anson, 1950.
2 Scottish Fisheries Museum.
3 FN, 19 Feb. 1921.
4 FN, 29 Jan. 1960.
5 FN, 1 Jan. 1921.

6 FN, 17 Sept. 1921.
7 FN, 1 Jan. 1927.
8 Angus, S., *Scottish Field*, Dec. 1975.
9 FN, 22 Jan. 1921.
10 Stewart, undated.
11 FN, 14 May 1921.
12 Sutherland, 1985.
13 FN, 29 Oct 1921.
14 Stewart, undated.
15 FN, 18 April 1936.
16 Stewart, 1993.
17 Goodlad, 1971.
18 Smith, 1985.
19 Newhaven Heritage Museum.
20 Smith, 1985.
21 Levy, 1988.
22 Lewis Association Report No. 5, undated.
23 Martin, 1981.
24 FN, 22 Feb. 1936.
25 Lewis Association Report No. 5, undated.
26 Stewart, undated.
27 Gibson, 1984.
28 FN, 11 April 1936.
29 FN, 2 April 1938; Anson, 1950.
30 FN, 15 Jan. 1938.
31 Domhnallach, 1987.
32 FBS Ann Rep 1912.
33 Bochel, 1979.
34 *Report on the Fisheries of Scotland 1939–1948*, Scottish Home Dept. 1949.
35 *Ibid.*

7 DISTANT WATERS

1 Wilson, 1968.
2 Two Hull trawlers, *St Romanus* and *Kingston Peridot*, were lost with all hands in January 1968 in Icelandic waters, probably through icing and capsizing. A third, the *Ross Cleveland*, capsized and sank in February; one man survived from the crew of nineteen.
3 Anson, 1950.
4 Ritchie, 1991.
5 Anson, 1950.
6 Ritchie, 1991.
7 Information from George Wood, Aberdeen.
8 Anson, 1950.
9 *Ibid.*
10 Stewart, undated.
11 Stewart, 1993.
12 FN, 13 Sept. 1952.
13 Anson, 1950.
14 FN, 6 Sept. 1974.
15 Anson, 1950.
16 Wilson, 1968.
17 Goodlad, 1971.
18 FN, 23 Dec. 1960.

8 CHANGES AT SEA

1 OSA, Gamrie.
2 Martin, 1981.
3 Wilson, 1995.
4 FN, 20 March 1959.
5 Wilson, 1968.
6 Wilson, 1995.

7   Anderson, 1785.
8   Information from Tom Ralston.
9   FN, 29 Nov. 1991.
10   FN, 28 Jan. 1966.
11   Goodlad, 1971.
12   Goodlad, 1971.
13   FN, 18 Feb. 1966.
14   FN, 22 April 1966.
15   FN, 28 Oct. 1966.
16   Wilson, 1995.
17   Ibid.
18   FN, 17 Sept. 1971.
19   FN, 30 Oct. 1959.
20   FN, 18 March 1960.
21   FN, 18 April 1975.
22   Wilson, 1968.
23   Wilson, 1995.
24   FN, 11 Oct. 1974.
25   Ralston, 1995.
26   Ibid.
27   FN, 16 July 1938.
28   Sutherland, 1985.
29   FN, 21 Jan. 1933.
30   FN, 30 Jan. 1998; 27 March 1998.
31   FN, 4 Sept. 1959.
32   Coull, J., 'Shell fisheries in Scotland:
     a case of transition from low to high
     value', *Scottish Geographical Magazine*,
     vol. 113, 1997, pp.168–76.
33   FN, 11 Jan. 1974.
34   Western Isles Council Fisheries Plan, 1989.
35   Gordon, 1996.
36   FN, 5 April 1991.
37   FN, 19 April 1991.

9   COD WARS

1   FAO statistics, quoted in *The Times*,
     3 Jan. 1972.
2   Rodger, 1997.
3   Elder, 1912.
4   FN, 8 Feb. 1936.
5   FN, 29 March 1952.
6   FN, 3 April 1959.
7   *The Times*, 22 Feb.1972. I have
     relied on *The Times* columns for much
     of the story of disputes, fishing
     limits and quotas during the 1970s.
8   FN, 15 May 1959.
9   FN, 3 Jan. 1975.
10   OSA, Rathven.
11   McGowran, 1985.
12   Wilson, undated.
13   *Acts of the Parliament of Scotland
     1424–1707*, Edinburgh, 1908.
14   Thompson, 1983.
15   Goodlad, 1971.
16   For example, FN, 10 June 1933;
     FN, 20 June 1936.
17   FN, 20 June 1936.
18   Ralston, 1995.
19   Information from Tom Ralston
     and Ian Stewart.
20   Cargill, 1976.
21   FN, 17 June 1977.
22   FN, 18 Jan. 1980.
23   *The Times*, 16 Dec. 1971.
24   FN, 16 Jan 1959.

25   *The Times*, 31 Jan. 1976.
26   FN, 7 Jan. 1977.
27   FN, 11 Feb. 1977.
28   Butcher, 1987.
29   Lewis Association Report No. 5, undated.
30   FN, 30 Dec. 1977.
31   Information from Tom Ralston.
32   *Daily Telegraph*, 30 Jan. 1979.
33   FN, 7 Jan. 1977.
34   Newhaven Heritage Museum.
35   *The Times*, 7 Feb.1980.
36   *The Times*, 9 June 1976.
37   *The Times*, 3 July 1978.
38   *The Times*, 25 May 1979.
39   Wilson, 1995.
40   *Caithness Courier*, 25 June 1986.

10   SAVING THE FISH

1   *The New Common Fisheries Policy*,
     Brussels, 1994.
2   Ibid.
3   Holden, 1994, is my major
     source for much of this account
     of the CFP.
4   FN, 26 Dec. 1997.
5   Information from the
     Scottish Office.
6   Edmonston, 1820.
7   OSA, Peterhead.
8   OSA, Nairn.
9   OSA, Cockburnspath.
10   Somner, 1983
11   Scottish Fisheries Protection Agency,
     Ann Rep 1996–7.
12   FN, 16 Jan. 1959.
13   For example, see *Scotland on Sunday*,
     16 Aug. 1992 and 24 Oct. 1993.
14   FN, 26 April 1991.
15   Campbell, 1995.
16   Holden, 1994.
17   FN, 6 March 1998.
18   FN, 4 Jan. 1991.
19   FN, 25 Jan. 1991.
20   FN, 27 Dec. 1991.
21   Information from Gordon Summers,
     Angus Council, 1997.
22   Information from Ross Macdonald,
     Aberdeen City Council, 1997.
23   Anson, 1930.
24   FN, 29 Nov. 1991.
25   *Olsen's Fisherman's Nautical Almanack*,
     1997 edn.
26   *Caithness Courier*, 28 Feb. 1996.
27   Hopper & MacDiarmid Report
     for Highland Region, *The Prospects
     for Fisheries and Aquaculture in the 1990s*,
     Sea Fish Industry Authority, 1991.
28   FN, 10 May 1991.
29   FN, 29 Nov. 1985.
30   Scottish Sea Fisheries
     Statistical Tables 1995.
31   Sea Fish Industry Authority Ann
     Rep 1995.
32   *Orkney Economic Review*, No. 16, 1996.
33   FN, 18 Oct. 1991.
34   Information from Iain Macleod, 1998.
35   Anson, 1969.

WEIGHTS
AND MEASURES

Over the centuries a wide range of weights and measures has been used by fishermen. I have not attempted to standardise or convert these in the text, as the words themselves are vehicles of history and carry a poetry in them. This glossary lists the main ones and indicates what they mean.

basket
The standard fish basket was one-quarter of a cran.

boll
A volume measure, usually of dry goods such as grain. There was some variation between districts, but a boll of meal usually weighed 140 pounds and had a volume of 145 litres.

box
Standard measure of volume of catch in white fishing. A box was equal in volume to the quarter-cran basket.

bushel
A volume measure, about 35 litres.

cran
Catches of herring were assessed according to the cran. This was a measure of volume, somewhat variable until in 1816 it was fixed as being equal to 42 gallons by the Commissioners for the Herring Fishery. This standard was revised again in 1852 and the cran was established as being 37.5 Imperial gallons of fresh fish. A cran contained roughly 1000 herring, although obviously this number could vary depending on the size of the fish. The weight of a cran is approximately 24 stone or 152 kilograms.

fathom
Nominally 6 feet, but most fishermen judged it as the span of their outstretched arms – slightly under 2 metres.

hundredweight
One-twentieth of a ton, or slightly over 50 kilograms.

last
Unit of weight or volume for large amounts of cargo, variously defined. A last of fish was 12 barrels.

league
Three nautical miles

ton
The Imperial ton is equivalent to slightly over 1016 kilograms.

tonne
Metric ton, or 1000 kilograms.

unit
A new measure of volume of catch, approximately one-sixth of a cran.

BIBLIOGRAPHY

Anderson, J., *Substance of a Report to the Lords of the Treasury of Facts Collected in a Tour of the Hebrides*, 1785.

Anson, P., *Fishing Boats and Fisherfolk on the East Coast of Scotland*, London, 1930.

Anson, P., *Scots Fisherfolk*, Banff, 1950.

Anson, P., *Life on Low Shore*, Banff, 1969.

Armit, I., *The Archaeology of Skye and the Western Isles*, Edinburgh, 1996.

Baldwin, J.R. (ed), *Caithness: A Cultural Crossroads*, Edinburgh, 1982.

Barrett, J.H., 'Fish trade in Norse Orkney and Caithness: a zooarchaeological approach',
    Antiquity, 71, 1997, pp. 616–38.

Bertram, J.G., *The Harvest of the Sea*, London, 1865.

Black, G.F., *The Surnames of Scotland*, New York, 1946.

Blaxter, J.H.S. & Hunter, J.R., 'The biology of the clupeoid fishes',
    Advances in Marine Biology, vol. 20, 1982.

Bochel, M., *Nairn Fishertown Weddings*, Nairn, 1977.

Bochel, M., *'Dear Gremista': The Story of Nairn Fisher Girls at the Gutting*, Nairn, 1979.

Bochel, M., *The Fishertown of Nairn*, Nairn, 1983.

Buchan, P., *Collected Poems and Short Stories*, Edinburgh 1992.

Buckland, F., Walpole, S. & Young, A., *Report on the Herring Fisheries of Scotland*, London, 1878.

Bunyan, S.A., *A Walk around Historic Dunbar*, Edinburgh, 1991.

Butcher, D., *Following the Fishing*, Newton Abbot, 1987.

Calder, J.T., *Sketch of the Civil and Traditional History of Caithness since the Tenth Century*, Wick, 1887.

Campbell, J., *The Fairtry Experiment*, Edinburgh, 1995.

Cargill, G., *Blockade '75*, Glasgow, 1976.

Christie, G., *Harbours of the Forth*, London, 1955.

Coull, J.R., *The Sea Fisheries of Scotland: A Historical Geography*, Edinburgh, 1996.

Cunningham, R.R., *Portpatrick Through the Ages*, Portpatrick, 1993.

Dobson, D., *The Mariners of Aberdeen and Northern Scotland, 1600–1700*, 1993.

Domhnallach, T.C. & Davenport, L., *Clann Nighean an Sgadain*, Stornoway, 1987.

Dorian, N., *The Tyranny of Tide*, Ann Arbor, 1985.

Dunlop, J., *The British Fisheries Society 1786–1893*, Edinburgh, 1978.

Edmonston, A., *Observations on the Nature and Extent of the Cod Fishery*, Edinburgh, 1820.

Elder, J., *The Royal Fishery Companies of the 17th Century*, Glasgow, 1912.

Fenton, A., *The Northern Isles: Orkney and Shetland*, Edinburgh, 1978.

Fraser, D. (ed), *The Christian Watt Papers*, Edinburgh, 1983.

Fraser, R., *A Review of the Domestic Fisheries of Great Britain and Ireland*, Edinburgh, 1818.

Gibson, W.M., *The Herring Fishing: Stronsay*, Edinburgh, 1984.

Gifford, J., *The Buildings of Scotland: Fife*, London, 1988; *Dumfries and Galloway*, London, 1989;
    Grampian. London, 1990.

Goodlad, C.A., *Shetland Fishing Saga*, Lerwick, 1971.

Gordon, J.D.M., Harrison, E.M. & Swan, S.C., *Guide to the Deep-water Fish of the North-eastern
    Atlantic*, Oban, 1996.

Gray, M., *The Fishing Industries of Scotland 1790–1914*, Oxford, 1978.

Gunn, Neil M., *The Silver Darlings*, London, 1941.

Halcrow, A., *The Sail Fishermen of Shetland*, Lerwick, 1950; facsimile edn, Lerwick, 1994.

Hallewell, R., *Scotland's Sailing Fishermen*, Anstruther, 1991.

Holden, M., *The Common Fisheries Policy*, Oxford, 1994 (revised by D. Garrod, 1996).

Hume Brown, P. (ed), *Scotland before 1700*, Edinburgh, 1893.

Johnstone, P., *The Sea-Craft of Prehistory*, London, 1980.

Levy, C. (ed), *Ardrossan Harbour 1805–1970*, Glasgow, 1988.

Lockhart, G.W., *The Scots and Their Fish*, Edinburgh, 1997.

Macdonald, D., *The Tolsta Townships*, Stornoway, 1984.

Macfarlane, W., *Geographical Collections*, Sir Arthur Mitchell (ed), Edinburgh, 1906.

McGowran, T., *Newhaven-on-Forth: Port of Grace*, Edinburgh, 1985.

McKean, C., *The District of Moray* (RIAS Guide), Edinburgh, 1987; *Banff & Buchan* (RIAS Guide), Edinburgh, 1990.

McKee, E., *Working Boats of Britain: Their Shape and Purpose*, London, 1983.

McNeill, P.G.B. & MacQueen, H.L., *Atlas of Scottish History to 1707*, Edinburgh, 1996.

Martin, A., *The Ring-Net Fishermen*, Edinburgh, 1981.

Martin, A., *Scotland's Past In Action: Fishing and Whaling*, Edinburgh, 1995.

Martin, M., *A Description of the Western Islands of Scotland circa 1695*, Donald J. Macleod (ed), Edinburgh, 1994.

Miller, J., *A Wild and Open Sea: The Story of the Pentland Firth*, Kirkwall, 1994.

Murison, D., *The Broch as It Was*, Fraserburgh, 1992.

Murray, M. (ed) *The Skipper's Notebook*, Anstruther, 1986.

New Statistical Account of Scotland, Edinburgh, 1845.

Pollard, A. & Morrison, A. (eds), *The Early Prehistory of Scotland*, Edinburgh, 1996.

Ralston, T., *My Captains*, Edinburgh, 1995.

Ritchie, G. & Ritchie, A., *Scotland: Archaeology and Early History*, London, 1981.

Ritchie, G.F., *The Real Price of Fish: Aberdeen Steam Trawler Losses 1887–1961*, London, 1991.

Rodger, N.A.M., *The Safeguard of the Sea: Volume 1*, London, 1997.

Sandison, C., *The Sixareen and Her Racing Descendants*, Lerwick, 1981.

Scottish Office, *Sea Fisheries Statistical Tables*, 1995.

Sinclair, Sir John (ed), *Statistical Account of Scotland*, 1791–9.

Slater, J., *Fishing Boat Names of the UK*, Edinburgh, 1997.

Smith, H.D., *Shetland Life and Trade 1550–1914*, Edinburgh, 1984.

Smith, P., *The Lammas Drave and the Winter Herrin'*, Edinburgh, 1985.

Somner, G., *Scottish Fishery Protection*, Cumbria, 1983.

Stevenson, S., *Hill and Adamson's* The Fishermen and Women of the Firth of Forth, Edinburgh, 1991.

Stewart, R., *Sail and Steam*, Moray, 1986.

Stewart, W., *A Fishing History of Lossiemouth*, Lossiemouth, nd.

Stewart, W., *Fishing in Scotland from the 16th Century to the Present Day*, Lossiemouth, nd.

Stewart, W,. *The Life of a Fisherman*, Lossiemouth, 1993.

Stromness Museum, *Harvest of Silver: the Herring Fishing in Orkney*, Stromness, 1976.

Summers, D.W., *Fishing off the Knuckle: The Fishing Villages of Buchan*, Aberdeen, 1988.

Sutherland, D.K., *Fisherlore of Avoch*, Avoch, nd.

Sutherland, I., *From Herring to Seine Net Fishing on the East Coast of Scotland*, Wick, 1985.

Sutherland, I., *The War of the Orange*, Wick, nd.

Sutherland, I., *Wick Harbour and the Herring Fishing*, Wick, 1984.

Tanner, M., *Scottish Fishing Boats*, Princes Risborough, 1996.

Thompson, P., *Living the Fishing*, London, 1983.

Thomson, J., *The Smuggling Coast: The Customs Port of Dumfries – Forty Miles of the Solway Firth*, Dumfries, 1989.

Washington, J., *Report on the Loss of Life and on the Damage Caused to Fishing Boats on the East Coast of Scotland in the Gale of the 19th August 1848*, House of Commons, London, 1849.

Waterman, J.J., *Aberdeen and the Fishing Industry in the 1870s*, Aberdeen, nd.

Wilson, G., *More Scottish Fishing Craft and Their Work*, London, 1968.

Wilson, G., *Scottish Fishing Boats*, London, 1995.

Wilson, H., *Nairn Fishermen's Society*, Nairn, nd.

Wilson, J., *Society of Free Fishermen of Newhaven*, R. M. Black (ed), Edinburgh, 1951.

Wood, G., *Torry: Past to Present 1495–1995*, Aberdeen, 1995.

INDEX